YATAKLI – VAGON
Turkish Steam Travel

George Behrend and Vincent Kelly

A Locomotives International Publication

Above: *2-6-2T no. 3558 on an Izmir Alsancak - Buca train passes 2-8-2 no. 46106 and 2-10-0 no. 56507 en route to Halkapinar.*
Photo: P. Ransome-Wallis.

Front cover, clockwise from top left:
A 'Churchill' class 2-8-0 shunting at Sivas (Paul Catchpole); The Blue Mosque, Istanbul (Turkish Tourism); Robert Stephenson loco at Izmir (Paul Cotterell); Mustafa Kemal 'Ataturk' at Kutahya in 1930 (National Library, Ankara); Banking engine at Bilecik (D. Trevor Rowe); Wagon-Lits no. 3312 at Istanbul Sirkeci station (J.H. Price).

Rear cover: *One of the handsome 2-10-2s based on Prussian Railways components, no. 57016, at Izmir Basmane, with a former Ottoman Railway Company 46101 class 2-8-2 in the background.*

Title page: *'Black Wolf'. Built at Eskisehir in 1961, Turkish Railways first home-built engine.   Photo: Courtesy of Tulomsas.*

ISBN: 1-900340-19-4   ISBN-13: 978-1-900340-19-9
Second edition. Published by Paul Catchpole Ltd., The Haven, Trevilley Lane, St. Teath, Cornwall, PL30 3JS, Great Britain.
(First edition published by Jersey Artists, 1969)
www.locomotivesinternational.co.uk
Printed and bound by Latimer Trend & Company Ltd., Estover Road, Plymouth, PL6 7PY.
British Library Cataloguing in Publication Data. A catalogue record for this book is available from the British Library.

YATAKLI - VAGON: Turkish Steam Travel

George Behrend and Vincent Kelly

Contents

Railways
Railways proposed

KARA DENİZ

AK DENİZ

KOTUR
VAN
KARS
ERZURUM
TATVAN
KURTALAN
ERZİNCAN
MARDİN
DİYARBAKIR
ÇETİNKAYA
MALATYA
GAZİANTEP
SİVAS
MARAŞ
ÇARŞAMBA
KALIN
KAYSERİ
OSMANİYE
SAMSUN
AMASYA
YOZGAT
TOPRAKKALE
ADANA
KARDEŞ GEDİĞİ
SAMSUN
ÇANKIRI
İZZETTİN
MERSİN
KARAMAN
IRMAK
ANKARA
ESENKENT
KONYA
FİLYOS
ÇATALAĞZI
MUDURNU
KALLIHAN
İSPARTA
ZONGULDAK
EREĞLİ
ADAPAZARI
AKYAZI
ESKİŞEHİR
BURDUR
İZMİT
ARİFİYE
BİLECİK
KÜTAHYA
İSTANBUL
H.PAŞA
SİNCEKÖY
TUNÇBİLEK SEYİTÖMER
DENİZLİ
BANDIRMA
MANİSA
ÖDEMİŞ
AYDIN
EDİRNE KIRKLARELİ
MAHMUDIYE
PEHLİVANKÖY
UZUNKÖPRÜ
BALIKESİR
İZMİR
PİTYON

4

Preface

One day in a conversation about travels in Turkey, fellow author Jim Horsford asked if I had ever read a book by George Behrend called 'Yatakli-Vagon', published back in 1969. As I had not, he lent me his copy and afterwards it took me a couple of years to track down a copy of my own, such was its scarcity.

Reading about the journey across Europe and around Turkey, so many incidents and comments evoked my own feelings and memories of two similar journeys made in 1977 and 1978. The impressions of long-distance sleeping-car travel, characters and places encountered, communist border control, and the whole experience of visiting non-tourist Turkey have all made this book a classic of its genre.

Furthermore, with George Behrend's renowned encyclopaedic knowledge of Wagons-Lits and Pullman cars and his attention to detail, we have an account rich in social and railway history. For these reasons I decided that this almost unobtainable book, which was originally published by the author himself, should be published again, even though 40 years have elapsed since George and Vincent boarded the Orient Express in Paris. The Author was astounded but delighted when I telephoned him out of the blue with the suggestion!

In 2006, as we prepare for this second edition, it is 150 years since the Ottoman Emperor first granted a concession for building a railway in Turkey so this is an appropriate time and an opportunity to mark the anniversary.

The book stands as a document of its time. Any attempt to update the text would have compromised the impressions and interrupted the flow of the account. This must be borne in mind by the reader as factual details are given which were pertinent at the time of the journey but which are now history. Reference to 'today' in many places means in 1966-67.

At the time of writing there were expectations of continued CIWL services in Turkey but the Company shut down its Turkish division not long after publication. They gave up the dining cars in 1970 and the sleepers followed around 1974. The cars used on the Direct Orient - Marmara Express ended on 19th May 1977. A CIWL dining car ran between Istanbul and the Turkish frontier at Uzunkopru in 1966 and it was probably this splendid vehicle, still in service but operated by the TCDD, in which I took breakfast when unknowingly following the author's route in 1978. By then a line had been laid to allow passage directly from Bulgaria to Turkey without passing through Greek territory via Pithion.

The original text was without the foreign accents that we would usually include in Locomotives International publications, however, they have been included in a list of places at the end of the book. To anybody familiar with the Turkish language the lack of accents might appear strange and it would not be possible to pronounce many place names correctly without understanding how the accents work, however, this is not a language lesson and it is not necessary in order to enjoy the book. A number of places are referred to by their older names or with now obsolete spellings, but reference to such changes were mostly already given in the 1969 text.

Readers familiar with the 1969 edition will notice that some reference notes for would-be travellers have been omitted - they would simply have been too misleading today. Some information in the appendices has been corrected or updated and George Behrend has provided a list of Wagons-Lits cars in the Turkish fleet. This replaces the full CIWL list in the original book and a more accurate, now definitive version of the complete CIWL fleet is included in his book "Pullman and the Orient Expresses". This is published by the Author and printed to order (details at the end of the appendices).

As many of the pictures from the 1969 book as possible have been included, all of them either taken by George Behrend or donated by official bodies, friends, and fellow enthusiasts, as credited. Nearly all the pictures have been reproduced from the original photographic prints, however, some are no longer available, in which case suitable substitutes have been used. A handful of essential views have been scanned from the original edition and a chance taken on how well they will reproduce.

Many of the photographic contributors have since passed on, amongst whom John Price deserves mention, a knowledgeable gentleman who was a lifelong Wagons-Lits and Pullman car enthusiast and spent over 40 years as editor of Cook's Timetable.

Finally, George Behrend especially wished that we should pay our respects to his co-author, travelling companion, and good friend, Vincent Kelly, who is also no longer with us, having died in Jersey in 1979 at the age of 44.

Paul Catchpole.

List of Abbreviations Found in this Book

BDZ	Bulgarian State Railways. Bulgarski Drzavne Zeleznice
BLS	Bern-Lotschberg-Simplon Railway (Switzerland)
BR	British Railways
SNCF	French Railways. Societe Nationale des Chemins de Fer Francais
CFOA	Ottoman-Anatolian Railway (Haydarpasa-Ankara-Konya)
	Old title: Société du Chemin de fer Ottoman d'Anatolie
CFR	Romanian Railways. Caile Ferrate Romane
CIWL	International Sleeping Car Co. Compagnie Internationale des Wagons-Lits.
CO	Oriental Railway (Plovdiv-Istanbul)
CSD	Czechoslovakian State Railways. Ceskoslovenske Statny Drahy
DB	West German Federal Railways. Deutsche Bundesbahn
DR	East German State Railways. Deutsche Reichsbahn
DSG	German Sleeping and Dining Car Co. Deutsche Schlaf - und Speisewagen Gesselschaft
F	Luggage Van (Fourgon)
FS	Italian State Railways. Ferrovie dello Stato
ISG	International Sleeping Car Co. Internationale Schlafwagen Gesellschaft
JZ	Yugoslavian Railways. Jugoslovenske Zeleznice
KSR	Yugoslav Sleeping & Dining Car Co. Kola za Spavanje Restauracje
LMS	London, Midland & Scottish Rly
MAV	Hungarian State Railways. Magyar Allam Vasutak
OBB	Austrian Federal Railways. Osterreichische Bundesbahn
ORC	Ottoman Railway Company. (Izmir-Aidin)
PLM	Paris, Lyons & Mediterrannée.
PKP	Polish State Railways. Polskie Koleje Panstwowe
RIC	International Carriage Regulations. Regolamento Internazionale delle Carrozze
SBB/CFF	Swiss Federal Railways. Schweizerische Bundesbahnen/Chemins de Fer Federeaux
SCP	Smyrma-Cassaba et Prolonguements (Izmir-Afyon, Izmir-Bandirma)
SEK	Greek State Railways.
TCDD	Turkish State Railways. TURKIYE CUMHURIYETI DEVLET DEMIRYOLLARI
UIC	International Union of Railways. Union Internationale des Chemins de Fer
WL	Sleeping Car (Wagon-Lits)
WR	Restaurant Car (Wagon Restaurant)

I   Introduction

Little Birds are Writing
Interesting Books,
To be read by Cooks
Lewis Carroll

'Does it', asks one potential reader who has seen an advance notice. 'Contain reliable information? Or is it merely a description of the author's journey across Turkey?' Perhaps this summarises the 1969 concept of travel books. Information and more information? Certainly; but instruction? No, certainly not.

Yatakli Vagon is Turkish for Sleeping Car. In the comfort of its compartments, this book ranges one thousand two hundred and thirty six miles beyond the eastern terminus of the Orient Express at Istanbul, a journey where steam will last well into the seventies. Details of the lines traversed and engines encountered on the journey, are given in the chapter for the railway enthusiast, and for those who cannot enjoy a railway exploration without an historical background to the system, a summary of the geography of Turkey and of the political events which created or affected Turkey's railways is given in the Appendix. There, too, is the list of locomotive classes with numbers, and details of the sleeping cars run by the International Sleeping Car Company in Turkey. For in Turkey, the Sleeping Cars are still provided by the Compagnie Internationale des Wagons Lits et du Tourisme, who, in line with the switch to mass travel changed their name in 1967 and dropped the 'et des Grandes Express Europeens.'

Though Turkey has entered the tourism market in a big way, the masses of foreign tourists who flock to Turkey, do not, as yet, travel to and through Turkey by train. So come with us, lie back and relax, while the scenery, instead of the autobahn, unfolds. Sip your apperitif without fear of prosecution for drunken driving or enjoy the full dining car services, which, if you follow our particular itinerary, are obtainable for most of the way.

STU class Yatakli Vagon. Photo courtesy of CIWL.

II   The "Proper Way", Paris - Vienna - Istanbul

It is like any other work of art,
It is and never can be changed.
Behind everything there is always
The unknown unwanted life.
Randall Jerrall: 'The Orient Express'

How lucky we are to be visiting Paris at all: it is part of the 'extra' holiday that train travel gives us. Visitors' Paris, as thousands of British, German and Americans see it, is quite different to Paris on the day of departure by Wagons-Lits to Istanbul. It would be pleasant to spend days wandering along the spacious boulevards, instead of having to keep one eye on the time, while doing so; to really relax over a coffee or a glass of beer at one of the tables on the pavement, or maybe to go for an excursion on the Seine in the Wagons-Lits Company's newly acquired river steamer, the 'Borde Fretigny' which can be hired for parties. The Company have a splendid service of outside catering for throwing parties or for business occasions, called "the Two Lions", after the heraldic animals that adorn their coat of arms.

The traditional way to go is to start from the Gare de l'Est and begin by visiting Vienna. This is the route of the original Orient Express, with Wagons-Lits sleeper running, in 1883 as now, from Paris to Bucharest, across France, Germany, Austria and Hungary. By this route today, we must change at Vienna for Istanbul. The use of the plural - we must change at Vienna, does not refer to one of the authors (George Behrend) being aware that Wagons-Lits travel is fit for, and often used by, royalty, but to the fact that both of them are travelling together. Vincent Kelly has the advantage of approaching the journey without any pre-conceived notions derived from pre-war conditions.

Of course it is not necessary for everybody to go first to Paris in order to visit Istanbul. For visitors from England there is the Tauern Express, a sleeper waiting at Ostend ready to take them through to either Munich or Salzburg; after a pleasant day spent at either of these places, the Tauern Orient Wagons-Lits car from Munich will convey them on to Istanbul, calling at Salzburg. Or in winter, from mid-December to the end of February each year the Wagons-Lits from London to Basle may be used, giving five hours in that fine city where three countries' railways meet, before the Wagons-Lits in the "Wiener Waltzer" waltzes through Switzerland and the Tyrol, over the spectacular Arlberg pass by moonlight, to reach Vienna in the morning. High supplements in the Night Ferry led to a reduction in the numbers of cars on the London-Paris service, but now that the charges have been reduced with an all-in fare of ticket plus supplement, the Night Ferry makes a pleasant prelude to starting from Paris, or going via Basle, and an alternative to travelling via Calais, the traditional departure point of first the Simplon-, and now the Direct-Orient Express, which we utilise on our return journey.

There is a much better reason than mere tradition for starting out via Vienna, from Paris. This way, you get breakfast and lunch on the train, unlike the Direct Orient; boarding the Balkan Express after half a day and dinner in Vienna, and choosing the sleeper marked 'Istanbul Express' (for such it becomes in Yugoslavia), breakfast and lunch are again available on the train,

and early dinner before the Yugoslav diner comes off.

The train route to Istanbul may be changeless, but it has countless variations on a theme, so that it is best to check with Cooks Continental Timetable exactly which route has the dining cars running. (Sad experience has taught that the best way to ensure the curtailment of an amenity is to put it in a book - the Yugoslav diner which had run to the Bulgarian frontier in 1966, is now detached from the Istanbul Express at Nis.)

Your travel agent will of course help you. But do not forget that everything possible is done to encourage him to send you by air - higher commission, educational flights for his staff and so forth; when you have successfully resisted the air, you must remember that as like as not he has never been by train to Istanbul. Before starting out, a few hints may be welcome. Smallpox vaccination is desirable, but further inoculations are not really necessary, unless you intend to hang about, roughing it at various places for several days, to photograph trains. The scrupulous cleanliness of Wagons-Lits sleepers is well known. But as you are on board for several days you need a few things for maximum comfort. An old pair of slacks, a shirt or blouse which does not show the dirt (for part of the journey is by steam) are useful for making forays though the ordinary coaches to the diner. A jersey pullover is essential for use on cold nights or sudden changes in temperature. Lack of attention to this is often the cause of upset stomach when abroad. That optional part of the conductor's uniform, a pair of slippers, is worth the weight of adding them to your luggage. Get a pair whose soles are strong enough to withstand walking on wet platforms or on the track, where you may wish to stretch your legs, or to reach the diner without clambering through the coaches.

Wearing travelling gear, your suit can hang happily on the special hangers with their rubber stops which prevent rattling, ready to step into, fresh and clean as the day you entered your cabin; cover it, in a plastic bag, or with your mackintosh. The shirt you intend to arrive in can stay, stowed and spotless, in your bag. In the delicious privacy of your sleeper compartment, furnished with a blind, changing clothes is no problem, even in the heart of a main line station.

You need too, that old fashioned aid to travel that everybody used to carry, a pocket knife. Failing that, a small knife, a corkscrew and a bottle-opener. Such implements when bought, will come in handy for picnics at home, or even about the house. A good idea is to get several of those stout bags for small change, which every bank keeps. Each bag is for a different currency, with one empty one for your English change once you have left the steamer (or started your journey by through sleeper). Hidden in your suitcase, there is little likelihood of their being stolen. Nothing seems to be more valueless than another country's small change; not even banks will take it. Have you ever tried to buy

anything in the heart of England, armed only with foreign money? It is a good idea to obtain small amounts of currency, during the pauses on your way. Get a few French francs before starting, as well as your travellers cheques. German marks and Austrian schillings are fairly easily obtained in Britain, also you benefit from a higher exchange rate, quite probably, too. Dinars are plentiful in Vienna. So also are levas, though it is strictly illegal to take them in or out of Bulgaria. The exchange rate for levas is very favourable outside the country, as they are no use to the money changers (who give an extremely bad rate for any surplus ones travellers may be carrying), and, of course, there is a risk of trouble with the Bulgarian frontier police. If they know you are in transit, they will not expect you to have any. Turkish lira are also obtainable in Vienna, or for that matter in Britain, if specially ordered. The amount you may take in is strictly limited, as is that you may take out. Lastly, you will need travellers cheques. These you can get from Cooks or from your Bank.

In Paris, it is easy to forget all the tedium of these preparations. The old buildings, the trees in the boulevards, which, somehow or other, have not all been torn down in the 1968 revolution, give the city an aura lost in many places in the west. The roaring Renault buses, with their open platforms, were still shouldering their way among the sleek modern cars when this was written, though they are going fast. Moreover Paris today is nothing like pre-war. Somehow, the French authorities have forced the property owners to clean their glorious facades and rid them of all the smoke of bygone eras. No horns blare; yet traffic moves more thickly than before, if (perhaps) less furiously. The great skyscrapers have only intruded into the Montparnasse area. So, unlike London, Paris has not lost its skyline (a London loss that with reason much upsets many people).

Dusk comes quickly, for the warm summer evening is threatened by clouds. The heat wave, that made the start of our journey (from Jersey) all that a holidaymaker could wish for, breaks with a deafening crash. Rain cascades upon the streets, upon shop awnings, and upon pedestrians believing that these give protection, whereas the water seems always to drip down their necks

rather than onto the pavement below. So not only is it good to be going, we are really going, instead of just thinking about it. Sections of the marvellous ticket that makes it possible, have, in our case, arrived from as far afield as Rome and Athens, though they are hundreds of miles from our itinerary.

The elegant Wagons-Lits Head Office, entered grandly from the Boulevard Haussmann (though it is always known as 40, Rue de l'Arcade), is the same building as was used at the turn of the century when Monsieur Nagelmackers had his office there, and something of the Victorian fearsomeness remains in its dignified elegance. Here the courtesies have been paid. Here we have been assured that the "tremblement de terre" has not interrupted the services. All is now ready for us to board the famous Orient Express, which leaves in the autumn of 1968, at 22.15, half an hour later than in the summer of 1966. It does not boast a diner in France. Dining cars are the bete noire of the Wagons-Lits today, instead of their pride and joy because, like railway operators everywhere, they lose money on them. If only we had all those station buffets, like British Railways they say wistfully in the Rue de l'Arcade, "that would be different'.

As the rain is descending in torrents, we pile into a taxi instead of the plebean bus. The forecourt of the Gare de l'Est is large and open enough to give anyone a soaking between the bus stop and the station building.

Towards the back of the train is the elegant latest type of sleeping car running from Paris to Salzburg, very popular with American visitors. Next to it is the more elderly car which on Mondays in 1966 covered the same journey. On other days of the week, Tuesdays, Wednesdays, Fridays and Sundays, it worked through to Bucharest.

Our own sleeper, for Vienna, is further up the Orient Express, identical with the others at first glance. Yet somehow, as we mount into the corridor, the whole bogus-romantic edifice crumbles, the excitement fades. Rain thunders on the roof as an English friend shouts an envious "Bon Voyage" through the door of the vestibule. Then swiftly and silently we glide out of the station, a nice, clean, electric train - so different from the gloomy sta-

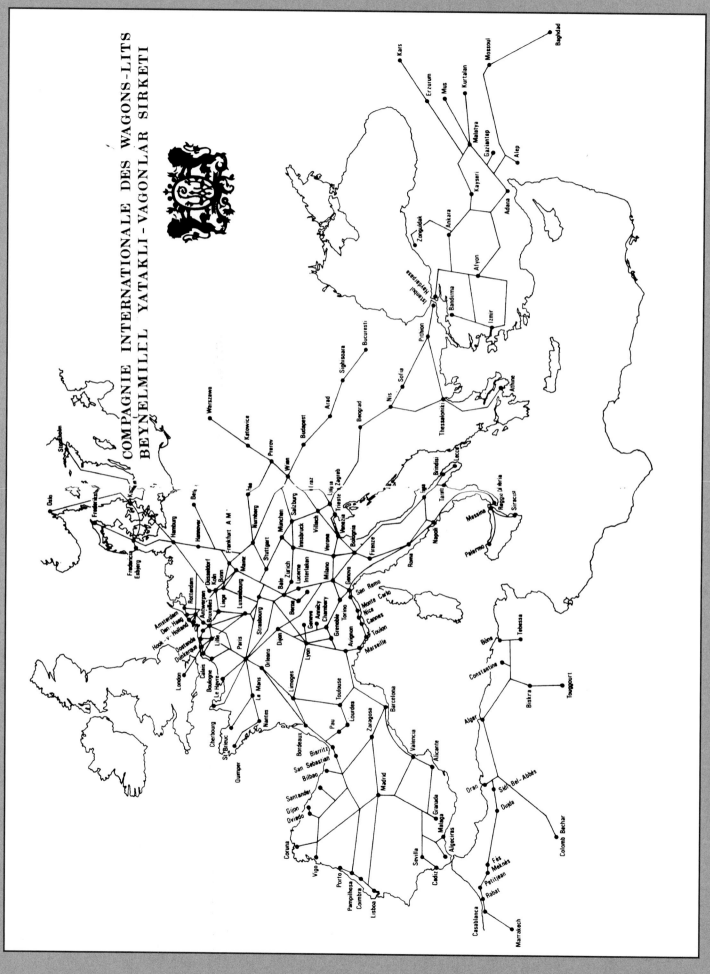

COMPAGNIE INTERNATIONALE DES WAGONS-LITS
BEYNELMILEL YATAKLI - VAGONLAR SIRKETI

10

tion with its smell of stale urine and diesel fumes from trains of other lines, the kind of thing that sends travellers scurrying into the airline offices, muttering darkly "never again."

Flip out the lights, raise the blind and peer a moment at the Parisian suburbs. Is this already Noisy-le-Sec? Perhaps; but here we are, anyway, started. It is too dark to see Noisy, as we rush eastward at a mile a minute and soon faster.

In the cabin, there is an extra notice, a sign of the times "The Company takes no responsibility for thefts". On the wash stand table is the enormous form in four languages, with which the Wagons-Lits have propitiated the Customs and Police of Western Europe. "Have we got a prayer mat with us?" The question has a new meaning this night. We deliver up the form and passports to the Conductor, and order champagne for this, the first of a dozen nights aboard various different cars. The Conductor is apologetic. This is an Austrian based car. So we have excellent Klosters White Wine instead. The train stops. Down with the window; a modern blue and white electric sign says: "Chalons Sur Marne". Already we have travelled over 100 miles! The French army are boarding the train in hundreds, returning from leave to French bases in Germany. Some how one can never go far in the Orient Express without reminders of wars......

Grey dawn over a grey German town. Modern buildings every where, mute witness to progress. High blocks of flats. "Karlsruhe" is obligingly posted up on a signal box. The Orient Express stops again, at the Hauptbahnhof, whence guttural German issues from the loud speakers. How different from the nasal nonsense of the previous evening, of which the words "en voiture", are the most easily assimilated. We glide out of the station, behind the blue German electric engine, and soon swing away from the line to Frankfurt turning east again from north, making for Stuttgart.

We pause outside the great Hauptbahnhof of Stuttgart, after circling the town. Down below is the big blue engine of the standard express class waiting to take us on to Munich, and next to it, the red dining car is belching smoke from its kitchen chimney. Evidently the German Sleeping Car Company do not put their latest restaurant cars on a service which runs so far outside the Fatherland, from Stuttgart to Vienna.

We run down into a corner of the Hauptbahnhof, opposite a wall. Principal stations in Germany are nearly always called Hauptbahnhof (literally "main" or superior station). Here the front sleeper is detached, its occupants graciously allowed to sleep in it until eight o'clock (this car was withdrawn in 1968). We are off again before six.

Out the way we came in, but down below this time, the ramp by which we entered rising on our left. We climb the small mountains that make the Stuttgart - Ulm section more spectacular than most of the German journey. They divide the Rhine from the Danube, forming a watershed. We doze as the plains begin again. Then the train stops first at Ulm, next at Augsburg, both spacious, intellectual-looking Bavarian cities. Bavaria begins at Ulm, where we cross the river Danube, placid and still. At Augsburg, the station announcer spits out the words "Orient Express", rolling off the destinations: "Munchen, Salzburg, Wien, Budapest". He puts such relish into the word "Pest", that you wonder whether this is because he only has the chance to say it once a day; or whether he is feeling patriotic, and would like every Hungarian worker in Augsburg to be banished instantly upon it.

Here is the line where the 125 miles-an-hour speeds were regularly undertaken for visitors to the Munich International Transport Exhibition of 1965. We glide along at a gentle sixty. It seems we are ahead of time, and Germany's very latest engines are not on view this morning.

The Munich-bound passengers will have taken up most of the seats in the diner, whereas after Munich we cease to be a businessman's convenient overnight express.

8.48 a.m. We draw ponderously into Munich's enormous station. Everyone else is hurrying into their offices, but we are still lounging in bed. Once again, as at Stuttgart, we must reverse. Trains galore run in and out of the station. Some are hauled by elderly electric shunters. Some are steam-hauled. Others again have diesel traction. Suddenly, I notice that our new engine is dark green, with OBB on the front, instead of DB of the German Federal Railways: an Austrian electric engine which takes us on all the way to Vienna.

From Munich, the Orient Express begins the prettiest part of its journey to Vienna, so there is little point in lingering in bed. Navigating through the Hungarians with their wicker baskets, in their overfull coach, we reach the calm of the DSG diner.

After Rosenheim, junction for the Brenner Pass, Italy and Innsbruck, the Simsee runs beside the windows, and the German Alps form a background to the ham and eggs, germanically underdone, that accompany coffee and rolls. The British tend to despise foreign dining cars, claiming they are too expensive. They are, of course, a part of this holiday of sleeping and eating, while magnificent scenery rolls past the window-which cannot be achieved properly by car; whilst at sea or in the air, the excellent meals are often taken without any scenery to look at.

The variety of the journey is an excuse for doing it in style. There is no need to spend 13.80 marks on breakfast, but you won't be able to spend any marks again on any breakfast in Germany, on this trip, so why not? Attack the cherry jam with relish, while the diner speeds past another lake, on the left. This is the Chiemsee, whose narrow gauge steam tram warrants a picture, though we rush non-stop through Prien, where it starts.

As the mountain foothills draw nearer, the activities of the dining-car attendants indicate that we should pay and go. The courteous Austrian Customs officials have already been along the train, for Munich is the last stop in Germany for the Orient Express. Tradition dies hard; whenever possible the few dining cars that still cross frontiers, do so without customers, even though duty is no longer charged on items carried by them. The diner's conductor is busy compiling his stock sheet and sales in German marks; after Salzburg he must start accounting all over again, in schillings.

We run through Freilassing, the junction for Berchtesgaden, and the last station in Bavaria. Six kilometres before Salzburg, our engine is back on its own tracks instead of foreign ones, and suddenly the Hohensalzburg can be seen on the right, as we thunder over the river Salzach The brakes come on with a flourish, to give us a fine view; a panorama of the festival city. The Hauptbahnhof has German trains at one end, Austrian at the other, and only international trains go through without reversal. In common with certain other places on our route, like Istanbul or Venice, Salzburg retains its own individual charm in this fast changing world of rationalisation. There are twenty minutes in which to buy postcards and send them off, and to regret that we are not stopping longer.

The charm of Salzburg's mountain scenery seems more apparent after we leave. For almost at once the mountains disappear, and with that sense of long-distance spaciousness and interminability which can so readily be associated with the old Hapsburg empire, the train runs almost imperceptibly from Western to Central Europe. As the train quietly pursues its way to the capital through the heart of Austria, pausing at various places of regional importance, such as Attnang Pucheim, Wels and Linz, it changes character in that subtle way which gives European Expresses their charm. No longer is it plainly international, but elegantly Viennese, except for those unfortunates going on to Hungary, whose bundles and baskets signify a harder life.

Luncheon in the dining car is quite different to breakfast. The crew are twice as friendly as before, recommending the Schnitzel with true Viennese relish, for they (like the veal steak) are Viennese, and very different from their glum, almost impersonal manner of breakfast-time, suitable for Germany. The menu, printed especially for DSG cars running outside their home country, covers operations in Austria, Holland and Switzerland. We take our places just before Linz, passing some old engines placed on a plinth, on the left outside the station. Occasionally, we come down to the great River Danube, but mostly it is out of sight. We run non-stop from Linz, through Amstetten, past Melk's lovely Abbey, and the important St. Polten junction. Before Vienna, the wooded hills begin, signifying an end to our journey towards this outpost of the western world, bounded on all sides by communist states. For a while, this last wooded section seems without end, before we run down past the beautiful Schonbrunn palaces into the gay, modern Westbahnhof, where Willi Brach nobly meets us.

Either you like Vienna, or you do not. It has an almost pedantic charm. There are the weinstube where they blankly refuse to give you beer, saying firmly "this is not Munich". The Viennese pretend they are still the centre of a great empire aided by the refugees from the old eastern provinces, who bring their specialist restaurants to add lustre to the native Austrian cuisine. The overdone gaiety is delicious, synonymous with well-contented living, free (at last) from Nazi domination and Russian occupation.

Like many tourists in Vienna, we pay an enjoyable visit to Grinzing. Wilhelm Brach points out to us an elderly gentleman of eighty-four, enjoying Viennese life as though he were but sixty and had not lost a vast estate near Cop (on the Hungarian border with what is now Russia, where they have a gadget for adjusting the wheels of the through oil tank wagons from Russian to European gauge). At Grinzing, fiddlers come and fiddle airs from the White Horse Inn, as if to recapture the best of the thirties, when one put off the inevitable horrors of mixed war and socialism, with this tinselly pleasure, as bogus then as it is today, though undeniably jolly. People laugh in Vienna as they sell their wares to the dour ones from beyond the curtain, who have little to laugh about.

Vienna is at once the end of the line for westerners, and the starting point and meeting place for eastern countries. In Vienna there are glorious trams, and a lokalbahn (electric). There is a 15-inch gauge steam railway in the Prater. And there is the modern Schnellbahn (fast railway), whose electric suburban trains run at frequent intervals, connecting various main lines.

Unfortunately the pouring rain caught up with us, and Vienna presented a sad aspect. One of those days when a journey by tram becomes blurred by such a torrential downpour, and other cars on the line can be seen but dimly. There are trams of all descriptions, new and old, even some genuine street-cars, obtained second hand from America. Because of the downpour, we omit visiting the Hofburg and the Spanish Riding School, and glance but briefly inside St. Stephen's Cathedral.

Time to go. Vienna's South Station, even newer than the West one, is perhaps even more ponderous. Though Vienna used to have several main line termini, the modern Sudbahnhof now links the former lines running east to Hungary and south to Italy, under one roof, though at different levels. The Wagons-Lits (from 1968) runs its station buffet. The heavy steel carriages of Austria predominate here, both their own and theirs derived from the unification with the German Reichsbahn during the Anschluss and the war. There are no other western carriages except those of Italy, waiting to start for Venice or Trieste. In the platforms of the high level part of the station, other trains, principally the 'Chopin', wait to depart for Czechoslovakia, Poland and Russia. U.S.S.R. sleepers mingle with the ancient car, recently returned from Turkey and modernised, which in 1966 worked the only Wagons-Lits service to Warsaw. The Balkan Express waits for us in the lower part of the station, next to the Venice train.

Wilhelm's fluent German is not wasted on the Wagons-Lits cleaner who takes our luggage into the car. He points out that the sleeper is right at the back of the train, and from the windows in the vestibule we shall have an observation view of the Semmering by night. Up at the front, the powerful electric engine that looks so like the one that brought us to Vienna, is of a class specially designed for this line. (Details of all the engines encountered on the way, are set out in the chapter 'For the Railway Enthusiast'.)

The absence of any number on the Wagons-Lits Conductor's tunic is confirmation that he is not of their Austrian personnel. He is a very independent Yugoslav, who clearly does not particularly like travellers from the west, particularly when they bear official-pattern tickets. He performs his duties in a manner that is impossible to complain about, yet with complete indifference. He informs us that he is going all the way to Sofia, which is a duty working non-stop for twenty five hours (longer than is tolerated in Western Europe, though we do not tell him so).

The sleeper is quite different to the solid mahogany one of the previous part of the journey. It has been refurnished with metal partitions and doors, enhancing the feeling of being shut into a sardine can, from which we are liable to be prized by every police force in Eastern Europe. Perhaps this is just a reaction to leaving Vienna behind, with its glittering gemutlichkeit, of abandoning all family responsibilities and penetrating into the unknown. It is the first time I have ever been to a Communist country, and western propaganda has done its stuff. The transit visa form, now abolished for British travellers and already dispensed with for Austrians, demanded to know if I had ever been to the People's Republic of Yugoslavia before; I dutifully put down 'No', for last time I was there, it was a Kingdom.

With effortless ease, we glide out of the station on an embankment above the city, due south, away from the Danube (which isn't blue but grey), entering a flat, dim, plain; the heart of lower Austria. The last landmark of any familiarity is the Lokalbahn depot, visited that afternoon. At the front of the train is an Austrian postal van, for this train also performs its function of

Scene on the Semmering line near Chixnitz-Barenschutzklamm, Austrian Railways. (Ö.B.B.). Photo: Ö.B.B.

internal life line, as did the Orient Express, from Salzburg. After some time on this great dim plain, we stop at a garish station serving an equally dim industrial town, Wiener Neustadt. No doubt it is a very fine town by day. At eleven at night it is soundless, and the station lights, harsh against the moonlit sky, reveal empty platforms. Somehow they have got rid of their occupations, and central Europe sleeps placidly, calmly awaiting the next upheaval, if any. (It came on 20th August, 1968 in nearby Czechoslovakia.) Meanwhile agricultural life goes on, and the crops from this fertile plain are sent up to feed the capital.

The implacable electric engine slips silently out of the large station, moving quietly towards Graz, its driver's home, and presently it stops again at a much older station. The mountains, which begin as suddenly as those in Wales, look mightily attractive. Why do not more people take their holidays here instead of in the Tyrol? Perhaps because tourists are a gregarious lot. Are there not wolves and bears in these great forests? Certainly there used to be.

Gloggnitz at midnight. One half expects to see Schweik, slightly tight, emerging from the station buffet, and boarding a train in the direction opposite to that in which he intends to travel. The place is mysteriously romantic. There is no hanging about, now, for banking engines. Again with effortless ease, different to the resounding struggles of steam engines, the engine attacks the great Semmering Pass. This is still the Austrians great route to the sea at Trieste, and there is plenty of goods traffic on the double track. At Bruck an der Mur, the Trieste Line continues south to Villach, whilst our train turns south-east. But long before Bruck I am asleep. Willi's excellent dinner vies with the glorious scenery over the Semmering, seen from the draughty vestibule of the sleeper, on the tip-up seat, forcing myself to stay awake to take in the view. After the great Tunnel and the descent to Murzzuschlag, sleep overpowers. It is a spectacular pass. The Semmering station, just before the Tunnel of that name, is 2,900 feet up. The ruling gradient is 1 in 40.

The line on to Graz is very beautiful. From Bruck an der Mur it is newly electrified. Its smooth riding soon has me fast asleep, assured that the demands of the Iron Curtain will wake me again.

When I do so, it is foggy. There are more mountains, damp in the early morning. Unquestionably there is a steam engine on the front of the train, but it is the horses and carts that convince me I have entered the People's Republic without knowing a thing. The Wagons Lits principle of not disturbing the clients whenever possible prevails even here. No doubt having a Yugoslav conductor helps. We seem to be at a small wayside station, on a single track; remote, almost Ruritanian.

For the first time, on this journey, the quiet sigh of the Westinghouse steam brake pump on the engine rends the morning air, and though to me it seems in place with the peaceful surroundings, the bells on the horses harness, the snap of a twig beneath the wheel of a bicycle whose owner stumps along a gravely track, pushing it, the whole scene takes on a new meaning, in the realisation that nowadays there must be people to whom gravel, push bicycles, steam engines and horses are all throwbacks to the past. So that when the whistle blows, echoing mournfully round the deep valley side, the whole ensemble of romantic foreign travel comes to life. Steam fizzling through the drain cocks up in front, drowned by the deep throated roar as the driver opens the regulator, may even have novelty in it for the travellers. The frantic increase of the Westinghouse pump as the brakes are released, will, on our journey become banal by its repetition, but now it seems exciting, though fast smothered by the powerful blast of steam and smoke up the chimney of this locomotive. No squashed-in Giesl ejector, with its thin hissing, crowns this engine. The sound from its standard kind of funnel reverberates all round the mountain, commensurate with the huge black locomotive that emits it.

An amplitude of such machines, pounding relentlessly up the stiff gradients, or, as in our present location, snuffing off downhill with an accompaniment of clanking coupling rods, will later leave us almost blasé about such sounds and smells. But now the wondrous noise is remarkable, for here for the first time the western traveller can behold a steam engine in its true surrounding, on the front of his express, roaming through a lugubrious forest, or sailing across great bridges, steam fluttering from the safety valves but not, as latterly in BR practice, from half a dozen weak glands as well! Here in the almost ethereal environment of high mountains and rushing streams, where every sound is amplified by nature, not a tape recorder, the engine is surrounded, not by hasty people in motor cars with cameras and other impedimenta, but its true setting, dominating the creaking carts and the high handle-bar bicycles, with an affable sense of benign power.

We run easily downhill and presently we stop again, this time outside an engine shed, where it is noteworthy how clean the People's Republican engines are. Spick and span, compared to many in the west. The people are walking to work or coming on old fashioned bicycles. There is a gorge, evidently some sort of junction. Curiously, it takes time for the penny to drop that this great viaduct we slowly traverse is the Most' in 'Zidani Most' (Iron bridge). Here we join on to the main route of the former Simplon Orient Express, between Ljubljana and Zagreb. Here too, we reverse again, and after coupling to carriages from Munich, we set forth for the first time on this journey, behind a diesel.

It is a U.S. diesel, from General Motors, and its chime whistle reminds us of it. Our line quickly leaves the mountains. At every unguarded crossing queues of carts are waiting to move off to the fields. A run of just under an hour brings us to Zagreb, Yugoslavia's second city. It is about 7.30 a.m.

Zagreb (or Agram as it was once called), is said to be a charming place; it is impossible to see anything of it, as we are in the middle of the through station, with wagons outside the window. Zagreb's particular charm at this hour, on this train, is that the modern dining car of the KSR, direct successor of the Wagons-Lits' old Yugoslav division, is hooked on here for our journey to the Bulgarian border.

From its wide windows an hour or so later, we survey the Yugoslavian plain. It still looks very much the same as thirty years earlier. The houses more battered, the roads immensely improved, very modern-looking buses occasionally on them. Lorries in plenty but very few cars. Ox-carts, buffalo-carts, geese in flocks, pigs roaming, cattle in large numbers, looking better fed than the people. All seen, shut off, through the modern plate glass windows of the swish diner for the elite. There are no police, nor soldiers, except for two who come in to drink a glass of beer.

Possibly wrongfully, I come to the conclusion that Slivovitz is the great leveller. Remove Slivovitz (Plum Brandy) from the Yugoslavs, and you have a country such as Britain might become if deprived totally of a tea supply. You don't need much Slivovitz: there is no need, for it is harsh and strong. But it sets you up, a barrier against all that mud and buffaloes which seem, from the train, just as depressing as of yore. How, does one begin to brainwash a buffalo? Does it pull its cart more willingly now that its driver is not being oppressed by a horrible absentee landlord, but instead is urged on by the ordinances of a collective farm? I doubt it. It dreams, like Michael Flanders' hippopotamus, of wallowing in the cool waters of the nearest river, with just its nose above water. On the train, where the conductor of the capitalist sleeper is bosom friends with the conductor of the communist diner, political divisions seem blurred In spite of the unease, the secret feeling of lack of freedom, that a westerner senses in communist lands, the people are friendly enough, even policemen at frontiers are human. It is obvious what they are thinking-hoping that everything will be in order so that without otherwise necessary delay they can get home, either to their wives and families, or off duty to the hostel, without the bother of reports and of grilling some unfortunate who has got into their clutches.

We reach Belgrade at one in the afternoon. From 1968 the train bypasses the main station and calls at Topcider instead, thereby avoiding the delay of reversing. Belgrade's great terminus is one of those where the junctions outside are deceptive, making it almost impossible to see precisely the point of divergence. There's a suburban tram, running on its own roadbed, intertwined with the railways for added interest. The station itself, like so many, is somewhat unprepossessing. After Belgrade, the train mounts into bare inhospitable hills, handy for the capital's radio masts. From here we descend quite sharply to the plain again.

There is a severe bottleneck along this line as all traffic from the west to Greece and Turkey, as well as all the through traffic from Yugoslavia to Bulgaria, plus the main national traffic from Belgrade to the south-east of the country, passes along this one single track. Work is in progress doubling it. Stops are frequent, to cross trains coming the other way, many of them filled with children, perhaps going to attend some rally. There seem to be a great many trains, some steam hauled, perhaps relief ones. The pattern of the trains has changed since before the war; owing to the greatly increased traffic, the long trains to Istanbul or Athens run separately, instead of dividing at Nis.

We pass non-stop through some station with a neat narrow gauge engine shed, filled to capacity with steam engines and a narrow gauge line veering off into eternity to the right. Could it be the line from Paracin to Zajecar?

Dusk is approaching as we come to rest at Crveni Krst, a place of cinders and no platforms. After a day of travel through rural Yugoslavia, past peasant women in black, men in dark clothes, and youths in jeans, it is a change to attain a junction. To the right, just before the station, the line bears off to Nis and Athens, past a large engine shed. There is twelve minutes halt here, for though it is still well within Yugoslavia, it is the last large provincial centre before the frontier, and the police come aboard to check passports of outgoing travellers, during the rest of the journey to the border.

By the time we leave this place whose name almost chokes you as you try to pronounce it, darkness has fallen; sure sign that the train is about to traverse one of the interesting and spectacular parts of the route. Instead of being able to see anything, there is dinner, before the diner comes off at Dimitrovgrad, the frontier town just inside Yugoslavia. In 1968 it proceeds to Skoplje and is detached at Nis (to which the train now runs instead of Crveni Krst).

The dining car's beer, brewed at Ljubljana, is particularly to be recommended. It tastes of hops, not chemicals, in an old-fashioned way. Possibly the brewery has inherited best German machinery from the days when Ljubljana was Austrian Laibach. The meal proceeds leisurely as the train climbs in pitch darkness through the Balkan mountains; several stops at upland villages prove not to be the frontier after all. Dinner is over, and we are snugly back in our cabin as the train lumbers into the single platform station, beside a long stone building, poorly lit and full of

The station at Zidani Most, Slovenia, on 27th August 1958. The train is a local service of 4-wheel coaches hauled by an Austrian-built tank locomotive, no. 18.005, dating from 1927.
Photo: A.E. Durrant.

uniformed figures. Policemen in brown, followed by more policemen in Prussian blue, and very ferocious. A peremptory knock, a demand for passports and the visas, which Bulgaria still requires, a long look at the visa and at the two portions detached when a visitor enters and leaves the country. The entrance piece is carefully removed and you are known for all time to the communists.

Up in front, the diesel engine has been taken off. The place abounds with large black steam engines, sizzling in the dark, for alongside the single platform line, there is a series of sidings and at the far end of the station, a big shed. One of the engines is attached to the front of the train. Its loud chime whistle distinguishes it from Yugoslav steam, and frequent use is made of this whistle as it bears us away up over the frontier, and down into its native Bulgaria. While the Yugoslav frontier town retains the name of the Bulgarian leader, Dimitrov, a memory of the period when the Bulgars, as allies of the Germans, took it over during World War II, the Bulgarian frontier retains its old Turkish name, Dragoman. Dimitrovgrad, before the War, was called Tsaribrod. Naturally 'Tsar-anything' will not do at all today.

In contrast to the meagrely lit remoteness of the Yugoslav town, Dragoman station is brilliant with modern fluorescent lights, there are several platforms, and goods trains of trucks of various Eastern block countries, waiting to depart. Dragoman is but three quarters of an hour's run down hill to the capital, Sofia. While the police report to their local base, our engine attaches some Bulgarian carriages for local passengers to use.

Here is the feeling of east meeting west, now that almost all the west, and Yugoslavia, uses Central European time, with very few exceptions. Between dim Dimitrovgrad and Dragoman, your watch is advanced one hour. Bulgaria is Eastern Europe and uses Eastern European time, like Greece and Turkey. Consequently it is just before ten o'clock at night when the Istanbul Express draws into Sofia, and the Yugoslav conductor, now separated from his colleague in the diner, pays strict attention to his duties. Though he has been at work continuously for twenty four hours, he comes along and makes up the beds before his Bulgarian colleague takes over at Sofia. During the war he had been in the R.A.F., flying Spitfires, and thus spoke English, as well as German and Bulgarian, besides his native tongue.

Sofia is quite a different station to others. Though it has innumerable platforms they are no wider nor higher than those used in Germany by the staff, for servicing the trains at large stations; perhaps six feet wide. Though all, except one, are without any covering whatever, their narrowness makes observations very difficult, even in daylight. Our train, which changed its name from Balkan to Istanbul Express back at Zidani Most, waits about half an hour in the station. This is teeming with people getting in or getting out, or just stretching their legs or changing money, for in Bulgaria you will recall, Levas may not be taken in or out of the country. The entrance is blocked, but my companion Vincent disappears through an exit, leaving all his papers aboard the train and ignoring my loud exhortations not to stray. On his return he nonchalantly says it is much more dangerous to shout, and attract the law's attention, than to meander off into the square. No doubt he imagines I will work some miracle to stop him being left behind. Our steam engine has snorted away and overhead wires stretch once more above the platforms, so we shall glide quietly and quickly off to Plovdiv, leaving late-comers stranded.

The chain which the Wagons-Lits Company has fixed to the inside of each cabin door, ever since corridor communications were introduced back in the nineties' is also a further western barrier against communism! By four in the morning, it proves its worth, for once again Bulgarian policemen are rapping on our door.

No easy-going collection of passports by the Wagons-Lits attendant is permitted here at Svilengrad, another gate in the iron curtain. The guards bang along the train, joyfully disturbing everyone in the wee small hours, almost as though they hope they can find somebody whose papers are not quite in order. I had quite forgotten that their particular interest in us, was because of our capacious tickets.

Outside, in the hour before dawn, the station seems to have a

Greek Kb class 0-10-0 at Pythion, SEK.
Photo: D. Trevor Rowe.

Cerkezkoy lies in Turkey between Alpullu and Halkali on the route to Istanbul. A Turkish 4-8-0 is simmering outside the shed
Photo: Paul Catchpole.

furtive abandoned air about it. Long before iron curtain days, its 'rush hour' was four in the morning, or earlier. For this reason pictures of it are rare, and nowadays, forbidden. There is a buffet, and a long low station building that is murky and low lying. Svilengrad evokes curiosity of timetable readers, and looks as curious in reality as in the imagination. Here Cyrillic lettering meets Greek lettering, incomprehensible to most of us.

Peeping out of the cabin door after the Bulgarian people's police have reluctantly abandoned the sleeper back to capitalism, I see the Direct Orient Express sleeper drawing out of the station, back towards Sofia. It would seem there cannot have been time to change conductors at the frontier. Total silence now descends over the further platform, which is bounded by a neat privet hedge. The Bulgarians seem to have finished with our train; but how we are going to move on is another matter.

Suddenly the silence is broken by a steam engine, which comes lurching round a bend, apparently from nowhere, at right angles to the hedge. Light from the firebox throws a silhouette in the earliest dawn, and in the remote strangeness of it all, it whistles hauntingly, romantically-and familiarly! I'd know that whistle anywhere. Spirited somehow out of some siding, our Greek engine has arrived.

Our engine hoots again mournfully, an utterly different sound from the Bulgar chime whistles. Then we creep out of the station, after a performance with the air brakes that is nostalgically pre-war. Somehow the modern valves cut out the sound of whistling through ones teeth.

At this point the traveller begins to look closely at the timetable. Three hours and ten minutes are devoted for this journey across a little part of Greece. A journey of just forty-five miles, unless the figures are wrong; they are not wrong. Timetables on this line, though, do not give intermediate stops.

We run along at a peaceful twenty-five miles an hour, the sleeper rocking gently, and all the while there is something else conspicuous by its absence in the rest of Europe; tiny lengths of rail. Tiny, for easy manhandling, instead of welded and placed by tracklayer. The clack of wheels over rail-joints has returned!

When I wake, we have stopped somewhere. What town? Goodness knows, it does not boast a station nameboard; poverty stricken and desolate it looks like innumerable Macedonian towns did, last time I was in them twenty-five years earlier. It has an engine shed and another of these Greek engines, placidly waiting outside it. Though there seems to be no motor road at all, only some dirt tracks.

The C.E.H. or S.E.K. as I always think of the Greek State Railways, seems much the same as of yore, though this line was only acquired a decade ago, which perhaps accounts for the steam, and the antiquity of it at that. In an earlier book I have written of the Greek capacity to stop for an eternity, and then suddenly to start off briskly for no apparent reason.

Edirne's Minarets are the first seen from the train. Courtesy of Turkish Tourism.

Why stop here? To change drivers perhaps? Or take water? Surely people do not drink Ouzo at this hour of the morning, even though the effort of going to Bulgaria and back, in the middle of the night, may need rewarding. Not until reaching Turkey could I find out that this place is Dikea.

In the town, people are moving about; so are their pigs and donkeys. The houses look squalid and neglected; we are indeed a very long way from Athens. Suddenly, we set off again, jauntily doing our twenty-miles per hour, which is much quicker than attempting to motor on the appalling roads. The meagre telegraph wires to herald our passage perch on stunted, crooked poles. The frequent level crossings of the tracks have a piece of tin plate cut in the form of a cross. Presently we come to a river on our left. Now whistling more loudly than ever, our train slows down, quite a feat considering the miniscule speed of normal motion; it would seem ready to stop at any second. We rumble over a great bridge across a tributary of the other river. This is the Arda, and beyond it, the level crossing signs are larger and wooden; the telegraph is supported on stiff straight posts. There are jeeps with soldiers patrolling, and last of all, the large station house at which we now draw up, has the large red Turkish flag, with Crescent and Star emblazoned on it, hanging down boldly over the platform.

The station has those high painted windows, seen on any Indian temple or mosque, the standard 'oriental' style as supplied by European designers. Just in case anyone might mistake the place for a Greek station, the words "TURKIYE CUMHURIYETI DEVLET DEMIRYOLLARI" stare at us from a large board. A smaller one says significantly "Welcome to Turkey" in English, French, German and Italian-but not Yunanistani (Greek). Though it is half past five in the morning, there are a number of small boys beside the train, looking poor, cold and hungry, as well they might be at this hour. The Turkish State Railways do not like the presence of these urchins at every stopping place, though there is nothing they can do about it. The

trains are an attraction, almost an event. Here at Edirne they were more ragged and ill-shod than anywhere else we went in Turkey. They give Turkish stations an unmistakable eastern character much more reminiscent of Egypt than of anywhere in Europe, save only that the high platforms built by the British in Egypt are missing here.

We wait in the station for a train to rattle in from the single line to the south, a crescent and star on every carriage window. The wagons have a great 'T' painted on them, and noticeably, there is not a single Greek truck in the station. Edirne Station is a very long way from Edirne itself, a common fault with Turkish stations. On the sky line, misty and mysterious, rise the city's Minarets. To someone arriving from Europe they have an air of utter strangeness, yet in harmony with the whole surroundings. Taking a closer look at the children I notice they are after all quite tidily if poorly dressed, though some run barefoot, unlike anywhere else visited in Turkey.

Edirne is the first town reached by motorists, and here every year the Turks hold their annual wrestling matches, the contestants stripped to the waist and shining in olive oil to make holds more difficult. The Turks say the Mosque at Edirne is the best preservation in all Turkey.

Our train loses no time in clearing out of the station once the line is clear, for driver and guard evidently do not care even for the short sojourn on hostile territory. Turkish troops are everywhere, in tanks or jeeps or marching. All are clad by the all-provider of N.A.T.O., the United States. For that matter so is the strutting corporal on our train who takes great pleasure in stumping up and down the corridor of the sleeper, waking everybody up. The railway guards in plain blue suits and peaked cap, with SEK clearly stitched on by hand, are very secondary creatures to the soldiers. A left-over from the days of the private Franco-Hellenic railway, is a large board with "Frontiere Grece-Turquie" on it, beside the track. On each side the fields are cultivated, and village herds are kept away from fear of straying. There is no fence, no apparent fortifications on the boundary itself.

Back in Greece again, it is easy to notice how much better the line was laid in Turkey; the bouncing motion begins again, and wobbly telephone poles again replace the straight ones. We stop at another rough-looking village, whose pathetic pill box in the village street looks as though it has been often in use. Our pompous corporal gets off and calls upon its soldiery, unshaven and in working rig; suddenly the Corporal descends to their level, placing his hands deep in his pockets and slouching off home.

Corn is laid on the flat floor for threshing. It has been raining and the corn is getting spoiled. Across the street a conglomeration of pathetic huts that serve for houses can boast a motor car. On the station, a board proclaims in Greek, that the place as New Orestias - it seems as "New" as William the Conqueror's "New Forest" in Britain.

We trundle away from the little village with its passing loop and come down to the river again, on our left. Pythion, the town to our right, looks quite large, and the station building is larger, too, than others in the area. Close by is a small engine shed, and a new Greek Customs House. The engine shed is positioned embarrasingly, amidst all this police activity, because of course it was there, long before Pythion became a frontier. To our left there are just weed-strewn sidings beside the river. They have a neglected air, though very much in use. There are no buildings at all on this side, just open country - giving a good field of fire; how ruefully uncivilised are our thoughts in this age.

A large Greek goods train makes ready to depart for Svilengrad on the line furthest from us; it arrived presumably over night from Alexandropolis. Next to it a smart black engine waits two tracks away from us, but drawn up level with our sleeper. Though it is quite obviously a German 'Kriegslok', the Crescent and Star below the cab window is plainly conspicuous. Next to the chimney there is a four-wheeled guards-van with 'Uzunkopru-Pythion' in Roman lettering, hanging on its destination board. It is the only Turkish truck visible in the station, and it is clearly going to be in the way when this, our engine, takes over the train.

More whistling occurs as the Greek engine at the head of our train, is uncoupled and moves off down the line. The Greek Railways shunter in turn blows on his whistle, and he shouts. He shouts at least three times and it is perfectly obvious to anybody with the slightest railway knowledge, even though he has not a word of either language, that the Turkish engine is now required to move forward to take the place of the Greek one.

But nobody shouts in Turkey; nobody shouted the entire time we were there, and no Yunanistani shunter is going to shout at a 'top link' Turkish engine driver. Inscrutable beneath an enormous peaked hat, the driver leans on the side of his cab, his wily looking eyes, separated by an enormous hook nose, stare at nothing on the ground below. Though he probably does this run every other day, he is not to be moved; he doesn't even blink. Whatever he thinks of the Greeks, he keeps to himself, while the young fireman is out on the side of the tender, shovelling back a little coal that has overflowed when coaling at Uzunkopru. It would never do if good Turkish coal spilled on to Greek soil: The Greeks would not hand it back again. The shunter comes and stands right underneath the cab so that the driver cannot fail to see him, gruffly muttering. In total contrast to the mournful hooting of the Greek machines, the Turkish engine emits a piercing shriek; for Turkish whistles are high pitched like French ones, bold and commanding.

The Greek shunter notices me laughing, and holds out his hands in a gesture of despair as the engine moves off, pushing its van before it. Obviously this happens every day, yet throughout the performance the Turk have not uttered a word.

Presently the little van which is provided to bring the Turkish police, customs men and train guards from over the border, is to be seen rolling back along the siding. It has to be uncoupled, and then flyshunted out of the way by the Greek engine which is still blocking the main line, before the latter can go off to its shed. It is hurled into the siding with ferocity, as though the Greek driver would prefer to push the obstructive Turk wagon into the river.

This frontier seems truly ferocious; everyone is armed, and uneasy. The Turks take over the train, and as they board the coaches, they pretend they are not being watched by Greek troops outside their Customs post five yards away. None of the officials says as much as good morning to them, as though they did not exist!

After holding us up as long as they dare, the Greeks allow the train to go. Two single lines run parallel outside the station for a little distance, but not under any circumstances are the Greeks able to run far along the left hand one. On the right the Oriental Railway has provided a large triangular track for turning engines, but only the Greeks are permitted to use it nowadays, and Turkish light engines must run backwards to and from their country.

On the line beside us is a through coach, marked Istanbul-Athens. The uneasy atmosphere at Pythion has reminded me that not so long ago, trains could only use the right-hand lane to Athens by day, because at night there were bandits. Until the traffic transferred to air, the Wagons-Lits ran a sleeper over the route, the passengers staying the night in it at Alexandropolis. Though I have never been down it, this line has very special associations for me. Were I to go along it far enough, I would come to that unguarded level crossing where, at the end of the war, a reconstruction train missed my army truck by inches, as I shot over the crossing at 40 m.p.h., never doubting that the railway was still out of use after German destruction.

We have turned east, away from Macedonia, and thunder into Turkey at five miles an hour, over a steel viaduct of so many spans that I lose count of them. At the Turkish end of the bridge, a sentry smartly presents arms to the train, magnificent in white blancoed web equipment and gleaming steel helmet. Here there are more barracks, close to a station called Demirkopru, which we pass without stopping. After four girder bridges in succession, the short run on to Uzunkopru seems quiet. We pass over yet another bridge, a foretaste of the great engineering feats of Turkish railways, so numerous as to defy full descriptions. The train rounds a bend into the station.

As at Edirne, the platform is crowded with boys, but this time they are selling various kinds of food, and water melons. The timetable pronounced that we were to spend the best part of an hour here, so I get down among the crowd to inspect the train engine and make sure it is going all the way. As I do so, an incredibly old locomotive, with fantastic chimney and outside coupling rods comes majestically down the other track, whistling the crowds from its path. When I return to the centre of the train, I find my sleeper has vanished.

Frantically walking down the train in search of it, I suddenly see it has been moved over to a siding, attached to an elderly Turkish second-class carriage; and on the carriage is written

4-8-0 no. 46008, as used for piloting Cerkezkoy - Halkali.
Photo: D. Trevor Rowe.

4-8-0 no. 46025.
Photo: D. Trevor Rowe.

'BUVET'. Here is a practice almost totally forgotten in modernised Europe. Instead of having to clamber along the corridor, the Turks trouble to remove the sleeper and hitch it to the buffet car, leaving it free of other passengers walking through it. This practice goes on all over Turkey, and very civilised it is.

After the rest of the coaches had been moved back to our train, the antique shunting engine makes ready to return for us, but suddenly went back to the rear of the express. Everyone seemed to be waiting for something, and soon it came, the second class only "Mototren" (we

Blue Mosque, Istanbul. Courtesy of Turkish Tourism.

might as well use Turkish idioms now we have arrived in Turkey), from Edirne to Istanbul. Much faster than our Istanbul Express, it is soon filled to bursting with the people on the platform. It was identical to that in which we later went to Konya. It soon drew away, leaving us to the leisurely shunting operations of this nonagenarian machine, one of the tourist attractions of modern Turkey, not listed in the brochures.

Uzunkopru is about 115 feet above sea level. Our train takes most of the day to reach Istanbul, setting off first up to the Ergene Valley, and calling at most places en route. Pehlivankoy, the first stop, has some past association which escapes me. Next Mandira is distinguished by being the only junction the whole way. Here the branch line from Kirklareli on the Istanbul main road, runs in, though the important junction station is Alpullu, ten kilometres further on, where there is another of these antique Oriental Railway shunting engines, still at work (in 1966).

Meanwhile breakfast is served by the attendant of the fusty-looking buffet car, in the Wagons-Lits compartment. The buffet breakfast is excellent and extremely Turkish, but it was not one of the services run by the Wagons-Lits Company up till 1966. There is tea, served in glasses. There is toast, butter, honey, cake, black olives, tomatoes and white mutton cheese (made from sheep's milk).

The train winds about, past great rolling fields of sun flowers, of sweet corn, and of melons. Often the country is simply grazing land, with herds of cattle, sheep and goats, together with great flocks of geese, but of course, no pigs (this is a Moslem country). The changeless arid-looking scenery, already gives the country a non-European look. The houses are mud brick, mostly single storey and primitive-looking. There are few trees, except at stations and settlements.

From Muratli, the line gradually climbs higher to Cerkezkoy, 486 feet up, which is about half way. (Cerkezkoy was the station where the S.O.E. was once stuck for a week in a snow drift in 1929). Here the Oriental Railway provided an engine shed, and from it comes our pilot, for the 1 in 66 climb over the hills to the sea of Marmara. Sinekli is the summit station, before the long

descent, also at 1 in 66. At many passing places we overtake car carrying wagons filled with German Volkswagen.

Quite suddenly the country changes, as an inlet of the sea appears on the right, behind another of the interminable ranges of hills. Our double-headed train sweeps round a long curve to sea level, entering the station at the head of the Istanbul suburban area, Halkali. Here overhead wires are apparent again, and the line becomes double track. There is colour light signalling too. Elsewhere when there are any signals, they are German pattern semaphores. But mostly operations seem to be by telephone and hand signals.

The suddenness and totality of the change in environment is very striking at Halkali. It seems to symbolise the clash of ancient and modern, noticeable all over Turkey. The two steam engines, for example, are not provided with a turntable; instead they disappear on to another great triangle track to turn, making it impossible to see their numbers. Meantime one of the three electric engines, which suffice to haul the long distance trains, has backed on to our train, and we are soon heading through a series of seaside suburbs, modern, new, well constructed, clean, and full of holidaymakers, who are served by the frequent local suburban electric trains. There are plenty of hotels and motels.

Just before Florya the line joins the sea coast of Marmara and on the left of the next station, Yesilkoy, is Istanbul's very busy airport. Istanbul itself, on its superb site overlooking the Bosphorus entrance, is but a little distance further on, though how far it is cannot be measured on this particular trip, in terms of time. Unlike the carefully maintained, reliable steam engines of the TCDD, which were to take us thousands of miles all over Turkey without failure, this precious French-built electric engine of which the Turks are not unnaturally proud, chooses to break down. So we sit just outside the city for over an hour, admiring the sea and some modern blocks of tall flats, while the small army of officials who accompany international trains in European Turkey give us a completely false feeling of Turkish trains being militarily controlled.

There are soldiers everywhere in Turkey; every station almost,

has its ramp for military tanks and lorries to be loaded. The officials guarding our train get very bothered by the inevitable bread-vendors who arrive almost at once, and nimbly climb the stout fence which is provided for this electric line through an urban area. The guards' duty is to prevent smuggling. At last a little Krupp diesel shunting engine arrives to tow us into the long-awaited terminus, at a funeral speed, while overhead the airliners buzz about, proud of their slickness. Perhaps the last few yards of the long journey to Istanbul are the most spectacular of all. The line runs down to the shore, immediately below the Topkapi Palace walls. Like the Germans, the Turks use right hand running, and from the window of the sleeper, on the right there are glimpses of the sea, of the old city walls, and of indescribable slums. Journey's end for all those books about the Orient Express; but we have only just begun our travels.

III The Eastern Express

I am a great train
lighted windows streaking the narrow dark,
berths opened out,
brown blankets spread,
circling towards the sun,
running,
running,
running,
into the long land,
into the eastern night

Richard G. Esler

Sirkeci Station is in a state of bewildered confusion. Travellers from the west disgorge on to the platform, and great queues form for the severe customs examination. It is severe, because many of the passengers are Turks returning from working in Germany, Switzerland and elsewhere, and are laden with dutiable presents. Foreigners are sympathetically sent through when they reach the head of the queue.

At this point, standing in the rear of the seemingly stationary queue, we try the efficacy of the splendid yellow permit. There was something about that permit, that seemed to my out-of-practice eye, to be exceedingly oriental. If it were not so powerful, would it not have been issued for our entire itinerary, instead of only from the frontier to Ankara, where we would, according to the accompanying letter, obtain another?

One flash of yellow card produces quicksilver results. Policemen without a word of anything but Turkish, hustle us out of a back way, and through the Customs. Stupidly, I pause to put away the precious document, which is our lifeline since it is attached to all the other permits covering our return journey. In a flash the Police barrier at the station exit returns to normal. My handgrip has no marks on it; so I must repair to the Customs man. He has suspicions of one tiny little bag for a whole month's stay. Can I speak Turkish? Regretfully I shake my head, and with an expression-Turks have very expressive features-which silently indicates that I am undoubtedly a liar, I am smuggling, but Turks are not allowed to impede tourists, my unopened bag has the chalked hieroglyphics slowly and reluctantly inlaid on it. I pass into the forecourt, where any pretence at westernisation has been abandoned. Taxi touts jostle for our custom, bundle us into an inoffensive, elderly post war American automobile, and, assuring us that the taxis are not dolmus or shared ones, the driver and tout set off.

Only after the tout has got out again does the driver repeat our destination. We move into a jumble of traffic. Buses, cars, horses and carts, trolleybuses; over extremely uneven, paved streets of stone sets, grimy, with weird smells. A high mosque is on the left. We swing over the Galata Bridge where the tramlines remain, and only the trams are missing to re-create the setting of Cairo in the late thirties.

People cry their wares, car horns blare continuously, everyone surges forward. Whatever Istanbul's individuality may be, the sense of pulsating activity, of busy people, of lively gay, active people, is uppermost. It is a city of sprawling communities, each one self-contained, and separated by water or hills from each other. Its first impression is decisively oriental, rather than Turkish; Mediterranean in outlook, though the Mediterranean is nowhere near. That the driver does not appear to know the way would surprise anyone unacquainted with the Middle East. The fact that he nevertheless goes straight to his destination after the discreet pause for his meter to tick up a bit, it is in keeping with the place. Less in keeping is that nowadays, after years of Attaturk, one does not bargain about the fare.

A plethora of servants is one of the features of Istanbul's hotels. To the western European, accustomed to indifferent service, this old fashioned attention is almost embarrassing. The personnel have a hungry look on their faces, though they are courteous enough. Our hotel is neither modest nor Americanised. It is distinctively European. After all, Istanbul never tires of pointing out that it is a European city, so what is so significant in that? All the same, to anyone who has never been east before, it is very difficult to remember that this town is not in the heart of Asia.

In beauty and setting, it is hard to surpass. Perhaps the most astonishing thing is the narrowness of the Bosphorus, also the fact that it turns and is full of blind corners. Not only is it a picturesque waterway, it is hazardous. One way traffic schemes have to be arranged for it, though the local Istanbul traffic takes no notice of this. Boats appear to be going in every direction at once on the Bosphorus, save only up it and down it at the same moment.

Off the shore, cruise liners ride at anchor. Russian tankers struggle upstream towards the Black Sea, homeward bound. This struggle is the next surprise, for the eight knot and more current can be seen, rushing down the Bosphorus to the Sea of Marmara. Only the Golden Horn is placid; and it is not golden, but murky.

Our Hotel, the Gezi Palace, looks out southwards over the car ferry terminal at Karatas, towards the Asiatic shore at Uskudar. The steepness of the hills enhance the background to the shipping. Dusk falls in the eastern manner, and after a stifling day, Istanbul is most beautiful at night. Noise from the night clubs loudspeakers goes on till two a.m. Dolmus drivers roar their engines for the rest of the night. Half-constructed houses, and waste ground with a detachment of the Turkish Army, complete with US trucks and military tents, pattern the landscape which also includes the Stadium, and the Dolmabahce Mosque. Lights are everywhere, on the Asiatic shore, on the ships dressed overall, in the European foreground, among the trees of Task Park, and from Leander's Tower, a little island off the shore on the Asian side. Not surprisingly there are books galore written about Istanbul, and this despite Rose Macaulay letting it be known that this is what so many writers write about.

More curious is the ease with which one can get lost. Tearing ourselves away from the view on the balcony, we feel sure that, if we set off downhill, we will come to the Golden Horn. Off we go, wrongly going west, and soon are among hundreds of small workshops where Istanbul's taxis are repaired. The paved road is exceedingly rough, there are puddles of dirty water, and we seem to be much better dressed than everybody else. After some while we do indeed reach the waterfront-at the only point where warehouses and shipyards do not occupy it, and here we have a brief glimpse of the Horn by night. Across it lies old Istanbul, where most of the Turkish people live, and where one civilisation after another left their mark upon the city. The whole place looks enormous now, whereas up at our hotel it seemed relatively compact and readily accessible.

Liner berths by Galata Bridge, Beyoglu, Istanbul. Courtesy of Turkish Tourism.

Certainly this part of the city gives it its true flavour, unlike the sophisticated area round the Hilton Hotel. Everywhere there are breads and cakes and lemonade, and melons on sale. There are water sellers, too, though these we encounter more often in the interior of Turkey. There are letter writers (or scribes), little cafes with Turks playing cards. There is a distinct feeling that these places close for only a few hours out of each twenty-four, if at all. Nobody takes any notice of us, nobody speaks anything but Turkish.

How we are to see the city is neatly solved for us by Cooks. Because of the earthquake at Varto, we find that our original route through Van will not be possible. So, circumnavigating the boot-blacks who are in profusion round Taksim Square, we repair to the Wagons-Lits Office in Cumhuriyet Caddesi, where Monsieur Erman re-arranges all our bookings. He also telephones to Haydarpasa, where the Company's Representative for Turkey, Monsieur Evliyagil, has his office. Their hospitality knows no bounds, and we are immediately despatched on some of the half day tours of the City. Costing about 30 Turkish Lira, they are far cheaper than attempting to visit the mosques and palaces by taxi, for the charge covers the entrance fees.

Sightseeing by conducted tour does nothing to dispel the feeling that grows on the visitor to Istanbul, that the city takes a long time to comprehend. The sense that you are only seeing the city's surface, in some ways is comparable to London. London is increasingly becoming an international city. Like London, Istanbul too is full of Americans, airmen on leave from the local US bases, and visitors. In our hotel there are some American civilian technicians who drive out expensively each day by taxi-cab, to install the electronic equipment in which they are expert.

What with the Americans ashore, and the Russian ships plying up and down the Bosphorus en route to Vietnam or Cuba, Istanbul has plenty of the reminders of that internationalism and sense of intrigue, which so disgusted Ataturk. Though he cleared the Turkish capital off to far away Ankara, the splendid foreign embassies have largely remained as consulates; that of Britain being particularly large, close to the main shopping street, the Istiklai Caddesi. Off this there is a small flower market, with a bar restaurant offering relatively cheap meals. Mostly Turkish Restaurants in Istanbul are in the grand manner.

The Liman Restaurant, down by the Galata Bridge at Karachi, opposite Sirkeci, has a particularly fine view of the shipping. Its cuisine, too, is excellent. It is handily situated for passengers visiting Istanbul by liner. Here we meet Monsieur Evliyagil for the first time, who explains to us that the tempo of the city, and indeed business life throughout Turkey, is largely governed by the difficulties of getting about. To have lunch with us, he has had to devote most of the day to find time to make the crossing, including waiting for the ferry, though the Bosphorus is only a mile and a half wide. The new bridge, when it comes, will certainly alter the whole atmosphere of Istanbul.

The city has existed in some form or another for 2,600 years, ever since 657 BC The feeling of occasion, of being at a cross roads in the centre of things imposes itself willy-nilly, even if the amount of history, and the numbers of different civilisations and races which have from time to time been in control, is so large that history is rather overwhelming.

Istanbul is very difficult to write about, except to urge you to go there. Like Venice, it has to be seen to be believed. Certain dates, such as the establishment of the capital of the Eastern Roman Empire by Constantine on 11th May, 330 (AD), (Constantinople) and the final overthrow of the Christians on 29th May 1453 by Sultan Fatih Mehmet, stand out in the history of the world, but to condense this two thousand year history of a city, where two million of Turkey's seventeen million inhabitants live, is not within this book's compass.

The Cooks tours are divided into four or five different drives, and an excursion by motor launch up the Golden Horn. The coaches pick up at the hotels, before proceeding to varied destinations. These include, on one afternoon tour, the Topkapi Palace, also called the Old Seraglio, where the Sultans lived and ruled from 1453 until about 1854, when they removed to the Dolmabahce Palace. The Topkapi Palace itself, fortified by an inner wall, which separates it from the old city, is placed majestically above the point where the Golden Horn runs out into the Bosphorus. Far down below are the boats - and the sidings of Sirkeci Station. Just to visit the various rooms, of different architectural styles down the ages, and admire the view and the varied arrangements, such as the splendid Turkish tiling surrounding the walls of the Harem quarters, is but a tiny part of the spectacle. There are enormous collections of wonderful Chinese porcelain, and in the Sultan's Treasury, an array of jewellery so magnificent and varied, that it can compare only with the treasures of the Vatican in diversity; and being Turkish, with many items from places further east, it is far more extraordinary. In add ition there are the clothes they wore, the scimitars of the Janissaries, their Turbans and embroidered velveteen or brocaded garments, which recreate the feeling of the barbaric hordes mercilessly supplanting Christianity with Islam - right up to the gates of Vienna.

Hard by is the former Cathedral of St. Sophia, later turned into a mosque, and later still transformed into a museum. To agnostic, humanists and atheists, a disused but magnificent church seems entirely in place. To Christian believers, troubled by the increasing lack of faith, it is surely a symbol. Here Byzantine man has glorified the Christian God, his successor has glorified Mohammed, and now it serves for foreign tourists to gape at, emptily.

In contrast, the Blue Mosque, visited on a morning tour immediately after St. Sophia, is a very holy place. Infidels, like us, are admitted only after removing their shoes and wearing slippers. Within there are many carpets overlaid upon each other, and the famous blue glass windows, and blue tiling and mosaic. Close to St. Sophia are the Roman Cisterns which are a monument to Roman architects in their longevity, and to their water diviners as a lasting source of supply. Roman cisterns played their part in Libya during World War II. The one in Istanbul features in "From Russia with Love", in which a Wagons-Lits from the Turkish Division, forms such a large part of the background to this well-known James Bond film. The morning tour also includes a visit to the Edirne Gate at the walls of the old city, before examining the former church of St. Saviour in Chora, or Kariye as the Turks call it.

Inside, the Byzantine frescos have been restored as far as possible to their former glory, and the mosaics of blue and gold are among the most wonderful in the world. Like so many churches in Istanbul, this one, which served the adjoining monastery, became a mosque, and the beautiful mosaics covered with whitewash. The rise of Turkish tourism has brought home to the authorities the need to preserve and display the glories of the former occupants of Turkey, so now, like St. Sophia, the building is a museum. The extent of the various works of art in Istanbul are, like London, or Rome, so great, that one feels one cannot hope to see everything, and one is slightly overwhelmed by the surfeit of sumptuously decorated historic buildings. It is somewhat a relief to be taken from Topkapi Palace to the Grand Bazaar. Here, in greatly extending covered alleyways are the booths of the various craftsmen-leather workers, beaters of copper and silver, the traditional inlaid brass work associated with the Mediterranean litoral,

more reminiscent of an Arab market or Souk, than of modern Turkey.

The vendors all speak some English, or have someone who does, and they press tourists to buy, as is expected. We are able to resist their tempting blandishments by saying that we cannot possibly take anything all round Eastern Turkey, and that we wish to see things, not buy them.

Istanbul makes much play of being astride two continents, and as most Europeans have never been to Asia, the afternoon excursion to Scutari is popular. On our afternoon, the Dolmabahce Palace on the European side, was open. From here the last Sultan departed in a British warship, and here, later, Kemal Ataturk died in 1938.

But as an extra charge was made to see it, none of the party agreed to go. In consequence we did not see the palatial Ballroom which should have been the climax, in May 1967, to an excursion from Paris to Istanbul.

The Dolmabahce Palace was the last used by the Sultans, until Ataturk forced the last Ottoman Sultan to depart, for Malta and exile. For a night in 1967, it almost attained something of its former splendour, for a Ball was arranged to be given by the City of Paris for the guests of the Train that never was.

There were to have been 150 of them, in an "Excursion Exceptionel" organised by Comte Guy de Casteja, who had arranged with the Wagons-Lits to plan it for him. It was to be a re-enactment of a group travel arrangement that took place between 15th and 18th April 1891. A Railway Cruise; but it never took place, for one of those unexplained reasons which, even today, gives the Company its air of faint mystique - the very opposite of Public Relations in the accepted sense. One of the Directors remarked to me several years back that the Company had no Public Relations, as the world know the term. He ought to know for he invented Public Relations himself, for the Southern Railway, in 1925, where he became the world's first P.R.O. This is now changed. The Company's P.R.O. is very go-ahead, the desire to modernise and the change of name has brought it about; or perhaps Sir John Elliot's presence on the Board has had something to do with it. At all events, though Sur Les Traces de L'Orient Express did not come off, in 1968 details of the allocation of berths in the ordinary sleepers was made public for the very first time, and is partially set out in the appendix!

Monsieur de Casteja's Cruise should have left on the 29th April 1967. But instead of taking three days, they were to have arrived in Istanbul on 11th May. Leaving on a Saturday night, they would have spent the Sunday in Munich, then gone overnight to Prague, spending all the rest of Monday 1st and Tuesday 2nd in Prague (sleeping in the train). Then on 3rd May they were to leave after luncheon, arriving about seven in the evening at Vienna. The 4th and 5th of May were to be spent at Vienna, and, one week after leaving Paris, they were to leave early Saturday morning for Budapest. The rest of 6th May and Sunday 7th were to be passed in the Hungarian capital, and on the evening of Monday 8th, depart for Belgrade, spending Tuesday 9th there. Then overnight to Sofia, arriving in the morning and leaving about 5 in the evening, with dinner in a Bulgarian dining car, the only one used on the train, apparently. On Thursday 11th May they were to reach Istanbul and stay until 15th when they would return - by air. The climax was the Grand Ball, the 'Thousand and Second Night, the Night of Paris" at the Dolmabahce Palace. The

Krupp diesel shunter at Haydarpasa ferry berth.
Photo: J.H. Price.

train was to be composed of Wagons-Lits stock only comprising Sleeping cars, a "wagon-boutique" and "L'Orient Express Sleeping Club" which was a voiture salon-bar, a spare one from the Blue Train, no doubt, for which the Company converted three Pullman cars. Unfortunately the coupon attached to the folder of the 1883 train did not produce (for me at any rate) the precise cars which would be attached. There were to have been happenings all along the route, and the Bar Car was arranged as a Voiture-Bar-Dancing, according to such information as was disclosed to agents. The decor, the atmosphere, the fetes and festivals of this 'Belle époque' were to have been recreated down to the minutest detail (i.e. Viennese Waltzes, Blue Danube, Tzigany music etc.) while the public's brochure referred to the Fairy Castle on the Bosphorus. The whole thing was to have been filmed as well.

From our hotel, the hills of Asiatic Turkey loom mysteriously by day, and twinkle with illumination after dark. On arrival at the Asiatic shore, only the Istanbul trams made any notable difference to the scenery, which looked otherwise the same as the rest of the city. Now the trams are gone. We found vast numbers of them in the depot which needed only some 25 cars in service, the remainder displaced from European Istanbul, but all were for sale. Later, after seeing over Haydarpasa works, in company with Monsieur Erman, we went to interview the head of the Istanbul Transport Company about their sale. We were received courteously enough, with the inevitable cups of Turkish coffee, but we were fortunate in having Monsieur Erman with us to interpret. The manager was clearly suspicious of all foreigners, whether interested in his old trams or not, and though we advertised their sale, in an appropriate place, even London wrote and said were we joking, because they had accepted our advertisement! We had visions of ardent tram enthusiasts writing off demanding lists of makers, dates, seating, trucks, the lot! This was not available, in fact only a few seem to have survived the scrap heap as roadside information kiosks at the frontier posts; yet even these may be a myth. Such is the way in which one can be flummoxed by Turkish conversation.

The afternoon tour to Scutari, took us first to the summit of Camlice Hill. Here there is a radar establishment, controlling the lower end of the Bosphorus shipping, for from it there is a view over all Istanbul, the Princes Islands, the Sea of Marmara approaches, and the Golden Horn. Then the coach took us along the Bosphorus on the Asian side past the fortress opposite the

Rumel Hisar fort, which between them guard the narrowest point, protected on both north and south by blind corners of the waterway. We went as far as Yenikoy, and on the return journey we were overtaken by a Russian cargo vessel, such is the speed attainable by shipping following the current.

Our return route took us through a tunnel under the Sea cadet college, the Turks equivalent to Dartmouth. This must not be confused with the quarter of Istanbul called Tunel. on the European side, next to Beyoglu. The Tunel Railway was built about 1925 and consists of ancient wooden coaches formed into trains, hauled up a steep incline from the waterside at Karakoy (near the Galata Bridge) to the top station Tunel, on the Istiklai Caddesi. Here the Transport offices are situated, and across the road, a large factory type chimney belching smoke, dominates the boiler house driving the stationary steam engine that works the Tunel Railway's cables. There is nothing like this, anywhere else in Turkey, which can also be said of all Istanbul itself. Even Cooks sightseeing tours are different at Istanbul from anywhere else in Europe. The coaches provided are newly built by Mercedes Benz, painted in a shade of royal blue in line with the company's colours, with Wagons-Lits//Cook on the side; for Cooks tours in Istanbul are made in Wagons-Lits own coaches, not those of some subsidiary or contractor.

Despite the overall sense of harshness, Istanbul seems a happy city. Life is harsh on the many Turks who pour into the city, and find housing problems; on the sick and maimed who have no welfare state; on the boatmen, plying every sort of boat, on the travellers in the long distance coaches, praying to Allah not to crash. Above it all there is beauty in the harshness, especially in the vividness of the colours - the Turkish Maritime Lines ships are blinding white, the sea deep blue, the land bare and brown, the buildings dazzling, and the orange coloured sunsets unbelievable. It comes up to expectations, even after thirty years of dreaming about going there.

The journey on the Turkish Blue Train is certainly the highlight of the whole visit. The vision of various people, far from Turkey, hinting "he only went to Turkey to go on it" - did nothing to tarnish the excitement of actually starting; though it must be admitted that they vied with the romantic scenery for capturing my imagination. The Bosphorus is one of these few places, like Venice, that does not disappoint in reality. The view is indeed very striking, and on the Haydarpasa ferry is more sensational than on the car ferry to Uskudar. This is because it crosses more diagonally, and nearer to the mouth of the Bosphorus, presenting a splendid vista of the Blue Mosque and Topkapi Palace.

On board the Ferry there is time to pause, away from the bustle of the city, away from cars, to ruminate for a minute or two on the almost eternally long time that civilisation of a sort has existed here. Europe, old and war-torn, visibly and actually recedes, the city's minarets rising in all their majesty, in the evening Mediterranean style sunset. It is a good idea to let imagination run wild on this last bastion of civilised Europe, still symbolised in 1966 by the word "Europeens" on the train about to greet us. For in fact this boat is but an unprepossessing ferry; possibly as romantic as the Wallasey sort in beat-struck Liverpool. In reality, the Bosphorus is choppy, the Ferry seems small. It will be nice to get ashore, without the diversion of an accident. The new bridge, in the planning stage at present, will be a great boon.

Turn and look the other way, at the imposing building that is Haydarpasa Terminus. So few are the large buildings hereabouts that Haydarpasa finds its niche in anyone's description of the city, whether interested in trains or not. Like St. Pancras in London, it commands attention, though (just like St. Pancras), perhaps it is not really worthy of the fuss it receives. Once the headquarters of the Anatolian Railway (and the Baghdad Railway) it is now housing merely the First Division of the Turkish State Railways.

The building's position makes it conspicuous, and the oriental-style windows of its pompous facade, if anything, enhance the nature of its non-Turkish origin. Inside, there are a number of island platforms, with borders of flowers, and at one of them, five sleepers and a diner are drawn up.

Pointed out by many to be the only train of exclusively Wagons-Lits stock, outside France or Italy, in fact the Anatolia Express has seven ordinary coaches and a van, marshalled beyond the dining car. This accounts for the change of name in 1965 back from "Ankara Express" to "Anatolia" which it was first called in 1926. In those far off days it was indeed made up of only the Company's cars. The sleeping cars themselves, gleaming and spotless, are a model of Wagons-Lits service. They are all full, too, and often supplementary cars are needed, though permission is not always given for them to be run. They were built specially for Turkey, in Belgium, just after World War II, and the fans in the cabins are a feature not found in the sleepers serving Sirkeci station. We hand over our railway ticket and permits to the conductor, and then wander off to explore the further side of the sleeping cars, thereby upsetting our official send-off party, whom we are not expecting, but who have come specially to tell us that our revised arrangements, due to the line blockage at Mus, are in order.

Next we are ushered into the diner, by the Chef de Section at Haydarpasa. He speaks French, and he has just time to tell us that one of the Controlleurs de Route, Mr. Halim Imre, is coming with us, when the train starts. Only then does he explain that he himself is not coming with us, and jumps off! Everything about this diner exudes old-style luxury, for which Wagons-Lits diners have long been famous.

What a dinner! It begins with toast and mutton cheese, accompanied by vodka. Then, excellent chicken soup, followed by tender escalops of veal, done in Parisian style, for the Turkish cooks of the Wagons-Lits were proud of their Parisian associations. The meat is marvellously tender, and done beautifully, with proper potatoes (memories of Egypt made me fear lest they be sweet ones), and Turkish red wine, called Dikmen, of Burgundy type, bottled in Ankara and grown in that district. The next course was as Turkish as the previous one pure French, light puff pastry, sweetened; quite the lightest I have ever tasted. Its Turkish name is baklava. I assume that this passes for the sweet, for the meal has already seen four courses, but no. The climax to this elegant repast is a superb peach melba, and everyone is offered two helpings. It is all quite splendid, in harmony with the glittering Birmingham brass of the heavy dining car which has proper chairs, and linen napery which gleams, bright as the glasses and cutlery. All contrast to the very dark night beyond the windows, obscuring the wild Asiatic shore.

Only by shielding the eyes against the reflection of all this finery, is it possible to peer out at the Sea of Marmara on the right. On the left there is the high rock cutting of the corniche. Outside, the mysteries of unknown Asia Minor; inside, "the luxury service that Turkey can do without".

Taurus Express beside the Sea of Marmara, 1958, with Henschel-built 2-8-2 no. 46052.
Photo: W. Middleton.

Left: Istanbul - Haydarpasa station, 1966 'Bogazici' diesel, and steam train.
Photo: P. Ransome-Wallis.

Below: T18 class 4-6-4T at Haydarpasa, used on suburban trains.
Photo: P. Ransome-Wallis.

Thus Turkey's Minister of Communications and Transport, referring to the Wagons-Lits contract, which, after forty years, expired at the end of 1966. I reflect on this as I enjoy myself to the full, conscious of the heavy deficit on the diners, which was shared 50-50 between the Company and the Railways, until, with the implementation of the new contract in April, 1967, the diners were wholly handed to the TCDD to run. Let us hope they are just as good as ever.

Although the Anatolia Express does not leave until 20.40, the inconvenience of finding the beds made up is avoided. This is done while the clients are dining. Turkish conductors work harder than their European counterparts, and the crack Anatolia Express is the only one where the total journey takes only one night from Haydarpasa. It takes twelve hours, so that there is ample time to savour the full splendour of this luxury train, which is so very inexpensive compared with those elsewhere. Calls are made at Bostanci and Pendik, two of the many suburban stations along the shore, but two hours pass before the train quits the Sea of Marmara at lzmit.

The Gulf of lzmit, some thirty miles long, is narrow, so that looking at most maps of Turkey, it is not easily realised what a barrier it makes to proceeding south from Istanbul. lzmit has a rail connected port, and the town also has a small chemical works. Swampy ground east of the head of the gulf keeps the railway going eastward to Arifiye, which is the junction for Adapazari, only five miles away down a branch.

Adapazari was the scene of an earthquake in 1967. This is an important market town, on the main Istanbul-Ankara road, and it is intended one day to make a new cut-off line on to Ankara, avoiding Eskisehir. In 1966 a contract for the electrification of the Haydarpasa-Adapazari line was let to a Hungarian firm, and when it is completed Arifiye will become an engine-changing point. At the moment, the Anatolia Express only stops two minutes at Arifiye, as there is no connection from Adapazari. Arifiye is just under three hours run from Haydarpasa, and by the time it is reached, most people are turning in.

Not travelling in the hindmost sleeper, we hear and see nothing of the great tank engine that comes on at Bilecik. In the dark we have left the Ak Ova plain behind at Arifiye, which is 118 feet above sea level, and climbed up the Sakarya valley, first through the Baleban gorge, then across the Akhisar plain, which grows tobacco, mulberries and plenty of corn, and then up another narrower gorge past Vezirhan, where the sides reach up 300 feet above the train to Bilecik, which is 965 feet up. The town is five kilometres to the north.

We now climb up the side of the Central Plateau which forms the heart of Turkey, rising some 1280 feet in 10 miles, up a gradient of 1 in 40. At Karakoy the banker comes off, I believe (it is very skilfully driven, achieving its object without disturbing the sleeper passengers), after which the line goes on rising more gently to the summit, a short way before Inonu station (2743 feet up). Eskisehir is some thirty miles further on.

Presently it is light again, and looking out of the window we have our first view of the real Turkey: arid and rocky, the Anatolian Plateau has great ranging fields of sparse productivity. We come upon a barracks where Turkish soldiery are doing physical training, naked to the waist although it is only a quarter to seven in the morning, and the upland air has a noticeable nip in it.

We pause at the station beyond the barracks, serving a town. This is Polatli, ninety miles from Ankara, and the last place of importance before the capital. No doubt this accounts for the army; handily available, but (politely) out of sight. There are several more stops on the way, and so there is plenty of time to get up, wash, shave, and have breakfast in the diner before arrival. After the manner of diners in luxury trains of the old days, this one runs all night, the crew sleeping on portable beds.

For breakfast there are the customary toast, cheese and olives, together with deliciously sweet, syrupy strawberry jam, and honey. There is also fruit cake. Turkey may be a poor country, but its people are so far the only ones I have met who put Marie Antoinette's dictum into practice! Black olives and fruit cake for breakfast apparently work as a way of slimming, too!

Outside the Anatolian plain rolls away to a crest on the horizon; half dried up rivers disect it. It is not easy to get a clear picture of the topography. The landscape seems endless. From time to time the train passes through a small crest, now in cutting, now in a short tunnel. Then the scenery repeats itself. Every so often the old line, built under a kilometre guarantee and therefore

Y class car interior with double windows, Anatolia Express.
(Intercommunicating doors open).

meandering on every occasion, has been abandoned for a newer track, shorter, with easier curves. There are lineside trees at every station, but these peter out between stations as the land is too barren to support trees everywhere.

Towards Ankara the line becomes more hilly, as the train follows the river Ankara valley. There are oil depots, factories, and other signs of approaching a modern metropolis. Roads are more plentiful, and all the main ones are tarred in this part of Turkey, while up in front, the mournful hoot of our engine becomes more prevalent than during the previous night. Punctual to the minute, the Anadolu Ekspresi (as the Anatolia is called in Turkish) slips quietly into its allotted

2-10-2T no. 5703, used for banking at Bilecik.
Photo: D. Trevor Rowe.

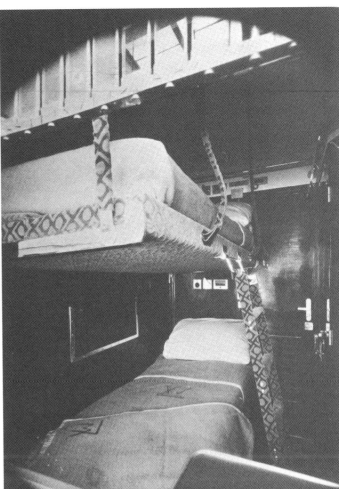

Y class single compartment, Anatolia Express.

Y class double-berth compartment, Anatolia Express.
Photographs courtesy of CIWL.

platform at Ankara - the grand one alongside the high booking hall. Large and overbearing, the station seems to symbolise the large and overbearing Turkish capital, which foreign diplomats describe as the dullest to which they have ever had the misfortune to be posted.

Not to visit Ankara, if only for a day, is to miss something of the Turkish character and way of life. Nevertheless miss it out by all means, if time is short: Turkish ports and coastal resorts strike me, at any rate, as infinitely more attractive. There is nothing really 'oriental' about Ankara; it is utterly Turkish. Compare, for

Bilecik shed and the Anatolian Plateau.
Photo: D. Trevor Rowe.

example, the placid, leisurely, ordered way in which the traveller is met by a porter, and his luggage placed in a taxi, outside Ankara's modern station, with the mad free-for-all with dragomen and taxi drivers jockeying for position, touting and hustling the passengers at Istanbul.

In Ankara all is spacious and serene. There are wide boulevards, stretching for an eternity, which you may cross without the constant fear, as in Istanbul, that you may be cut down by a passing motorist. On the boulevards, there are excellent shops, though most of them turn out to be branch establishments of Istanbul houses. The taxis in Ankara do not overcharge as they sometimes do at Istanbul, and the hotels are generally less expensive. They are none-the-less excellent modern establishments with every kind of European-style comfort. The Barikan is a typical example, with an open air bar and a garden restaurant, where your mutton is grilled, Turkish style, on a spit. The restaurants too, are numerous and excellent; but the atmosphere is totally lacking in gaiety. Instead, it is intensely purposeful. The city hums with studiousness; new and large, its greatness is physical, strong and hard like Attaturk, the man who created it, whose regulation portrait hangs dutifully in every one of the offices that are the reason why most visitors find themselves in the city. People, in Ankara, are very busy governing, and there is a great deal to see to. Clean, tidy and restrained (even in its Coca Cola advertisements), set down apparently miles from anywhere, Ankara cannot in any sense be regarded as provincial, like the small fortified citadel which is now Old Ankara.

Every other town has old associations, ancient history shared with many other races, such as Hittites, Greeks, Armenians, Nestorians, Romans. Ankara's sights for visitors include the sombre mausoleum of Mustapha Kemal Ataturk, whose spirit pervades his capital still. Though communications are long and difficult over mountainous terrain, though much power is vested locally, nevertheless the regional centres are as tightly knit to the capital as in Britain. There is something perhaps mid-western, about the dusty, spacious streets. There are uniforms every-

A view of Ankara Station! Photo: P. Ransome-Wallis.

where. Surrounded by hardworking, industrious Turks, foreigners visiting Ankara for this, that, and the other permission, are left with the feeling that there is a lot more going on than perhaps they know about. The Turks deliberately created Ankara to break free of the cosmopolitan atmosphere of Istanbul.

In the city there is an intense feeling of security. There are ubiquitous armed policemen, a reminder that the Turks came safely through what they call the 'Revolution' of 1960. But the policemen are cheerful, the citizens helpful and the traditional Turkish courtesy and kindliness extends also to the officials, all moving at their own pace in their own way, and arriving at their own conclusions, which they may, or again may not, choose to impart! For example, we had come all this way to emphasize the opportunities of railway travel in Turkey to foreign visitors, especially those who take an enthusiastic delight in railway matters on all sorts. Yet no mention at all was made of the existence of the miniature railway outside the station in a nearby

Childrens' Railway, Ankara. 2-8-2 no. KL 46002. Photo: D. Trevor Rowe.

park, nor would we have known of it, but for a chance remark made in London.

The straightforward layout of the railway lines at Ankara station, symbolise the city, where Eastern and Western Turkey join. Eastern Turkey has been shut for many years to foreigners, whereas Western Turkey has been systematically developed for tourism.

On arrival at Ankara, we repair to the Wagons-Lits Section office, whence telephone calls are made, prior to visiting the TCDD Headquarters, which are situated alongside the station building. In the main hall, incidentally, there are some splendid models of locomotives and equipment. First we visit Fahir Bilce, the Turkish State Railways indefatigable Secretary General, who has time for everybody, and does his own work by the expedient of being in his office for fourteen hours a day, or longer. He it was who issued our yellow permit which had worked such wonders at Istanbul, in passing us through the Customs. We emerge from our visit armed with a further yellow permit for travel all over Turkey,

except where the Varto earthquake had disrupted the lines near Mus. We are also provided with a visiting card in French and another in Turkish, with some Turkish inscription on the back, commanding whom it may concern to telephone to the Secretary General over the railway network, immediately. In fact we did not have to use it once. There was of course the custom of serving Turkish coffee to us, in tiny cups, brought in by one of the 'passage hangers'. Every official seems to have a retinue of people loitering in the passage outside, who barricade him and his secretaries from outsiders. Fahir Bilce disregarded the system to some extent, and people constantly drifted in and out of his office.

We also visit Mr. Hekimgil, then Secretary for Tourism, who is grander than when he visited Jersey, when he was kind enough to suggest the project. When we have got the better of his "passage men" and actually meet him, we find his attitude to rail travel in Turkey more understanding than that of some people. It is regarded as additional to the recognised ways to go about Turkey, by air, car, bus or ship. Having paid our courtesy visit, we are

directed to another office to another official of Tourism.

Our first destination is Kars, centre of one of Turkey's least developed areas. It is quite obvious that the Tourism authorities are none too keen for us to see it. Nevertheless the official assures us that there is an hotel there, and they will reserve rooms in it for us on the next day, whilst we are travelling, since it takes some time to ring through on the telephone to a city 855 miles away to the east. If necessary they will arrange for the Governor to meet us in a jeep. This strikes me as an excessively hospitable welcome, when all I want is the name of an hotel, which for some reason is not on the hotel list. "It is the Kars Hotel" he said.

Eastern Turkey is not for those who cannot bear the unexpected, the unusual. For those whose idea of a holiday is simply to go to some beach and laze in the sun, where everything is laid on exactly like the brochure, the places described further on in this book - Izmir, Kusadasi, Mersin, for example, are ideal. If anything, they turn out to be slightly more luxurious and sophisticated than the modest brochures suggest. Nowadays there are very few areas left to 'explore' by train in any degree of comfort, for there seems to me to be really no comfort in going to a place where the inhabitants are hostile to foreigners, and where the police are officious; Eastern Turkey is not one of these.

We leave the luxurious Barikan Hotel for the station some two miles distant, in a taxi which costs about seven shillings. We arrive about quarter to eight in the morning and on the platform we again meet Mr. Imre, who is apparently coming with us on all our journeys by sleeping car. The 'Dogu Ekspresi', overnight from Istanbul, arrives on time, shortly before the Anatolia Express is due, so it cannot use the grand platform by the main entrance, but is allotted one of the others. The train's name, 'Eastern Express', imparts a vague feeling of adventure. No sooner has it come in, than shunting begins, so that the leisurely half hour shown in the timetable for people to get in or out of the sleeper, which of course is right at the back of the train, is reduced to a few minutes at the platform. The Turks apparently run their trains Russian style, that is, one train to each long distance destination, or sometimes two, in each twenty-four hours. The shunting enables extra coaches for Ankara passengers to join the train.

Up in front the diesel of Western Turkey gives way to a great steam engine. Eventually all these will burn oil, but for the moment on this part of the system, many still use coal.

We are still waiting to start, when the Anatolia Express draws in from Istanbul, and eventually we set off about twenty minutes late. In the suburbs of Ankara, some small boys were amusing themselves, throwing stones at passing trains without getting caught. They score a direct bullseye on our sleeper, fortunately without breaking the window-pane. The nice little cast brass notice "Pencereden Sarkmak Yasaktir", which finds its place beside the others, the familiar standard kind that say "Dangerous to Lean Out" in English, French, German and Italian (as you can see any day in the Night Ferry at Victoria), takes on a slightly different meaning; not that it stops us leaning out.

The buffet car, which separates us from the train's ordinary passengers, is one of the Turkish State Railways converted second-class coaches, which the Wagons-Lits company worked up until 1966. Turkish coffee, served from it in the compartments, makes a welcome break and also serves as an opportunity for Mr. Imre to introduce another of the Controlleurs de Route, the roaming inspectors of the Wagons-Lits who ensure that all is in order. The limitations of our phrase book are soon apparent - it gives everything possible that a motorist may by remotest chance need to know, but to try and explain in pidgin Turkish that our sleeper is, as it happens, one of the first all-steel blue and gold cars built in Leeds (England) for the original Blue Train from Calais to the Riviera, takes an astonishing length of time. This kind of thing appears to interest the two controllers, both of whom have been twenty five years with the Company, but are only vaguely aware of what happens outside Turkey.

The topography remains confusing. Much of it is rounded hills, almost desert, hot and arid in summer, snow-clad in winter. The principal river is the Kizil Irmak which sweeps upstream in a crescent shaped course, only partially suitable for the line to follow. There are three rivers called Irmak, just as there are three rivers called Avon in Britain. There is nothing extraordinary about this, for Irmak means river in Turkish, just as Avon (Afon) does in Welsh.

There is also a town called Irmak, junction for the line to Zonguldak, which follows the Kizil Irmak down stream at first. Our route lies at first upstream, and then to cut off the corner formed by the river's crescent shape, it goes up a tributary past Kirikkale. Here there is a munitions factory, and an interesting collection of ancient four-wheeled coaches to take the workers from the station over the Government line into the works.

A few tunnels bring us into the valley of Delice Irmak. Though the line undulates, the rises and falls are only a few hundred feet, in the first 300 kilometres from Ankara. To get back into the Kizil Irmak valley, after Pasali, it drops down nearly 1,000 feet, and once in the valley, life looks much more fertile. The hedges of poplar trees, and great dusty fields, some full of melons, others of sun flowers, others again of maize, alternate with barren fields and those areas where Angora goats scratch a living among the scrub.

In the villages, the harvest has been gathered in, and threshing is going on in the same manner as in biblical times, driving oxen dragging a board round and round on the hard earth floor, to smash the husks against each other, and release the grain. After this ancient and arduous labour (complete with gleaners) the corn is put into ultra-modern, gleaming aluminium silos! These are found at every stop. The villages are thus able to store food and either receive it if they are deficient, or send off any surplus. The silos are Government owned and controlled, mostly through the Villayet or provincial authorities. All are served by railway sidings, and it is easy to see how the railways are the lifelines of the country.

Eastern European time, two hours ahead of Greenwich, means early nights. Three kilometres before Bogazkopru we come to the apex of the triangular junction with the line now taken by the Taurus Express to reach Adana, which forks to our right. Our line runs into Bogazkopru station where it is joined by the third arm of the triangle, fifteen kilometres before the important town of Kayseri.

Thirteen miles away, the Erciyas Dag, a distinctive mountain (see photograph) rises 9,400 feet above the town. The plain down below is fertile, because of the streams flowing from the mountains, which are a continuation of the Taurus chain. The ford across the Kizil Irmak here, and the junction of the two routes just mentioned, made Kayseri important centuries before the railway age. There are large cotton mills, and other factories, though the town is also a great market for the area. In the plain they grow vines, wheat and barley, also sugar beet and rye. The Turks are great people for sugar growing, which they use liberally in coffee, and in Turkish Delight. These two national dishes are so much taken for granted, that one forgets that the ingredients have to come from somewhere.

Kayseri was at one time the capital of Cappadocia. It has had a harsh history, becoming Christian in 257 AD and subsequently massacred by Persians, plundered by Seljuk Turks and Mongols, but in the late nineteenth century Christians were still surviving in small numbers. The name Caesarea, given to the town by the Romans, seems to have survived too, though the Turks give it their own spelling and pronunciation.

We do not see much of the place, because it is dark, The town's lights give the impression of a large sized place, and indeed it has several good hotels. The visitors come to see Urgup which has a number of early churches, hollowed out of caves, and adorned with sixth and eleventh century frescos, and also the curious rock formation at Goreme, as the district is called around Urgup. These are conical shaped rocks, sometimes with a flat stone on top, and early Christians used them as homes, hollowing out living space in them. The nearest station to Urgup is the one after Bogazkopru, going towards Adana. It is therefore necessary to hire a car or go by bus, to visit these caves and churches. The latest tourist hotel, opening in 1968, is built in cave style; taps in the bedrooms spout red and white wine as well as h. & c.!

In the Dogu Express, dinner is served after leaving Kayseri. The buffet car has a very limited seating capacity, as most Turkish folk bring their own food with them when travelling; so half the car is given over to ordinary second-class passengers. Tomato soup is followed by shaslik (mutton on skewers) with black olives, rice and salad. For sweet, there is a combination of water melons and ordinary melons. The Ankara Kavak white wine is available, and Turkish beer; also bottled water. Turkish beer is a good substitute for water in places where the bottling is doubtful. On the dining cars, the water is only put aboard at Haydarpasa.

The hot day and the delicious meal combine with the leisurely pace, 30-40 miles per hour, to induce sound sleep. Looking out next morning, the scenery is completely changed. We are travelling along the Atma gorge of the upper Euphrates, where the scenery is not merely impressive, but frightening. There are bridges of every description; stone, reinforced concrete, underslung, and box-girder; there are frequent tunnels, too. The success of the engineers in forcing a railway through this mountainous and earthquake-prone terrain is more apparent, perhaps, than in the Alps. In Switzerland or Austria, there is a greater sense of magnificence, than of struggle.

The echoing rock walls reverberate to the lusty passage of our locomotive. Here the inhabitants live in wooden houses sprung from the rock, picturesque but primitive, and very different from the mud-brick dwellings of the plains. The name of this particular village is not shown, though it is probably Bagistas.

After an extremely tricky piece of gorge, the valley widens out at a more fertile spot, Eric, where we stop again. Stops are frequent, on average two per hour. For livelihood, the inhabitants here rely on sparse fruit trees and a few cultivated fields.

Some ideas of the engineering features of this line may be gained by mentioning that there are fourteen tunnels in the 17 km immediately preceding Eric, and a further sixteen tunnels in the next 50 km to Erzincan.

By breakfast time we are on a great plain, with Erzincan at this end of it. The plain is surrounded by mountains at a distance, but it is flat and rich, and continues most of the way to Erzurum. There is no road through the gorge by which we have come, indeed there is barely room for the railway, which requires the constant attention of platelaying and engineering staff. At Erzincan we rejoin the road, and the large town has many modern government buildings. Once it was an Armenian town, until the massacre; the Turks in turn suffered grievously in the 1939 earthquake when 10,000 people died, and much of the town was destroyed. It has been restored with a Turkish doggedness and perseverance that becomes more noteworthy, the further one penetrates into the interior of their large country. Surrounding the town is fertile land, with orchards as well as fields of corn.

The two hundred kilometres on to Erzurum takes up the morning. About 11 a.m. near Askale, Mount Ararat briefly comes into view on the right. Its snow-covered peak is unmistakable, but it is so far away, that it is easy to understand how it can also be seen in Russia. Lunch is served early, as the dining car does not go beyond Erzurum. Though we understood he was accompanying us everywhere, we learn that Mr. Imre is not going any further

either; we discover that he has never been to Kars. Steak and chips - 'Mode Paris', as Mr. Imre puts it, throw us into total confusion as we try desperately to translate these words, and can find neither 'Mode' nor 'Paris' in the Turkish part of our dictionary. There follows beans, hot peppers, stuffed meat, pastry and spaghetti. Mr. Imre who has donned a white apron and cooked the steaks for us himself, has effectively given us the impression that we will not eat again, until rejoining the diner the following evening.

As we approach Erzurum, it is noticeable that the city has much more primitive mud hut dwellings than the single storey mud brick houses met with so far. The bullock carts have solid wooden wheels, as they have had since time immemorial. Motor cars are few. Erzurum is six thousand feet up, standing on a hill slightly above the station, dominated by a large mosque. As a cross-roads, it is an old and important centre, for here our route crosses the road from Trabzon, on the Black Sea Coast, to Persia.

Erzurum is the capital of Eastern Turkey, so it has an airport and a large garrison, mostly quartered in the great citadel. It also has a large new and modern university, named, of course, after Attaturk. When it was opened on 15th November, 1958, the Wagons-Lits ran two special trains, one from Haydarpasa and the other from Ankara. In the second of these, which had five sleepers and an ex-Pullman diner (No.4052, a Wagons-Lits Co. vehicle built originally for the Paris-Calais Golden Arrow) Mr. Imre presided over the kitchen. 35,272.75 liras were apparently spent on food and drink on the journey!

For Turkish students, the great thing is to go to Istanbul university. Here all the delights of the city are theirs for the asking. Though the education is a good one, to get sent to Attaturk university, Erzurum, is what the students really dread. For the place is harsh-looking, rough and scruffy. There is absolutely nothing to do there apart from work, though no doubt as a capital it boasts a good restaurant or two. Perhaps the great mountains to the south have something to do with the shut-in, banished feeling that Erzurum ought to shake off, but somehow does not.

Withal it is not a bit as one imagines, from reading Buchan's Greenmantle, and without Greenmantle would the Anglo-Saxons remember Erzurum? What appalling hardships everybody must have suffered in World War I, boggles the imagination, when the place at peace looks as hard as this city does. The snow would soon be coming, and up in the mountains lay Varto, victim of what at the time was the latest earthquake.

Leaving Erzurum, where a forty minute pause is included for shunting off some of the coaches (including Mr. Imre and the buffet), our lightened train starts off almost through the town, with houses on each side of the track. Almost one could say it runs through the street, though there is no street. Here we leave the Euphrates, the Kara Su (black water) as the Turks call it, and climb round some of the hills that enclose Erzurum's valley. The hills are covered with Turkish troops on manoeuvres, and how they have persuaded their six-wheel American trucks to disperse over the rocky ground without overturning, is a tribute to their skilful driving. Obviously bored stiff, and waiting to bivouac by their lorries for the night, they take pleasure in waving to us as we go by. The soldiers are almost all conscripts, and are never aloof from the people.

We pass through some tunnels and descend into the Araxes valley, going along a plain which seems even greyer and dustier than the Euphrates valley. This is because the surface is mostly covered in lava from the extinct volcanoes of these parts, which form most of the mountains. Most noticeably, the river is flowing away from Turkey - that is, in the same direction as we are travelling.

Our sleeper is now almost empty. The conductor, a young man who speaks only Turkish, has withdrawn to the end of the car, where he stays firmly in his corridor armchair. In the third class compartment next door, the sole remaining of the three occupants is a man with a limp. He explains that he lives in Kars, and offers us various items to eat. He thrusts some caraway seed bread at us, which we have seen dropped on the ash-ridden ground by the vendor at a wayside station from whom he bought it. Along with his bread-fruit, it zooms out of our window, the instant his back is turned in the corridor, a shoddy western way of accepting his gen-

General view of Kars from Citadel, looking south. The railway station is in the far background (and inset right). Courtesy of Turkish Tourism.

erous Turkish hospitality. All Turks seem to have an interminable capacity for eating, and he is no exception.

The man tells us he is a retired army captain, but for one retired, it is extraordinary how he seems to know everybody along the line. Station masters greet him personally, at almost every stop, while between stations, the Captain keeps making forays into the first class half of the car, beyond our compartment, where a lady in black is travelling alone.

After Horasan, our line leaves the river, which continues its way to Erevan, and climbs north, into the mountains, which begin as rounded hills. The bed of the former narrow gauge railway is easily seen beside the line, though later on our larger requirements necessitate moving away from the old course of the former railway. It is easy to see, from the topography, why the Russians chose a narrow gauge for this military supply line to Erzurum; they must have had a terrible time building it by hand.

The retired captain indicates to us that the lady speaks a little French. She too, it seems, is staying in Kars.

"Are we sure there is an hotel?" she asks us.

"Oh, yes", we say reassuringly, "quite certain. The Tourism people have telephoned for reservations . Nevertheless it seems an odd question.

"We will share a car if you wish", says the lady next. The idea of having someone who speaks a little something is attractive. The sun has gone down behind the harsh, bare mountainside. As we climb, the staccato beat of the steam engine is loud in its efforts up the grade.

The lady explains that she has come on the train from Istanbul,

and that she is going to stay with her relations for a fortnight. She does not know where they live in Kars, and she must find them in the morning. This sounds a little mysterious; still, I thank her for suggesting that we will share a taxi to the hotel; there is probably only one.

"Taxi?" she says disdainfully, with all the pride of Istanbul, "There are no taxis".

"No taxis? But you said share a car".

"No, no; carriage; horse-cab" she withdrew diffidently into her cabin, while I thought of western tourists who paid, in far off Vienna, to show off by hiring a horse-cab instead of a taxi.

At - was it Topdagi? - we wait at the head of the pass for a train coming the other way. Quite suddenly fir forests have begun. Perhaps this part of the country was Russian until 1918, and so the Turks have not yet cut down this forest. For Kars too was Russian until then, when the Bolsheviks made peace with Turkey after the revolution, and handed it over.

We plunge into a long tunnel, stuffy and smoke laden from the train we have just crossed; then we emerge among the fir trees in the moonlight. In this remote forest there are certainly wolves, and bears too, very likely. Miles from anywhere we stop; then cautiously go on again, past a red oil lamp, dangling from a post. Somebody must have lit it, though there is no other sign of human life at all - not so much as a hut or even a tent beside the desolate railway. It is altogether eerie, and presently the train stops again, by another red lamp.

"All descending goods trains must stop dead here", is what it would say, on a nice metal board, if this were the West of England or Wales. The Turks did not find any need for a notice, you would soon be really dead if you did get out here. No wonder the train takes an hour and a quarter for this part of the line. Every other line in the Turkish timetable shows the distances; not this one. Even Cooks Timetable - dare I point it out - appears to have a misprint in the distance from Horasan to Kars, which is all of 180 miles.

Round a bend, below us, some twinkling lights appear ahead. We run into a station with a large goods yard. This must be Sarikamis, once the starting point of the narrow gauge, and the terminus of the Russian gauge (5 ft.) line from Leninakan through Kars, which the Turks have converted to standard gauge, as far as the frontier.

After a pause here, the train sets off again into the dark, for the final stage, taking but an hour and twenty minutes, including two stops. Our bags are packed, ready to leave this hospitable and familiar sleeper for the strange unknown. As we rumble on over the rail joints every thirty feet or so, the words at the beginning of Grand European Expresses come ruefully home to roost "In the days when horse and mule drawn cabs were found in the station yards..."

At the third stop, the train appears to be in a siding. There are no lights to be seen at all, anywhere. The young conductor puts his head through the open door of our compartment:

"Kars , he says laconically, taking one of our bags to the end of the corridor. We tumble out into the dark, to pause uncertainly among the cinders. The Turkish lady beseeches us to wait. She is surrounded by a vast array of packages, a tidily large sample of the "flesh-pots of Istanbul", reminding me of the way we used to load up in Cairo for life up the desert.

Two young Turks appear from nowhere, and the Captain despatches one of them in search of the carriages. There appears to be no sign of life at all - no lights, no people, no horse-cabs. After the bright interior of the sleeper we slowly become accustomed to the pale moon and the stars; gradually we are able to see more clearly the dim outline of some trucks on the adjacent line. We wait for a very long time, and the conductor courteously waits with us. I notice that he does not bother to put his kepi on, which at other stations would be a serious offence. He smiles broadly: "Kars", he says again, in a tone that fully makes up for his inability to communicate with us. It is becoming evident that nobody save fools like us, goes to Kars if they can possibly help it, only junior sleeping car conductors who can't help it; even Mr. Imre has abandoned us at Erzurum.

"Please wait", wails the lady again, in French. I wonder whether Kars possessed such a thing as a station house and if the governor's jeep is also waiting. At that moment the young Turk returns, and after an altercation in that language, we move round the end of the trucks. There does seem to be a well built stone station, right at the other end of the train; a solid edifice against the snow which hangs about Kars for half the year, and built of course by Russia.

We stumble about in the darkness over the rails and rough ballast and I cannot help wondering if we are being led straight into a den of thieves. For now we stop again, in the shadow of some building. There seems to be in front of us a large open space of blankness. The Captain has temporarily disappeared.

"I am Armenian", the lady says to me in a sad voice, filling me with alarm, for all I know of Kars is that every Armenian in it was massacred by the Turks at the time of the first world war.

"The Turks hate the Armenians; they do not like foreigners of any sort" she adds comfortingly.

"Where are your relatives?" I ask her. Her French is not the easiest to understand; neither is mine.

"I don't know; I have never been to Kars before. Are you sure there is a hotel?"

By this time I am 75 per cent sure that the hotel is just as likely to exist as that the Governor's jeep is waiting for us.

Hoping that I do not sound too doubtful I again say, "Yes, Kars Hotel". Beyond the Plough and the Southern Cross (can I really see both at once here?) I look down on to dim outlines of horse-cabs beyond the open space. Shadows loom as the patient nags toss their heads. The Captain rejoins our group and says something to the Armenian woman who turns to us: The carriages are here she says simply.

There are loud cries of "Osman". Is that his first name, or is this the Turkish for garry-driver? Further cries of "Fai-Tonne". Except in Istanbul where everybody talks at once, nobody shouts in Turkey; so if anyone is so misguided as to do so, no one takes the slightest notice.

All at once the two young Turks descend on our bags and lead off unexpectedly to the horse-cabs while we stumble behind across the dark, bumpy piece of ground. All it wants now is for me to break my ankle and be stranded here. We cross it without mishap, and on the far side the young Turk urges us into the dark cavern that is the back seat of a Victoria, under its hood.

"Kars Hotel" we say to the driver.

"Kars Palas" answers the driver triumphantly, whipping up his horses. Off we bump, over the uneven stone sets and through some deep gutters, running almost head on into another Victoria with no lights, rushing up to the station for its share of hapless passengers. In the eerie moonlight, our driver honks on an ancient, feeble, tin bulb-horn, straight out of Kipling's 'Stalky and Co.' - a cross between an old bicycle horn of the thirties, and those of very old cars. Though neither of us admits as much, we are both certain that the palatial nature of the hotel which Ankara did not care to mention, is the same as the squalid-looking mud huts that line the street down which we are proceeding. We wonder why the Armenian woman, who had been so keen to share our conveyance, should have suddenly disappeared without explanation....

He guggles and he struggles, and he will not stand nor sit,
But he gives an imitation of an apoplectic fit
I am not very captious, and I wish not to complain-
But what a crying grievance is the Baby in the Train!
J. Ashby-Sterry

Our fragile conveyance by now had moved into the centre of Kars. Here the dimly lit streets reveal stolid stone houses of obvious Russian origin, while the usual mud hut constructions are evident down the side turnings. A few cars and the occasional bus or lorry from the outside world, mingle with the horse and ox traffic of the town.

Our driver whips up his horses and we rattle past the Europ Palas Hotel. bright with lights within, and, a car or two without. We swing round a corner into another main street, over a cross roads where the lighting becomes even fainter, and turn suddenly in the road. "Kars Palas", announces the driver.

Five minutes later, Vincent returns from an exploratory visit.

"We are not staying there" he says firmly, as he climbs into the horse-cab. In the feeble light I have at last found suitable phrases in the book "Yok Kars Palas, Kars Oteli" I say to the driver, who does not care to understand my lamentable Turkish, but grasps that "No Kars Palace" means more fare for him. He takes us to another of these Turk dosshouses (marked "very modest" in the hotel books), which for so long have formed a barrier to travelling in much of the country. Hence the development, in tourist areas, of camping sites and motels, away from the towns, and, when possible, by the sea.

Vincent comes back from the establishment at which our driver has now stopped, even faster than from the Kars Palas. I notice that he no longer laughs at my general foreboding moodiness, no longer jokes that I was 'windy' of visiting Eastern Turkey because of the earthquakes.

I realise that this infernal driver has not the slightest notion what we want, and will drive us round and round Kars all night if necessary. "Europ Palas" I say to him severely, thankful that this hotel not merely exists, but is modern enough to have a sign which I can read from a passing horse-cab.

The driver now appears to be going the wrong way, but Vincent assures me that I am but the victim of my own imagination. From the rear, the Europ Palas looks quite as gloomy and uninviting as the others. "I'll try this time", I say hopefully, and go in.

Through the door a staircase leads to the hotel reception on the first floor. It is perfectly clean, modest and comfortable-looking, with spotless white sheets on the beds. But the beds look like hospital beds, and why, I wonder uneasily, are they in the passages?

"You have a room for me?"

"Yok".

"Telefon Ankara".

"Yok".

The charm with which these people said No, made me glad I did not have the Armenian lady in tow: I wonder how she was getting on. I tried again, but these beds in the corridor were ample proof that they meant what they said.

"Can I stay in your hotel tonight?" - At last the confounded phrase book actually had the right phrase in it.

"Yok".

"Can you speak English?" Desperately the phrase book played its ace.

Well, the tourist people had been against our coming to Kars. They had done everything possible to get us to go somewhere else, save actually to tell us that Kars was full of refugees from the Varto earthquake. I thought of the Director of Tourism in London, smiling one of those Oriental smiles that indicate an understatement: "You will have an adventurous time", was his comment when Kars was mentioned.

"What about the Kars Palas?" I asked Vincent.

"Well", he says, with not much enthusiasm in his voice. "As a last resort I suppose we could try it. But be prepared to rough it. It's pretty squalid in there".

Now, knowing his usual indifference to the creature comforts this particular "modest" establishment must have been "very modest" indeed!

Apparently on his brief excursion, after climbing up a rickety, dubious-looking staircase he walked into an uncarpeted, dimly-lit lobby, the bare boards of the floor scuffed and battered by years of heavily-booted traffic. On each side of a short passage were several doorless dormitories each containing about fifteen beds, all seemingly occupied - but it was difficult to be sure of this in the dim light of the passage's single 15 watt bulb.

The smell of the place was tolerable, but it was quite obvious that it had vintage quality about it. A connoisseur, put to it, might reasonably presume it to be a combination of rotten fruit, unwashed bodies, sweat, garlic and cats, and an obviously over-worked lavatory adding its own particular odour.

Explaining his presence there, as best he could, for his command of Turkish was as inadequate as mine, he decided that at this stage of the evening we might, with luck, still have time to find a less "modest" hotel. The two middle-aged men, playing cards at the reception desk, look rather relieved when he retreats down the stairs, glad to get back to their game, and not wanting the trouble of dealing with two non-Turkish speaking foreigners.

The "Kars Oteli" had a cleaner air about it, and even ran to carpets on the floor, but the vehemence of their protest that there was no room in the inn discouraged any idea of bargaining with them.

The situation, in a horse-cab in the dark, and no hotel, seems much worse than actually it is. One could disappear here for weeks before anyone knew about it. Would they set on us? "The Turks do not like foreigners" - that woman had said, less than an hour ago.

The thing to do, evidently is to go back to the station. There, at least, a comfortable bed awaits; the only thing is, it is not avail-

able. When we say "Gar" to the driver, for once he instantly understands, and takes us immediately to the nearest police station. All are agreed that wherever else we might sleep, it is absolutely forbidden to do so in the station. It is high time to act, fast, for if we do not succeed in returning before the night train leaves for Erzurum, the station will be well and truly closed, instead of just barred to us.

Suddenly I remember our brief cases, most generously given us by Mr. Erman, and with relief I trot out the only Turkish words I know, for which I do not require the wretched phrase-book. "Yatakli-Vagon" I say hopefully to the gendarmerie, who shake their heads vigorously, and then I flash the brief case, with "Wagons- Lits/Cook" stamped on it. We assure them that we only wish to visit the Sleeping car "Yok Yatmak Gar" ("No sleep station".) Self assurance returned as the policemen accepted our masquerading status. Later on we formed the opinion that they had never met any real Wagons-Lits/Cook officials, who assiduously follow Mr. Imre's example.

The garry driver gives us a final fright by taking a different road back to the station, but after what seems like an eternity, a particularly bad bump seems comfortingly familiar, while the driver honks his horn again and lets his poor horses walk the rest of the way, over the rough stones. The station appears to be in pitch darkness, and I fear the last train must have left. But there is a pressure lamp burning in one of the offices, and inside are a number of railwaymen. They are quite sure that they know what I want, and in two minutes one of them, armed with a lamp, is conducting me through the night train which is about to start, to reach the one by which we had arrived.

We clump along the cinders, and as I feared, the Wagons- Lits is in darkness, so we climb up and knock. Inside a dim light shows that the conductor has not yet finally retired, but is saving the batteries. In fact, though he receives us in his underwear, and points out it is forbidden, I think he is half expecting us, for our beds are already made up!

We are hardly settled in our compartment before the sleeper

slowly begins to move. We are indeed fortunate to be aboard. Had we arrived but a few minutes later, would not all those station officials stared uncomprehendingly at us, and courteously said "Yok"? We did not move far; enough to be beyond the station, out of range of the public, but not of the mosquitoes breeding in some muddy pools, part of a rather squalid suburb which we saw with the dawn next morning.

We are woken by a cleaner, who chooses to begin his operations at five o'clock. Then we are shunted round the ordinary coaches to the rear of the train, and drawn slowly back into the station, this time stopping beyond the station house. The conductor indicates by signs that we must take all our luggage with us and present ourselves to the stationmaster. Although this is not explained, presumably it is to give the lie to any suggestion that we have stayed overnight in the sleeper. Accompanied by the conductor, we have not been in the station office long, when in walks the Armenian lady, escorted by the Captain! She seems as put out to find us at the station as we are surprised. Did she find a hotel? Yes. Was it the Kars Palas? No, another. Was it all right? She indicates by a grimace that it was not and adds that the Captain has nobly housed her for the night. In her black raiment the lady is expressionless, as the Captain, who again seems to know everybody, hustles her along the platform, while we are presented to the stationmaster. Our papers are quite in order: it is now perfectly all right for us to leave our baggage locked up in the sleeper by the conductor, who then goes off to breakfast at the kiosk which dispenses strong and sour black coffee, and breads which would be appetising if they were not so fly-blown. Kars is a flies' paradise.

Before exploring the touristic attractions of the town - for Kars even has a tourists map available - the very ordinary little train of three ancient four wheelers and a single bogie coach requires investigation. Its ex-German engine, pointing east, has removed the bogie coach, solemnly to add one more little four wheeler, a Saturday ritual laid down, but apparently quite unnecessary, for the few peasants aboard. I notice that unlike the rest of the train, which has Kars-Akyaka on it, the bogie coach bears the placard

'Kars-Hudut' (Hudut meaning frontier). For this is Saturday morning and on Saturdays only the train is said to go on to Akhurian, though in fact only this composite first and second class coach, next to the engine, does so. I also notice that only the Armenian lady and the Captain are in it.

There is no mistaking the look of agonised consternation on their faces, as I proceed - admittedly in something of a hurry, to photograph it. The sky is dark and dust laden, adding to the air of sinister mystery of the lady whose relatives obviously do not live in Kars at all - massacred long ago if ever they had, I thought. Foreigners without a special permit have been barred from Kars until very recent years, but in democratic Turkey, you cannot be arrested just for looking at a train.

My harmless investigation obviously agitates them, but as they must surely have found out that "I am something to do with the railway", I peer learnedly at Turkish inscriptions marked "Fren" which obviously refers to the brake, when all the time the reason for the lady's escort, not to mention all the bundles and packages and suitcases of the previous day, provokes my curiosity.

The Armenian woman, obviously uneasy at the prospect of the forthcoming frontier crossing, comes to the window: "This is not the Istanbul train" - as a child could tell from the ancient four wheelers, and the engine, pointing the wrong way! "I am going to the Soviet", the woman hisses at me in French, and then, loudly, says "goodbye" in French for me, and in Turkish for anybody standing by.

This iron curtain crossing is no place for foreigners without visas, so I am left to ruminate on whether she is escaping out of Turkey, to claim the widow's pension which the Armenian Soviet Socialist Republic pays to such Armenian refugees from Istanbul as manage to get into the country; if she is really just visiting; or visiting with a purpose, and if the Captain, for all his plain clothes and his limp, is not retired a tall!

Reading the foregoing anecdote, stuffed full of Bond-style clichés, evokes the criticism that it sounds as though we had made the whole thing up. How easily we might have done. Yet in fact, all this really happened, exactly as we have described. The Armenian lady and her escort, and as you may imagine, this story-book-come-to-life atmosphere, seemed at the time as unbelievably unreal, as it does to see it set down in print.

To add to the faint air of mystery, the timetable says the lady's train goes to somewhere named Sinir, though this is marked on the map as Kisilcakcak (probably Akyaka in disguise). All these different names are too much for the local railwaymen of Kars, who settle for plain Hudut (Frontier). Though there is a through sleeping car waiting at Akhurian to take Russian diplomats and others on to Moscow, it is not, as far as I am aware, a much-frequented entry point to Russia for visitors from the west. Recent British visitors to Soviet Armenia have been remarkably few. Therefore, the arrival of a copy of Peter Pears' "Armenian Holiday" meant rather more to me than to most of the recipients. This privately circulated account of his holiday with Benjamin Britten in August 1965, is a personal diary; they stayed a long way from this end of Soviet Armenia, south east of Erevan at the Armenian composers' summer colony, high above Dilidjan. This part of Armenia seems much nicer than Kars. From Erevan, he writes of the journey to Dilidjan, 3 or 4 hours away by car. "Some roads in the U.S.S.R. are perfectly good. Others are in the process

of being made, and in this vast process vast holes are simply left for cars to break their axles in, until the time comes to fill them up. There was a lot of traffic, about 95 per cent of it trucks and lorries, carrying stones, cement, machinery, up and down from the hills, which most of the way were brown and parched. Gradually the crops got thicker and better... On we went, up into the mountains. The wild flowers grew more and more extraordinary every mile.

The description of the colony, seen after the clouds had cleared, is the very opposite of Kars. "Glorious green woods of all sorts of trees, oak, sycamore, beech, birch, crowned above the trees by sunny downs, with sheep and cows visible on the sky-line". Armenia is portrayed as gay, civilised if primitive, its people courteous, progressive and happy.

The food seems very similar to that in Turkey, perhaps Armenian gastronomy has been inherited by the Turks. The churches dating back to the sixth century, are still used, though "their religion has shrunk much. Church bells can be heard but rarely".

Kars has at least six churches, the most interesting one being tenth century. Kars Tourism is very active here, preventing one taking pictures of the square building with nave, chancel and aisles all the same size. Where the altar ought to be are reminders that this is a Turkish Museum, not a church. Beautifully built of stone, it stands firm as a rock and indifferent to the changing world that has put it out of use.

Our horse-cab journey into Kars by daylight is very different to the previous one. I find a crowd of children on the platform, eager to practice their class-room English on Vincent, and extremely keen to acquire his phrase book; exactly how he has collected this large crowd during the short space of my looking at the train for Russia, I do not discover. We move off accompanied by a large lout who speaks no English, who domineers a younger, brighter child, who does. "Kars is our least developed place" we were told, apologetically, in Ankara, and it would seem that the younger inhabitants are aware of this. Living in these sad mud huts, (which have the advantage of being relatively safe against earthquakes) keeping clean and tidy must be very difficult. Yet these boys are well and neatly dressed, and quite sure they are going to improve things when they grow up. The stone built houses of the former Russian Armenians give a glimpse of what has gone, and makes the desire for self improvement in living conditions so ardently desirable.

Kars lies where it does, because the Kars river here makes a deep gorge in the lava ridden plain, protecting the citadel, whose walls are high above us as we stand outside the church. The river Kars flows east, to turn south into the Arpa, the frontier then bears east towards Erevan. Kars itself, with stone buildings, and horse-cabs, is superior to its neighbouring mud hut villages, yet in these surroundings where one feels one has gone back at least to the end of the nineteenth century, save only for the occasional car, lorry or military truck. Istanbul gleams like a star, and London, like a galaxy. The concern for cities and bright lights as a goal to aim for - a goal so sought after in Britain, here takes on a new meaning.

The younger of the two boys is delighted to learn that indeed we have been to London. "Do they", he asks wondrously have many phaetons in London?" How hurt he would have been had we told him the truth - that London did not even retain any victorias for tourists, at fancy prices. Picturing his face at the sight of

London Transport's great red juggernauts charging down Whitehall in the rush hour (and even these are out of date, doubtless to be replaced by one man single deckers) I found myself at a loss for words. Vincent tactfully replied, "No, not many, but the Queen has a few".

Before heading for the station our young guide takes us to a restaurant, where, in the usual hospitable Turkish way, we were invited to inspect the kitchens. Everything looked clean and wholesome; the Turks are very fussy about food hygiene, just as, in most restaurants, there is linen napery on the tables, not the plastic or ersatz paper of Western Europe. Great steaming pans of stew were bubbling on a large coal range, with its chimney at the back. All simmered in a tomato-covered sauce making the choice almost as difficult as from the menu which was in Turkish only: curries, lamb, beef, peppers, all at amazingly cheap prices. Moreover, all this was waiting to be eaten at ten thirty in the morning; imagine trying to have luncheon at such an hour in Britain!

The lean nags whose flanks look cruelly beaten, wait placidly outside the station where the yard is being re-paved - the reason for the curious empty space of the night before. Storm clouds, already gathered in the morning, now loom ominously, and it is almost dark, though the Dogu Express is timed to start at noon - five days a week. On other days it goes no further east than Erzurum.

We again have difficulty in saying goodbye without being parted from the phrase book. Their eagerness to learn is touching; their generation will make Turkey the great nation, Ataturk dreamed of, and nowhere is one more forcefully reminded of how hard a place the world is, than in Kars. Coldest of all the Turkish provinces, dusty and hot at other times, it is poor land, and painfully close to the barrier between west and east.

A great dust storm is gathering, on the ground as well as in the sky. What a haven of comfort waits at the end of the train. Hail stones clatter on the roof of this stalwart, English-built sleeper, they bang against the familiar gold lettering on the sides, and beat down on the poor cab horses, who stand miserably on the rank, their backs turned to the dust and hail, while their driver crouches in the cab, under the hood. Before our eyes the alleyways of Kars are turned to thick mud. And in the middle of it all we suddenly set off, the wind and lashing rain, drowning the whistle at the other end of the train.

Without first going east, the thrill of proceeding west, romantic alluring, civilised, is just not understood. Something to make fun of, perhaps. This elderly and common place sleeping car, trundling through this remote part of Turkey in a hideous dust storm has all the grandeur of the original Blue Train, and fires the imagination, bearing us back to the civilisation of which it is itself a part. Until you have seen a dust storm that brings darkness at mid-day, you will just scoff at its eeriness. Varto and its earthquake seem very close.

Everywhere cakes of dung are laid out to dry - and are getting wet. The fertiliser that would so improve this dusty soil, is carefully gathered for fuel, an evil smelling business. The journey across the plain takes an hour and a half, with one stop, at Selim. This place consists of a lonely stone-built station house. There are some flocks of sheep, and cattle, miserable from the storm. But why we choose to stop here, rather than one of the other little places is anybody's guess. There are no other trains in the district at this time.

After Sarikamis, the storm abates. The long climb looks more spectacular by day, through a typical frontier country of inhospitable rocks, fir trees, scree, and rough vegetation. There seems to be no human habitation, nor flocks, as there are everywhere else on the way to Erzurum. The Erzurum side of the pass has a strange rough beauty, for the brown earth huts look attractive in the rich warm glow of the Turkish sunset, when seen from a distance.

The troops are still deployed on their hill, apparently indifferent to the weather, as we approach Erzurum, whistling loudly. On this Saturday night the station is alive with people; there is no feeling of remoteness here, as faintly exists in Kars, whose "touristic attractions" do not extend to picture postcards. Here you may not only buy a postcard of Erzurum, but find a stamp and posting box as well. The shunting engine comes to remove us without delay from the madding crowd on the platform, who are waiting impatiently for the extra coaches which are put on here. These are standing next to the diner, its windows shining a bright welcome, on a nearby siding. There is no mistaking the clank of the engine's coupling rods as it approaches our train. In far away Erzurum, here are the authentic sounds of Crewe, in the flesh, the very same sort of engine as that on which a certain John Axon met his death heroically at Chapel-en-le-Frith in 1957, when his goods train ran out of control through faulty brakes. A radio-ballad, a new fangled piece of British folklore, and was invented specially for the Axon feature, and has immortalised this event. As the sleeper moves off towards Kars again, into the dark, its door open so that sounds and smells of Sir William Stanier's freight engine predominates over everything else, it is hard to remember that this part of John Buchan country is not, after all, the Scottish Highlands! When we set back onto the diner, the standard Turkish whistle brings back reality; I half expected one of those horrible hooters, which the LMS imported from Scotland on to their entire system. Perhaps this book will get across to the Turkish Tourism department, the fact that the State Railways have such a ready-made attraction for British tourists, who nowadays have to be content with long playing records of them.

We move off again, eastwards out of the station, attached now to the dining car and the coaches, to enjoy a further half-mile run with an engine whose like in Britain has disappeared. Then we are shunted back onto the Express, the corridor connections made, and Mr. Imre bounds through to see to his charges. No, he has never been to Kars; but come along and have some dinner!

We set off confidently into the dark, behind a fresh engine. Not many of the passengers who have crowded on board our train are taking dinner, but those who are, clearly thoroughly enjoy it. The menu is much the same as luncheon in the car, the previous day, and generously served. One of the contrasts of this desert-like countryside is the way that people eat in anything but desert conditions. Though Mr. Imre is still sure that we have been starving in Kars.

We turn in early, so as to be ready to leave our comfortable sleeper at Sivas at seven-thirty next morning. Our intention is to travel to Samsun, on the Black Sea, in the day train which takes from nine in the morning to eight at night to get there. Samsun possesses the last remaining narrow-gauge line of the State railways, starting at the town centre goods station and running through the street to the station, apparently, before crossing the edge of the delta of the Yesil Irmak (Green River) which flows out into the Black Sea at "Wednesday", Carsamba, as it is called in Turkish. The first five miles are along the coast, but then the line has to turn inland as the delta is marshy.

Our intentions were thwarted, and so this fine area of Turkey, much pleasanter than the Anatolian Plateau, eluded us. One day perhaps, we shall return, and go, by sea for choice, along the Black Sea coast to Zonguldak, Samsun and Trabzon (Trebizond) by the Turkish Maritime Lines. Because the Turks are so busy developing their Aegean and Mediterranean Coasts, this area is a sort of reserve of tourism attractions, at present not neglected, but not yet fully developed. There are fair hotels at most of the ports, and of course it is also possible to travel by road. But I think if I were to go again, I would plump for a ship. Looking at my Wagons-Lits timetable of 1938, I notice

Minibus leaving Erzincan. Courtesy of Turkish Tourism.

regretfully as I write this, how a comfortable sleeper of the varnished teak variety, plied between Haydarpasa and Samsun, and another one ran between Ankara and Zonguldak, in the good old days. Though ships are still needed for supplies, many people nowadays go by air.

While pondering on the lack of sleepers to Samsun, where Kemal Ataturk was posted by the Ottoman Government, just after World War I, as Inspector General of the Turkish Third Army, I fall soundly asleep, waking only when we stop about midnight. I look forward to seeing this Black Sea area and also, on the way, Amasya, an ancient town with its citadel high on a rock above the deep gorge of the Yesil Irmak. This is the place from which Kemal Ataturk started his operations, because the port of Samsun was subject to visits by British Army Officers from the occupying force at Istanbul. About two in the morning I again awake, and I become convinced that the station outside the window is the same as that I had noticed at midnight. I fall asleep again, certain that whatever else might befall us, early rising would not be needed; we will not now reach Sivas on time.

Sure enough, next morning we are still there, and 'there' turns out to be Erzincan. The storm which in Kars had seemed so sinister, has done its work, and caused a landslide in the gorge of the Kara Su (Euphrates), that had looked so dangerous on the journey eastwards. While we breakfast in the buffet car, another train comes slowly into the station, headed by an engine running backwards. It, too has a dining car, and a sleeper, and the crews join us. Their train was the Erzurum Express, running between Erzurum and Ankara, daily, but leaving Erzurum at midday instead of six in the evening. They had got stuck further up the line, and our train engine had been sent forward to retrieve them.

A friendly group of Turkish officers on leave invite us to pay large sums and motor by taxi to Ankara, explaining that to provide a connecting road service to Sivas, the minibus drivers work ceaselessly, without sleep. Minibuses are dangerous they said,

with the drivers hurtling over the edge: it is important to get away early, in a proper car. As we wish to go on from Sivas to Samsun, not Ankara, we thought we might later continue by train. But by mid morning came the news that all trains would be stuck at Erzincan for three days. The dining cars shut down immediately, in a state of siege except for the staff, and we are told there would be a bus at six. The foresight of the Wagons-Lits Co.'s Turkish representative, Mr. Evliyagil in providing us with Mr. Imre as an escort, now becomes apparent. We stay in the train, whose odour is becoming increasingly unpleasant, and in due course Mr. Imre announces lunch. The buffet car attendant serves us, the conductors of the two sleepers, and the conductor of the Erzurum Express buffet.

The bus turns out to be a small Volkswagen minibus, and as there are many, rather important looking gentlemen stranded at Erzincan that day, we think it resourceful of Mr. Imre to get us on it at all. We pile in, our luggage stacked precariously on top, and start off on what is to be an interesting journey, to say the least. Crammed together like sardines, we are fortunate to have secured the seats directly behind the driver which give us slightly more leg-room than the rest of the passengers. Even the centre aisle is packed to capacity, with people sitting on camp-stools or whatever else they can find to soften the jolting.

An hour or so later, after the road has risen steeply, and we have arrived in hair-pin bend country, we realise that we also have a very fine view of the road. As it is now dark we can only see as far as the edge of the precipice, but occasionally a twinkling light far below, gives us an unnerving idea of how high we are. The driver had already done the round-trip to Sivas that day, and on some of the more nerve-racking bends we pray that he will stay sufficiently alert to manoeuvre us safely on to the straight. Our fellow-travellers seem to have the same idea, and some of them have decided that the only way to keep him awake, is to sing, and keep him continually supplied with cigarettes. One of the most strident of the singers, is a fierce-looking hawk-nosed man, who was a refugee from the earthquake at Varto, who had lost everything there, all his family and his business. He seems uncommonly cheerful under the circumstances, but Mr. Imre later explains to us that he thought the mans business had been rather shaky to begin with, and he was quite happy at the prospect of starting a new life in Ankara.

Three hours after leaving Erzincan, the driver brings the bus to a halt outside a forlorn looking little cafe, and we all troop out, except for several women, who remain seated in the bus. The cafe, belieing its dingy exterior is brightly lit, and clean; in fact, the cleanest we have encountered yet in Eastern Turkey. Whilst we enjoy several cups of strong sweet coffee, our driver tucks in to a large plate of Pilav. We notice that everyone else seems to have lost their appetites. The driver having finished his meal, we continue our journey, now beginning to stiffen and ache because of our cramped positions, and the prospect of another six hours of this is somewhat daunting.

The driver seems to be getting anxious about the performance of his bus, and true enough on one of the steeper gradients it fails to make it. Osman the driver's mate, is ordered out to lessen the load, and although only a boy, and light weight, this seems to do the trick. Unfortunately for Osman, the driver makes a rather fast getaway and thinks it wiser to keep the bus rolling until he reaches the top of the hill. Safely there we wait for his mate, but as the minutes tick by and there is no sign of him, we look anxiously at our watches, knowing how little time there is left to connect with our train at Sivas. Five minutes go by, and then Osman, furious, arrives panting out of the darkness, his first action, to give the bus a vicious kick.

After a highly emotional argument with the driver in which everyone else joins in, good relations are restored with Osman, who is no doubt relieved, that we are now rolling downhill towards the Sivas plain.

Mr. Imre has been constantly looking at his watch ever since we left Zara, the town on the Sivas plain where the mountain road ends. Nor does he fail us, even though the minibus in a final act of defiance, runs out of petrol a few miles outside Sivas. Fortunately the driver has a reserve can. After nine hours we bowl through the town, the driver's home town, to the station square, where his next load of unfortunate passengers are already waiting for another trip. He starts back again within half an hour, spent, not in rest, but in piling bundles on the roof.

The station boasts a train which arrived at half past six. The Dogu Express is due to leave at 8.10, and the sleeping car, garnished for a through run to Kars, is rapidly made ready by the conductor for the return to Haydarpasa. Thanks to Mr. Imre, there are berths in it for us. We relax for half an hour or so in the station buffet over a coffee, regretting our bad luck in not seeing Samsun, and not being able to look at the Sivas engine works, which serves all Eastern Turkey. These workshops make many other things besides repairing engines, for they are one of the few steel plants in Turkey. Because of this, visitors are not permitted into the works. The railways are regarded as an asset for use of the nation, as the erstwhile Minister of Transport in socialist Britain, Mrs. Barbara Castle, has in mind in her new nationalised Transport Bill.

The tall factory chimney, with star, crescent and "TCDD" dominates the rear of the railway station yard. There are a number of interesting engines shunting rolling stock, but in the short time available, it is impossible to see much. With the Tatvan line blocked at Mus, and now the stoppage on the Erzurum Line, the station is full of wagons that have been delayed. Like so many important places in Turkey, the station is a straightforward affair, not a terminus, and devoid of junctions. Trains from Ankara to Samsun reverse here, and the one we ought to have taken steams in, from Ankara, just before we start.

Two stations up the line, eighteen kilometres from Sivas, is Kalin, where we look rather guiltily at the Samsun branch, curving away to the right. "Yok Samsun" was the sum total of most of the conversation at Erzincan prior to the bus trip; and not since 1955 has it been possible to go there by Yatakli Vagon. After the cramped jolting of the minibus past fearful precipices, the 'luxury' that is always attached to sleeping car travel, takes on its true meaning. Our journey back to Ankara was uneventful.

Because Turkish Express trains do not run every day, it was impossible for us to plan our itinerary in any other way. Our extra day in Ankara is again spent in a round of visits. The official from the Tourism Office whom we saw immediately before leaving for Kars, has himself gone on leave; while Fahir Bilce, in an expansively hospitable mood, insists that I should call in his office whenever I wished, disregarding his 'passage-man'. Not only does he most kindly introduce me to the planning department, at work on the Adapazari electrification project, as well as to the Directeur of Traction; he also insists on my photograph being taken with him, in his office. When I ask this affable Secretary General, who seems to know everybody and everyone all over the system, I find that he, too, has never been to Kars.

The TCDD are delighted that the next stage of our journey is to be in their crack train, the Bogazici Ekspresi (Bosphorus Express). This 'Mototren' takes only 8¾ hours for its daily run between the capital and Haydarpasa, reaching Eskisehir, 263 kilometres from Ankara, in three hours and thirty-nine minutes. Fitted with air-conditioning, all the coaches have numbered and reserved seats. For this train reservation is essential; the Mototrens have priority and reach their destinations on time. One of the coaches is fitted out as a dining saloon, which serves breakfast as soon as the train starts. Up to the end of 1966, the Wagons-Lits operated these diners, though not those in the second-class-only diesel trains.

After only one stop, at Polatli, and a few unofficial pauses to pass trains coming the other way that make way for us, the 'Bosphorus' draws into the ultra-modern station at Eskisehir, shortly before midday. It is hot and dusty on the platform, and jet fighters from the nearby air-base, scream angrily overhead. Eskisehir is the principal railway works of the TCDD, also with a tall tower or chimney, very like the one at Sivas. The station is on the left of the line facing away from Ankara, with the works on its left. The rail entrance is from the line to Konya, which forms a Y junction with that to Haydarpasa. Istanbul - Konya trains have always had to reverse at Eskisehir.

Turkey strikes the visitor as prolific in unskilled people. Messengers and porters are available in abundance everywhere. One of these is summoned by the stationmaster, who takes me through a labyrinth of pathways to the heavily guarded works main entrance.

Lunch for Turks seems to be as important as for Frenchmen, and it being lunch-hour, the works manager is quite unable (or

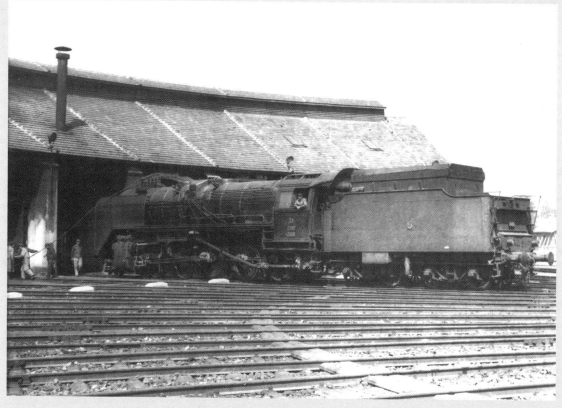

unwilling) to show me round. Slowly the works are going over to building new diesel locomotives to save foreign exchange; all the diesels go for repairs here, and eventually all steam overhauls will be done at Sivas, officially from 1972 when all steam engines are to be withdrawn from lines west of Ankara. This is a new departure for the works which has only built one new steam locomotive (Black Wolf). Sivas also built a new locomotive, not to be outdone, called Grey Wolf. Sivas is in fact a larger repair works than Eskisehir.

Eskisehir station restaurant is cool and inviting as I return, hot, cross and frustrated; the food is cheap and well cooked, the premises spotless. Our Konya diesel train leaves just before two in the afternoon. The one coming the other way arrives first, and gives an inkling of what we can expect. People burst forth from it, as more dive for the doors to cram into it. For the Konya line,

once the main route from the Bosphorus to Syria, has been deliberately run down to branch line status, and only the daily diesel and one all stations train, which goes all night, serves the route, though there is plenty of goods traffic.

The only space available in the train is in the buffet section, on an extremely small three legged stool, low on the ground, portable and uncomfortable. It is designed to induce the occupant not to linger, but to return to his seat. This works very well in a half-empty train, but ours has people in the corridors between the carriages, and more standing between the seats. It is impossible to see out well, owing to the frosted glass of the buffet window. From our side of the train it is just possible to see that we leave past the round-house running shed, which has plenty of steam locomotives in it.

The countryside quickly changes from the almost level

plateau, to rocky outcrops, escarpments, hills and little valleys. Though it stops at almost every station, the diesel train runs at quite high speeds between them. In the heavy, sunny afternoon, life goes lazily past the window, and as lazily, sheep graze on the sparse foliage beside the track; the sudden application of full brakes and frequent whistling, brings all the dozing passengers to life.

We stop for some minutes for no apparent reason. Outside the train, there is nothing to see but a flock of sheep, munching the stubby grass. But the shepherd boy is standing by one of his flock which is not eating, and whose fleece is beginning to dye an ominous red. I recall that though I have twice mentioned how nobody shouts or makes a scene in Turkey, I have omitted to mention, that all the engines and diesel trains are fitted with a cow catcher, save for the oldest steam engines which normally only shunt in station areas.

My limited Turkish cannot describe the scene. "Sis-Kebab" brings floods of laughter to the dining car crew inside the car; outside it is more serious. The guard is talking to the shepherd who calmly accepts the inevitable. It is the will of Allah, and it is nobody's fault, except the sheep's, of course; thus we are on our way again. The one and only train must not be too late, though there seems little reason for the train running when it does, save for connections at Afyon, further on. As there is only one train it would be full whenever it ran. What uses up time is the tendency of Turkish trains to take the wrong turning at junctions, in order to serve the first station down the line, before returning all the way back to the second arm of the triangular junction, to rejoin their real route! This is all shown in the timetable as though it were perfectly straightforward.

Our train has two drivers, as between them they are working for thirteen hours, with no break except for a brief ten minutes at Eskisehir and Afyon. The second man is already in the cab at the far end of the train, ready for the triangular progress with which we visit Kutahya, from Alayunt, instead of going directly down the Konya line. About an hour later, Afyon's citadel towers above the plain in which the junction station lies. It gets its name from the Opium (Afyon) that grows on this marshy plain, which stretches into the distance, a change from the undulating plateau country which preceded it. On the right the mountains loom large. The two routes to Izmir, one ex-French and the other, made by the State Railways, to join on to the ex-British railway, start from the junction by the way we came in, curve off on our right round to Afyonkarahisar Town station, serving the town community better than the junction does. Twelve kilometres beyond here, the routes actually divide, and 'double single' tracks are provided, to obviate any need for a manned junction. About half our passengers disembark, to board another railcar that is proceeding down the Aydin line as far as Nazilli, passing Denizli on the way. Close by Denizli is Pamukkale, where there is one of those petrified waterfalls achieved by deposits of calcium, born along in the stream. There is also the site of Laodicea, which became Christian in the lifetime of St. John, and also Hieropolis. All these attractions are accessible from the well developed Aegean coastal area of Turkey, and Pamukkale figures in the Tourism brochures.

Afyonkarahisar is just over 100 miles from Eskisehir, and 169 miles from Konya. Among other things it boasts a drink (called Afyonkarahisar), presumably made from opium, worthy of a special space in the Wagons-Lits bills, but unfortunately we did not

General view of Eskisehir. Courtesy of Turkish Tourism.

have the opportunity to try it. Leaving Karahisar, "the citadel of the black castle", behind us, we now veer eastward through a flat plain which gradually becomes more marshy. Then it grows dark, so we do not see the climb over the Bozdag mountain before reaching Konya. The summit is 4,373 feet, and the line falls steeply at 1 in 40 to the Konya plain; Konya is about 1000 feet lower. In early days goods trains had to be divided on this stretch, when running northbound up from Konya to Eskisehir.

Memories of this train in the dark fuse into a kaleidoscope of cramp, frequent stops, bowls of steaming stew, and the grand camaraderie of the buffet car crew of three, the youngest of whom frequently asks if we can speak Yugoslav. What unexpected questions Turks do put to travellers! It seems he was born in Yugoslavia to Turkish parents, who were left over from the old Ottoman empire and who fled to Istanbul when Yugoslavia went communist. Safely naturalised, he has already been back to his former home as a tourist! He is a friendly soul, who insists on coming with us when at last we roll into Konya about nine o'clock at night, and places our luggage for us in a horse-cab.

This is a far superior phaeton to the one at Kars. Its bell rings merrily-no husky horn playing here - no wobbly wheels, and rubber tyres instead of iron ones. It slips along the smooth road, the lean nags trotting briskly under the full moon, a welcome break after the buffet car. Our hotel is typical of Turkey. Some three years old, its modern plumbing works fairly well, though there is the usual lack of plugs to bath and basin, as Konya is a holy place and devout Muslims only use running water.

The great attraction of Konya takes place in December, when the Mevlevi order of Dervishes perform, in the Tekki or Palace of Dervishes, the Whirling that has made them famous and that

Konya. Whirling Dervishes Tekka in far background. Courtesy of Turkish Tourism.

Attaturk tried to ban. Attempts to get them to whirl at a more suitable time of year to suit tourists has not been too successful, from a religious viewpoint, so for the rest of the year toy dervishes perform by proxy, whirling by electric motor in every knick-knack shop, until even the most uninterested tourist begins to feel giddy, sickened by their continual gyrations, now fast, now slow, now uneven, depending on their batteries. Even when closed, the dervishes in the brightly lit windows of the shops continue to whirl dizzily all night!

The sense of reverence which Konya yet retains, akin to York or Winchester in this respect, was enhanced on the day of our particular visit by the funeral in Ankara of the Turkish President, General Gurel. Without any explanation, shops were shut, giving us great difficulty in buying food for the next stage of our journey, while restaurants point blank refused to serve wine at table to anybody.

Konya is a few hours journey by bus from Ankara, and buses ply frequently between the two cities. The main road leaves from the north end of the town, skirting the little hill known as Alaeddin's Hill, from the time of the Seljuk Turks who made Konya their capital. The Seljuks established themselves firmly in 1097, but Alaeddin's reign was later, from 1219-1256. Nowadays the foot of the hill is occupied by the Officers Club. These clubs are found all over Turkey, but by the time we reached Konya, we had learnt, the hard way, not to attempt to enter them. They look like the best restaurant in town - no doubt they are; but instead of commissionaires on the door, visitors encounter a polite but firm Military Policeman.

The only passenger train of the day, or night, on the Konya - Ulukisla stretch of the former Baghdad Railway is supposed to leave at 9 a.m. We trot hopefully to the station. Some Kurds squat on the platform, while Turks in European dress, oscillate between the nice new station building, airy and modern, with a knife and fork in marble where the refreshment room ought to be, and the

cavernous, flyblown edifice where it actually was, in 1966.

Due to be pulled down, it contains a frieze of the Baghdad Railway, showing colour scenes of the formidable crossing of the Taurus mountains. Trains of the 1920s are shown popping in and out of tunnels above superlative gorges, for this building was the headquarters of the line. It is not possible to leave the station as no one seems to know when the train might arrive, though shunting operations, blocking the main line, indicates that a good long wait is probable. The general air of departed grandeur is reflected in the engines waiting at the shed. For the engines are mostly those which were the elite passenger ones, formerly used for crack trains like the Anatolia Express. Now they pull goods trains; our train when it arrives, is too heavy for them, and the usual mixed-traffic sort is at its head.

Engines are changed at Konya, and though we can see the new one making ready to take over, the actual operation occurs while we are scrambling for seats. The Turkish Railways have excelled themselves by leaving a compartment locked up, all the way from Haydarpasa, which by a combination of the display of Fahir Bilce's visiting card and our yellow pass, is opened for us; (Konya is after all the place where hills are named after Aladdin). No sooner are we installed, when we are joined by a sergeant returning from leave, with wife and baby. They are travelling over 1000 kilometres to Diyarbakir, and the sergeant at once begins rigging up a hammock for the baby. This makes it impossible to get in or out of the compartment without crawling underneath. But it does leave us with the compartment to ourselves.

The sergeant and his wife are most hospitable and, as always on Turkish trains, their food supplies are lavish. Pastries and melons are thrust upon us, as for thirty nine miles or so we crawl wearily across the Konya plain, to the defile between the Taurus foothills, always visible on the right, and the Kara Dag, an extinct volcano on the left. A fairly wide valley leads us into the Karaman plain. Here, 100 miles from Konya, we turn from South east to

North east.

Mountain roads through the Taurus, climbing a pass about 5000 feet high before descending to the Mediterranean, give Karaman its importance as a cross-roads. The train, following the earlier route near the Cilician gates, keeps to the plain, then passing through some of the Taurus foothills, reaches a further plain, marshy this time, of which the principal town is Eregli. Though some houses are still mud brick, they are ever so superior to those of Kars. They are well built and stout, with two storeys and a proper roof, snug among the groves of fruit and poplar trees.

It is harvest time and the stop here is memorable for the apples. They are brought to the train in baskets, buckets, tin cans, even wash basins; great golden fruit, glowing in the evening sun. Almost all the apples are instantly bought by the eager passengers, though the more venturous vendors board our train and scramble along the corridors among the several beggars whose terrible deformities make their own mute appeal. Begging is forbidden in Turkey, but Turks are by nature kind and generous and everyone gives something.

Meanwhile the baby, squalling from time to time, swings in its hammock, while the sergeant insists we eat some Eregli apples. All the way, we keep running by passing loops, where the points are just left beside the track. For war-time traffic they can be quickly put back into use. It has taken until evening to cover the 224 kilometres to Cakmak, the station after Eregli; for our train is a local one. Cakmak is 200 feet above Eregli and here the line turns in earnest to the Taurus crossing. In the next eighteen miles it rises 1200 feet,

The Baghdad Railway in the heart of the Taurus Mountains. Courtesy of Turkish Tourism.

mostly at 1 in 40. So a pilot engine is required and this wastes a lot of time by first going to the rear of the train. The apple vendors are wandering about on the adjacent track, with the station building beyond it. Here we have to pass the one and only passenger train coming the other way, which they wait for eagerly.

But at last the pilot engine has been manoeuvred to head our train, whistling at the apple-merchants. The up train arrives, and soon we are storming up the hill to Kardesgedigi, the junction with the line from Bogazkopru and Ankara.

The lonely station house with a few trees, looks as though it were miles from anywhere. In fact Ulukisla, the important station at the top of the Taurus pass, is only 4 kilometres away, tucked out of sight round a bend, and much more sheltered than this bleak junction.

Here we are clearly in the way. Our train runs into a loop. The pilot immediately is uncoupled and returns to Cakmak for the goods train that has been following us from Konya. Beyond the baby's hammock are two further through lines, and beyond them again the station house. Into one of these lines runs a curious local train of light steel railcar trailers hauled by a diesel locomotive different from those in use elsewhere, with a steeple cab. This train does not even get into the timetable! It too seems to be waiting for something - and sure enough, the Ankara-Adana Mototren called the Cukurova, comes through the station without stopping. This diesel set is the same sort as the Bogazici; but it only runs twice weekly, and takes 12¼ hours, which is quicker than any other train.

After its departure we move on down to Ulukisla, where another long pause ensures that the really spectacular part of the journey will be done after dark.

The delay this time is not for engine changing, for engine and guards work through from Konya, their home shed, to Adana and back. Merely we shed a few carriages, from the rear of the train, which are destined for Erzurum, which, if we had arrived on time

would leave after only 56 minutes delay. The local train to which they should be attached is itself given two hours at Ulukisla in which to recover from late running if necessary, but today there is no sign of it. The darkness is unfortunate, for the descent of the Cakit stream is most spectacular. Kardesgedigi is 4,816 feet above sea level, and Yenice, just 112 feet-one hundred and ten kilometres of descent in tunnels, corniches, and bridges over side-ravines, while above the Taurus line, the mountains rise 3,000 feet. The narrow valley has pine trees in it, and about 35 kilometres down lies Pozanti, which has a small shed for extra banking engines.

Descending the Taurus gives a sense of overwhelming engineering achievement, where even those not really interested in railways must perforce be moved, as gorges, viaducts and tunnels succeed each other. We stop occasionally at remote mountain villages, where the moonlight is a much stronger illumination than the single oil lamp, flickering on the platforms of the little stations. Ten kilometres of continuous tunnels, interspersed by bridges over side ravines, are a feature of this part of the line, whose engineering is quite as breathtaking as that of the Alps or the Cevennes. Indeed it is so vast a succession of man-made works, that an ordinary embankment above the great Seyhan plain, onto which the train at last emerges, comes as quite a change. We quickly descend the sloping embankment, to reach ground level at the junction station of Yenice.

Here we must reverse direction, leaving the sergeant to go on towards Adana. A choice of trains awaits us, both going to Mersin, only 42 kilometres away. We pick the diesel car and trailer, which are French built and older than any of the other diesel trains we have so far met, which roams swiftly away towards Tarsus and the sea. It is followed later, by the steam train, which is a mixed one, chiefly made up of goods wagons.

Tarsus is the only place of note on the journey across the flat cotton fields. Its twinkling lights reveal the place to be another mud-hut settlement, and looking much the same, I imagine, as in St. Paul's day. Such a hard birth place and limited prospects make his conversion to evangelism and his urge to travel, the more understandable.

The white lights of the Mersin port installations, and the many cars flashing along the tarmacadam coast road are a change from the almost deserted villages in the mountains, or even of Tarsus. Our railcar deposits us at the clean little passenger terminus, away from the sea front. There are palms on the platform, and taxis outside. The weather is far warmer than on the plateau. So we take a victoria, which still has its hood down, for the pleasant drive between the stone-built houses of the well-lit port, under the stars of the clear Mediterranean night.

Mersin is the pleasantest place we have so far struck, since leaving Istanbul. Though it is not yet greatly frequented by tourists, the Toros hotel offers a European style welcome to visitors, who are dining on the terrace in the open, next to the beach, with a fountain playing. There is a change in atmosphere, a barrier between Turk and foreigner, as there so often is between English speaking people on a seaside holiday abroad and the local inhabitants, whom an older generation would refer to as natives. The Turkish waiters, deft and obsequious seem withdrawn and disinclined to talking.

Tarsus; birthplace of St. Paul. Courtesy of Turkish Tourism.

Mersin beach looking east to the docks. Courtesy of Turkish Tourism.

V Up the Taurus, Mersin to Izmir

Beyond the town there lies the open country,
Where, gathering speed, she acquires mystery,
The luminous self-possession of ships on ocean
It is now she begins to sing - at first quite low
Then loud, and at last with a jazzy madness -
The song of her whistle screaming at curves,
Of deafening tunnels, brakes, innumerable bolts.
                                        Stephen Spender

Mersin and Iskenderun have both applied for permission to become free ports, as have Izmir and Istanbul, and Trabzon on the Black Sea. The Turkish south coast is becoming a tourist resort, but not as quickly and extensively as the Aegean coast. Southern Turkey is appreciably hotter than the other coastal places, and so has a good chance of developing winter tourism. It is forgotten that, though it is on the north side of the Mediterranean, the latitude is that of Tunis. The Gulf of Iskenderun provides a warm spot, protected by high mountains which block the winds from the north, while the island of Cyprus, forty miles off shore and slightly south-west, gives a break to the westerly winds rolling down the Mediterranean. Cyprus offers much (including a sterling holiday) when that unhappy country is not engaged in or under threat of war. Tunisia also offers much to the sun-seeking tourist. Southern Turkey offers something more, something that all those other places do not have; accessibility by Wagons-Lits.

An airport taking the largest international jets has been established to serve the Mersin - Adana area. Adana and Yenice already have the famous Taurus Express, running for almost forty years, three times a week from Istanbul (Haydarpasa). The entire journey including the four nights on the train from Britain or France can be paid for in Sterling, though of course the stop-over in Istanbul cannot. Everyone wants to see Istanbul anyway. Mersin is not merely warmer than Istanbul, it is half the price of staying there.

One of the facets that differentiate this part of Turkey is the Arab television, beamed across the corner of the Mediterranean from Beirut. Of course you can go right through to Beirut by the Taurus Express once a week, if you so choose; though for the choosing you have another night in the sleeper, and no diner in Syria or Lebanon. Beirut is apparently not the cheapest of holiday resorts either.

Southern Turkey has a charm different to the other regions. Warm, open and unpretentious, it contains many relics of civilisations going back 3,000 years. It has a complicated history, conquered at various times by Assyrians, and Persians, and then Alexander the Great. Then the Romans came; the Arabs also moved into the area from the south, and the Armenians from the North East. The Seljuks took over control of Cilicia in 1077 AD; and in the 16th century it became part of the Ottoman Empire. Later, as we set out at the end of this book, various Western Allies thought they would like to carve up the more fertile parts of Turkey after World War I, and Antioch only reverted to Turkey in 1939.

Nevertheless Mersin is not cosmopolitan like Istanbul; nor pompous and official like Ankara, nor remote, poor, proud and friendly, like Kars. Mersin is amiable and happy; Adana is the centre of the region, but Mersin is as important. Its port has the largest of all the grain silos dotted about Turkey. Oranges, lemons and bananas are grown; inland there is cotton. To the west, Roman baths and Greek temples wait to be explored. Taxis to do this are not particularly dear; self drive hire cars have not yet reached this part of Turkey, which is a pity.

Alternatively you may laze on the beach, admiring the British looking, British built and former Royal Navy warships, which the Turkish Navy keeps ready for any bother in Cyprus. There are open air restaurants, cafes and apparently two night clubs (not explored by us). The local information office of Turkish Tourism is run by Dr. Cemil Toksoz, who is the author of a little book obtainable here called 'Cilicia in History'. It conveys the sense of continuity of life which goes on in the area much as it has always done. No doubt the many remains, smashed and largely uncharted by archaeologists, contribute their quota of antiques which are illegally smuggled from Turkey to be sold in America and elsewhere. Many of these ancient sites are on the road to Silifke, where the mountains come down to the sea, 57 kms. west of Mersin.

Mersin's clean streets lead to the well-laden market in Silifke Street; selling local carpets and cloth; copperware, ox-harness and so forth. It exists for the people, not tourists. One could linger in Mersin a week or a year; such is the sense of lengthy history, it wouldn't make much difference. The port lacks bustle, and it is perhaps this that brings a tinge of regret on leaving. Mersin is altogether an affable place.

Tarsus, on the other hand, looks as unattractive by day as by night. What with Mark Anthony meeting Cleopatra here, not to mention St. Paul, whose birthplace can be seen, it is steeped in history. More recently another meeting between heads of state took place in 1945, between Sir Winston Churchill and the President of Turkey. Churchill landed at Mersin and the meeting took place in a train, at Yenice. Ataturk's elegant carriages were used, presumably to bring the President from Ankara. The rendezvous was held on the west curve, now torn up, that gave access to Mersin from Ankara, without reversal. I seem to recall reading somewhere that Churchill had to wait for his arrival. But at least he did not have to wait seven hours, as we do. Anticipation of the romantic thrill of pounding up the Taurus in the express of that name, perforce begins to wane. We pass the time conversing with two Turkish youths from Mersin, going to Istanbul to take their entrance exam to the University. This is a slow process as there is only one dictionary; the youths are twins, Ahmed and Mehmed, and so identical in looks and behaviour, we keep getting their

Borsig-built 2-6-0T no. 3403, a former Anatolian Railway locomotive.
Photo: P. Ransome-Wallis.

Mustafa Kemal 'Ataturk' at Kutahya in 1930. Photo courtesy of Milli Kutuphane Anakar (National Library, Ankara)

An official works photo of Ataturk's special train.
Courtesy of Linke Hofmann.

names wrong. In the intervals of waiting for my turn with the lexicon, I become obsessed with the notion that life would be easier, if only they had had their names embroidered on their collars like Tweedledum and Tweedledee.

After the tenth glass of tea in the fly-infested buffet, the sun goes down. It is one of those heinous waits when the train is expected any time, and it is therefore impossible to go away. Local trains come and go; long goods trains arrive from Adana and depart fussily for Mersin, while we curse our luck at again being deprived of seeing the marvellous mountain section by day-

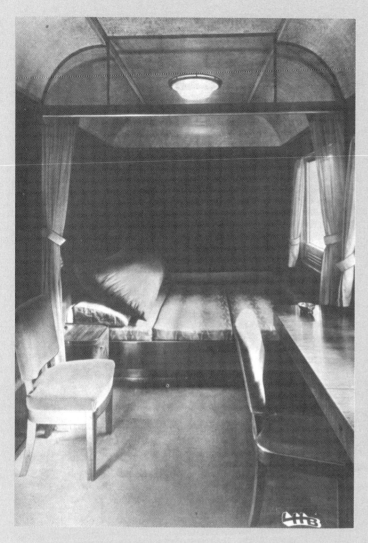

Three views of the interior of Ataturk's personal saloon. Above are his sleeping compartment and the on-train bathroom, while his study is shown at left.
Courtesy of Linke Hofmann.

light. When at length the quivering blob of the headlight turns out to be the great train, hauled by two enormous engines, romantic anticipation has completely given place to profound relief that the train turns up at all!

Like a great illuminated slug, it creeps into the station, and suddenly there is need to hurry. The indefatigable Mr. Imre, who had been sent by the Company to join the train at Adana, jumps down on to the track to welcome us aboard. He is almost impatient with me for pausing in front of the evocative destination board with "Baghdad—Istanbul (H'pasa)" on it.

A whistle from one of the engines to indicate to the driver of the other one to start, and we are off, majestically, discreetly, gracefully; the braying of a startled moke is drowned by the staccato exhaust of the two great engines getting a run at the hill, as the mud huts of Yenice are left behind. There is no difficulty in finding the right word for our progress, it is neither sedate, nor discreet, nor, let's face it, particularly smooth; the word is Grand, as our elegant conveyance clatters over the points at the end of the station, where the junction with the Mersin line is located.

Although it is after eleven o'clock at night, there is a full dinner waiting for us - not in a "B-Mixte" converted second class carriage, but in a real WL dining car, whose familiar Birmingham brass fittings gleam their own magnificent welcome.

Inside the diner besides Mr. Imre, we find also the Chef de Section of Haydarpasa, who has been on a visit to the Company's Syrian Representative. With him is a young man about to be promoted to Controleur de Route. In contrast to the hurry to get on board, here all is calm. There is all night, if necessary, to dine, for the train is self contained and the sumptuous diner runs through from Gaziantep to Haydarpasa. Old fashioned it may be, intolerable today in countries where working hours and wages have shortened and increased respectively, it remains splendidly enjoyable. The diner has double luggage racks for hand baggage, said to be called "Pullman" racks and to be designed by Lord Dalziel himself, when he was Chairman of the British Pullman Car Co. and President of Wagons-Lits; they are still (1968) to be seen in the cars of the Brighton Belle, the electric London - Brighton Pullman train. I explain how the lower, small rack is for umbrellas to go with the bowlers businessmen in London wear. This greatly amuses the Turkish Wagons-Lits officials, who take a personal pride in the whole train.

They are more than ready to answer my queries, for is this not far better than bouncing all night in a minibus? Mr. Imre had retailed our misfortunes at Erzincan to

Above: Taurus Express destination board, Voiture-Lits no. 3441.
Photo: J.H. Price.

The Taurus Express from Gaziantep uses modern rolling stock.
Courtesy of Turkish Tourism.

53

his colleagues, and we are now accepted as one of the family, not visiting foreigners requiring their courteous assistance as hitherto. In reply to the question whether the Turkish dining car crews went all the way to Baghdad in the war, Mr. Imre answers that not only did they do so, but very often he was the chef. Now the car goes no further than Gaziantep, perhaps it is appreciated more. Certainly the evening passes in an atmosphere of amiability worth of the glittering surroundings of this relic of a bygone age, this too-expensive diner. The thought that in far-off Madrid, Company's Representative for Turkey, Monsieur Evliyagil, was at this very moment bargaining for its existence with the Director General of Wagons-Lits and the Turkish Railways delegation, who were both attending the international Timetable Conference, is banished by the reverberant roar of the two ten-coupled engines pounding through the succession of tunnels.

The jolliests of repasts must end, and when we step into the vestibule swirling smoke and smuts drench us. We are reminded that the Taurus Express is a Turkish train, and that Turks leave the corridor connections open for increased ventilation. Inside the sleeper, everyone has gone to bed. The stout conductor looks a romantic figure from the past, in his seat in the dimly lit corridor, from which most of the lights have been extinguished. The noise of the locomotives is louder than ever, the air rich with sulphur and coal-dust. The brise-bise of brown blanketing material which helps to deaden noise and keeps in heat and stops condensation, covers most of the windows, though it is folded down by day. Instead of seeming lugubrious, brown now appears exactly the right colour, for it does not show the dirt at all.

The sleeping car is forced up the hill at a relentless fifteen miles an hour, to the accompaniment of the struggles of the engines. Who wants a gramophone record, when they can come and hear the real thing - and smell it into the bargain? There seems to my trained, but out-of-practice ear, to be a third engine, banking the Express at the rear, and since we are only one sleeper and a van away from the back of the train, small wonder there is so much din. Now the speed drops further, the exertions die away, and we come to rest at a little country station in the Taurus mountains. Three ten-coupled engines taking water is quite a sight today. Alas, there is time only to pull the ring to try to lower the window, heave on the handle in the accustomed manner, and let out some of the worst of the smoke in the corridor.

From the corridor, there is little to see, except for the charming rhododendrons growing on the platform; the sound of rushing water mingles with the panting of the Westinghouse brake pumps. When the drivers are ready there is another sound, almost forgotten in these days of diesel or effortless electric haulage, whistle-crowing for the banker to get ready to push again. There is no doubt now about how many engines; all three of them blast away, reverberating round the mountains. Where else, outside the Iron Curtain, does this happen nowadays? The stupendous pounding of the three locomotives, climbing the 1 in 40 hill, in and out of the tunnels, will attract the enthusiasts from far and wide, now steam has made its bow in Britain.

No wonder that for the Taurus Express, the Wagons-Lits Co. ordered the SG class of sleeper. Though there are none as such left in Turkey, the SGT with third class berths as well as first and second, were reconstructed from them and from other S class sleepers, by the expedient of removing some of the compartments, and using the extra space as individual wash-rooms. This is our first night in an SGT, and its amenities can never be more appreciated than after snorting up the gradient. To the accompaniment of all these puffing locomotives contented sleep comes faster than ever.... The achievement of engines and crews exudes a sense of elation, felt despite the desultory remarks about Turkish trains from the upper berth, where the window with its blanketing remains tightly shut.

A long stop, and the stuffiness of the compartment wakes me. Dawn is breaking; up front there is an unmistakable diesel puttering. I wake as from a dream; though the soot all over everything is real enough. We set off, backwards, past a board proclaiming "Bogazkopru", confirming that we are not going to reverse further than to take the connecting spur of the triangular junction. The sense of change which vanished steam brings home, leaves behind it an air charged with sulphuric nostalgia. As we inch round the sharp curve of the spur, and the familiar red diesel is easily seen from the window of our cabin, I think of all those people filling their sitting rooms with the sound of Peter Handford's gramophone records, free of all grime; we have the grime without the sound.

After breakfast I notice a tired Turk in the blue uniform used by dining car crews, sleeping on the conductor's corridor berth. "Post-man" says our stout, jolly conductor cryptically. Together they have been from Haydarpasa to Baghdad and back. But on the return journey, it seems that TCDD personnel take over the Wagons-Lits baggage car at the frontier, to deal with the internal mails and parcels, and in desperation the "Bagagiste" has taken refuge in the sleeper after his sixth night on the train.

The baggage vans, or "Fourgons" as they are always known in Wagons-Lits parlance, are another reminder of bygone days, when a rapid transit service was operated all over Europe. Many of the Fourgons, like ours, had a mail compartment. The Taurus was the last of these services to be extended. New Fourgons-Postes were supplied from Paris in 1939, ready for the projection of the line to Mosul in Iraq. Today it is almost the last run to have a mail contract; though the Portuguese also use Wagons-Lits to carry their Lisbon mail in the Sud Express to and from the French frontier. In spite of all the upheavals in Iraq and Syria, the Taurus service has gone on, for nearly thirty years now, in the best International Sleeping Car tradition. At the time of our journey only the Postman and the Wagons-Lits Conductor were allowed over the frontier, because of the typhoid epidemic. Apparently the car ran empty in Iraq, with no local passengers. The conductor assured us that there was in fact no typhoid raging in Baghdad; but the Turkish Government were frightened of it reaching Varto, and were taking stringent precautions. Our sleeper becomes the centre of the coterie of Wagons-Lits personnel on board, as we are between the diner and the Beirut - Haydarpasa sleeper. The latter was reinstated, first to Tripoli and later to Beirut. The line had ended at Tripoli until the British Forces extended it during World War II. In pre-war days an old teak WL sleeper made a connection from Aleppo to Tripoli; but now all the sleeping cars and conductors come from Haydarpasa.

There is an air of erstwhile glory in the sleeper's mottled plush, and in the heavy brass ashtrays in the diner; the brass spitoons are fortunately no longer needed, though perhaps they ought to be retained in the third class. Looking round the compartment there are many reminders of an age of ebullient affluence and snobbery, when the car took people to Diaghilev's Ballet Russe at

Monte Carlo, where one of the ballets was called "Blue Train", with decor by Picasso! Does anyone now really use the hook for a fob watch, still carefully upholstered in a little piece of mottled plush to match the seating? In this age of austerity and atom bombs, most of the passengers seem to be military on leave, or business men, rather than diplomats, international opera stars or nobility. Here in Turkey, the good manners of the people reflect the sense of etiquette and good behaviour demanded of the pre-war clientele. Imagine, today, if customers were forbidden to bring all their baggage into a compartment! Here in Turkey there is still pride in the service, the same pride that ensured there was no compartment-sharing, during the war, by allied and axis customers. The Taurus Express was the one best patronised by the allies, though the Germans sent agents on it, with the sole purpose of examining unattended baggage, or picking up careless talk. They themselves preferred to use the Anatolia Express on their journeys from Ankara to Istanbul.

The unexpected ringing of the luncheon bell rouses me from these ruminations of earlier journeys along the line. That we will not reach Ankara before midday is good enough for Mr. Imre to insist that his charges (and thus himself) are given further hospitality in the diner before being set down. This is our last whole day as guests of the Company in his care, though it has no bearing on the matter of luncheon. Late running of the westbound Taurus seems to have been going on for over twenty years, and the Turks are quite used to it. Their own express trains run punctually enough, but with international ones it is a different matter. In fact we only have three hours to wait in Ankara, before leaving again.

The Izmir Express Wagon-Lits is run by the Ankara Section, and is one of the Y class cars which are also found on the Anatolia Express. Because the International Fair is being held at Izmir, the sleeper is running daily, instead of three times a week. This is another of the several unadvertised surprises which makes the TCDD so much better in fact than in the timetable! As the Fair is due to end the day after our arrival, the car is half empty, and we are given single compartments. The car is much newer, and rather more elegant than that of the romantic Taurus. It is one of the batch specially built after the war for the Ankara Express. The Ankara Section is tiny compared to Haydarpasa, and such stores as are needed for running repairs are kept in an aged teak diner (No. 1396), which is stabled at the end of a siding. The twisted nature of its bodywork is easily apparent; but so few old Wagons-Lits cars have escaped the scrap heap that the preservationists may well have their eye on this one.

The Izmir train - called the Izmir Express (Turkish for Smyrna) - is timed to leave at 17.40, which is a very reasonable hour to start an overnight sleeper journey. It is drawn into the station about an hour before departure time by the diesel express engine that takes it all the way. The Ankara Chef de Section is there to watch us start, and no sooner have we done so, than Mr. Imre appears to announce "Afternoon Tea".

This relic of the late 1920s is the least remembered one. Afternoon Tea is an essentially English institution, much publicised in the days when Lord Dalziel was President of the Company. The Ege Express in 1966 is one of the three remaining trains of 1966 with a proper Wagons-Lits diner, not a buffet converted from a TCDD carriage, so tea is proudly served to us, in a British built car. The Turks of course grow their own tea as well

as coffee, though it is always served in glasses with lemon.

Soon after starting, we pause for the Bogazici Express from Haydarpasa to pass without stopping; because of this we are booked to call first at Etimesgut, only 18 km. from Ankara, out of a total journey of 800 km. (500 miles). Dinner begins after Polatli, reached at 7 p.m. (19.00 hrs.) and the diner's conductor, proud of his twenty-five years service with the Company is determined that his Ankara-based car shall be just as good as any from Haydarpasa.

We stop for eight minutes at Eskisehir, and then follow the Konya line again to Alayunt. During the night, the Express leaves the old Konya line at Kutahya, which is 3,251 feet up and climbs down from the plateau to the plain of Balikesir, which is only 430 feet above sea level. From the summit 3,396 ft. at Kopruoren (24 km. from Kutahya), the bare plateau gradually descends, the railway following first one river, then another, and some tunnelling is necessary in this process, which takes place after passing Tavsanli. This station possesses an engine shed and is junction for a modern branch line to Tuncbilek, 14 km. long. After passing some 3 or 4 tunnels around Demirli, the line passes various lignite mines at Degirmisaz and Balikoy. The ruling gradient is 1 in 60 easing on the last stretch to 1 in 66. The line winds about with sharp curves and many more short tunnels. It was the first to be built by the TCDD after nationalisation, and was completed in 1932. Most of the way the line follows enclosed, wooded valleys, after leaving the plateau. There are 39 tunnels on this stretch altogether, of a total combined length of just over 6,000 metres.

At Balikesir, reached at half past three in the morning, we join the formerly French owned line from Izmir to Bandirma, which we follow in the next chapter. This takes us over from the Balikesir plain to the rich valley of the river Gediz at Manisa, which we reach at about seven o'clock. The richness of the Smyrna region is astonishing. The land is abundantly fertile and the climate favourable. Figs, olives, vines, corn, oranges, lemons, walnuts, maize, sesame, tobacco, cotton and liquorice are produced in it, not to mention dairy products. There are proper brickworks, but many houses are built of stone and are two-storey. To anyone who has first visited other more barren parts of Turkey, and also been to Greece, the Graeco-Turk wars fought for the possession of this gloriously rich area becomes still more understandable. A person with the most cursory knowledge of agriculture, food production and economics, cannot fail to be impressed by the proliferation of growing crops. All the good things in the dining car seem to have their origin here. When so much of Turkey seems to consist of harsh, bare valleys, or dusty plains that are snow-bound half the year, it is only on visiting Western Anatolia that you understand how they manage to live so comparatively well.

The feeling of difference is continued on the railway. The Aegean area services are still shown separately in the timetable, in 1966 all save the Ege Express and the railcar trains, were steam hauled. Some of the local trains that run the suburban service between Menemen and Izmir are still composed of very elderly-looking, four-wheeled carriages from diverse lines. The stations still reflect their former French ownership in a variety of little ways, such as concrete railings, level crossing gates, huts, and so on.

Suddenly Izmir's landlocked gulf sweeps into view on our right. The train calls at Karsiyaka, the northern suburb of Izmir connected by ferry across the bay, as well as by railway, which is an 11 km. journey. The size of Izmir, second in importance only to Istanbul as a port, is grasped as we proceed to the terminus, through Turan and other suburban stations. Near Cinarli the suburban line to Bornova runs in on the left and the line becomes double for the last 3 km. past Halkapinar, where the former French railway works and engine sheds are situated, and over the famous level crossing with the Izmir - Aydin railway, into Basmane terminus.

The station is small and insignificant by modern standards, which is perhaps why the Alsancak station, nearer the docks and quite as big, is also retained, though only secondary lines use it. Basmane is much more central for the residential part of the city.

Izmir is much less noisy than Istanbul; it lacks the troublesome bustle that surrounds the former capital. Above all, Izmir is placid, almost pompous; a superior city. The waterfront is reminiscent of Salonika; its gardens have a large statue of Ataturk pointing out to the sea, into which the Greek armies were hurled in 1922. Here the resemblance to Greece ends. All is calm and orderly. There is no raucous singing or drunkenness in the little water front bars. Many of them serve only tea or coffee or the ubiquitous lemonade; Gazinozu.

Manisa.
  Courtesy of Turkish Tourism.

Manisa station with 56500 class engine no. 56545.
  Photo: P. Ransome-Wallis.

I think of toil by rail and boat,
And crackle at the table d'hote;
Of passes steep that try the lungs
And chattering in unknown tongues
                    J. Ashby Sterry

Izmir has a great deal to offer the conventional tourist. Among the attractions not so far advertised, is the Fire Station where the Fire Brigade exhibit an old Merryweather of 1875, and newer motor appliances including a Saurer-mounted engine. The conventional amenities are growing, as are the hotels. There is the great Efes (Ephesus) Hotel, round which other hotels, like the Kismet, are situated. This one is quite as comfortable as the Grand Efes, but cheaper. Leaving our luggage in the lobby, in the care of the somewhat startled management who were not expecting Mr. Imre, we go off to explore the town with him.

Izmir is considerably more 'Tamam' (in English "O.K.") with him than any of the other outlandish places - particularly Erzincan to Sivas. that he has been obliged to visit in the course of his escort duty with us. He walks us briskly southwards along the waterfront, where one of the larger liners of the Turkish Maritime Lines, was loading and discharging motor cars, before leaving for Istanbul.

Further on is the central bus station and No.25 takes us up to the Kadife Kalesi, an old fort to the south of the city with a superb view all round. To the north the Kultur Park or International Fair Ground is prominent. Also visible is the Basmane Station. Trains seem to be continuously whistling, which is odd, as none seem to be moving there, nor on the Aydin line, on our right. The old Roman Forum site is plainly seen in the foreground.

Returning to the city, we explore the narrow streets of the bazaar, where prices seem to be higher than in Istanbul, which is surprising, as prices elsewhere are lower than in that city.

After some deliberation we stumble on a restaurant where the menu suits Mr. Imre's good taste. It includes a fish shashlik, pieces of fish grilled on skewers with the usual bay leaves, tomatoes etc., and considered a treat by the Turks; a speciality only to be had in Izmir, apparently. The Izmir white wine seems better than that served on the trains, which comes from Ankara. Afterwards Mr. Imre leaves us, saying he wishes to sleep as he has to change trains at Eskisehir at 3 next morning. He departs rather suddenly, and we do not see him again.

The International Fair at Izmir which takes place each year is excellent by standards of such fairs elsewhere. The Kultur Park with its restaurants and interesting antiquity museum is a permanent feature open all the year. The Turkish visitors are immensely taken with the closed circuit television, with camera turned on the crowd, in the Soviet Pavilion. They point excitedly to themselves on the T.V. sets, which Turkey did not possess in 1966. Foreign visitors interested in Turkish Steam Travel, are equally attracted to the miniature 15 inch gauge railway. This is also permanent, unlike the foreign pavilions, and is most realistic.

The engine is an authentic model of the standard mixed traffic class locomotive, and looks as though it were built to scale in Eskisehir shops, like the model passenger engines at Ankara. It has an authentic whistle, which shrieks all round the park at the innumerable level crossings with pedestrian walks. It is this that had been confusing me, up at Kadife Kalesi, for the park has many trees, and the line is invisible from the fort.

The carriages form an enormously long train in authentic style, and the passengers are smothered in authentic coal-dust, since they are open type, as at Ankara (see photo on page 30); the whole line exudes an authentic smell of hot oil and sulphur. There is a passing loop and a small engine shed near the principal stopping place, but trains run in one direction only, and only one engine appeared to be available. When working, it runs for long hours without respite - as on the TCDD; though it does not run every day, and often not at all when the fair is not in progress, save on special occasions.

Most people who stay in Izmir visit Pergamon and Ephesus to see the ancient monuments. Pergamon is not on the railway and it is not very feasible to take the train to Selcuk from the Alsancak

View of Izmir looking north from the Kadifekale Castle.
Courtesy of Turkish Tourism.

A diamond crossing is formed by the tracks leading out of Izmir's two terminus stations, Alsancak and Basmane, and was in steam days one of the most photographed railway locations in Turkey.

Left: A Hanomag 34001 class 2-6-0 approaching Izmir Alsancak, showing here the carrying wheels added to this class of locomotive to reduce the axle weight.
Photo: D. Trevor Rowe.

Right: For comparison, another of the Hanomag 2-6-0s, seen at Ankara with the carrying axle removed.
Photo: E.L. Bell.

Humboldt-built 2-8-0 no. 45132 leaving Izmir Alsancak.
D. Trevor Rowe.

2-10-2 no. 57018 approaching Izmir Basmane from Manisa.
Photo: D. Trevor Rowe.

Left: Corpet Louvet-built 2-6-2T no. 3513 on an Izmir suburban train.
Photo: P. Ransome-Wallis.

Below: Izmir fair by night in the Kultur Park.
Courtesy of Turkish Tourism.

TCDD 2-10-2 no. 57008 at Halkapinar.
Photo: P. Ransome-Wallis.

Station, to visit Ephesus, as it is 3 kilometres further off to the south east. One can hire a car or take a taxi or use one of the many bus services. Ephesus is extremely well documented, as it is one of the largest and best known ancient Greek cities. Continuing efforts have been made in the 1960s to restore it, both by the Turkish Government and many foreign archaeologists. Many of the statues are in the museum at Selcuk, which itself has ancient remains. Other Ephesus relics are in the Kultur Park at Izmir.

The best way to get a view of the whole city, whose size is striking, is to enter from the top road, which leads to the House of the Virgin Mary, where she is said to have been taken by St. John. This international shrine is cared for by nuns, and the Turkish Tourism Department have made it possible for most visitors to read about it in their own language. Even Greek notices are permitted here.

By sending your taxi round to the main entrance of the old city it is possible to explore the entire ruined streets without retracing your steps. There are theatres, gymnasia, a market place, the city wall, villas and houses - even a ruined brothel!

The main road to Kusadasi passes the main entrance. This resort is 16 kms. further on, and it is easy to see how far the sea has receded, since the days when Ephesus was a port. The Ephesians originally colonised Kusadasi, then called Neapolis, with islanders from Samos. This Greek island is within sight of Kusadasi, which has a deep water quay. The village attracts many liners whose itinerary comprises many more Greek monuments than just Ephesus.

Close to the quay the caravanserai has been developed as a hotel, by the Club Mediterranee. Many more new hotels, motels and camps make the village one of the best known Turkish holiday resorts. It is possible in 1969 to spend all-inclusive holidays there, with direct flights from London to Izmir. The hills, running down to warm, sandy beaches, form a beautiful background to this peaceful resort.

On our return to Izmir, we pass several camel trains. Camels are only found in the Izmir area, as it is too cold for them on the Anatolian plateau. Camel fights, like Turkish wrestling, are among the spectacles provided for the tourists.

Though a wide variety of steam is on show at Izmir, where all loco-hauled trains except the Izmir Express use steam engines, the 'Marmara' diesel train, not to be confused with the Marmara Express (so named only in 1967) is one of the second class only type, similar to the one we took to Konya. This time we are scrambling in at the terminus, and the first twenty minutes of our journey are again occupied in skirting the Gulf of Izmir and making a leisurely stop at Karsiyaka, where many more people squeeze on board our already full train. Another twenty minutes brings us to Menemen, reached three quarters of an hour before Manisa.

The figs, orange and lemons, which grow in abundance, gradually cease to surround the line, and the rich plain of Smyrna slowly peters out after we leave Manisa, 164 feet above sea level.

The hills are not nearly as harsh as the great central plateau of Anatolia, as we slowly climb up to Akhisar, 331 feet, where there is another important commercial centre. Cloth, cereals, tobacco, olives, grapes are among the products of the locality. At Donertas, 137 kms. from Izmir we reach 778 feet up and drop gently down into Bakir valley to Kirkagac, which has another rich plain surrounding it, and next, Soma where the station is across the river from the town.

After this the line gets harsher, and climbs at 1 in 50 to get over the watershed between the Aegean and Marmara seas. The coaches are so full only those near the buffet can get any lunch, though valiant efforts are made by one of the stewards to sell drinks to the passengers further down the train. We are finishing our leisurely meal with a cup of Turkish coffee, while the train pauses for the regulation thirteen minutes at Balikesir, 241 km. from Izmir, 101 km. from Bandirma (station), and 430 feet above sea level.

Balikesir is an air base, and many Turkish Air Force personnel, going on weekend leave to Istanbul, come aboard our train. Luckily some people have got off, though most passengers are going all the way.

It is curious how Turkey grows on one. Exactly what is so likeable about the country escapes the westerner. Though we have been in Turkey for a month, we seem hardly to have scratched the surface; but should we ever be allowed to penetrate in depth?

We leave the railway by which we arrived from Ankara, turning off to the right across the Balikesir plain, while we ourselves drop down a little and then climb up to nearly 1,000 feet before dropping down to Yenikoy, 764 feet, high and barren, in the hills and Omerkoy, 348 feet, where we are booked to pass the Marmara railcar coming in the reverse direction. All the trains serve the steamers. We are preceded by an all-stations, the steam train leaving Izmir at 7 a.m. and arriving ten minutes before us. On the other three days a week, when the boat does not run, the two diesel trains forming the Marmara Mototren make a journey in the afternoon; on Saturdays, there are no trains. There are extra trains between Izmir and Balikesir, and Izmir to Soma.

Mustapha Kemalpasa station is a full 20 km. away from the town of that name, where some curious goings-on connected with the robbery of Turkish Art Treasures, were revealed in a British Sunday newspaper soon after our return to Britain.

Hereabouts are rich farms, miles of land with no buildings, and hardly any trees. The area is not far from Lake Manyas, to the west. We wait some time at the next station, alongside a goods train going the other way, which also dozes in mid-afternoon. Stationmasters and understationmasters come and rouse the driver and guard into activity, and the great steam engine takes the road again, slowly, to enable all the various attendants travelling on it to rush out from the station house and board its vans. Like the camels round Izmir, goods trains seem to move imperturbably, slowly and sedately to their destination. They usually arrive within the next twelve hours. Delays are not usually due to the operators, who keep very good time when they can. Breakdowns, mishaps and irregularities are rare, though through carriages run vast distances. Obviously in this case, the boat has been late arriving at Bandirma.

The extent of the Sea of Marmara is not really well shown in some atlases; but the outcrop or peninsular, shaped rather like a mushroom, that protects Bandirma on the west, is clearly marked on the southern shore, towards the centre of the sea. The sea on the west or left of this "mushroom shaped projection", appears from our carriage window, near Aksakal station where we meet the Mototren coming the other way. At the next stop, Sigirci, we meet the local all-stations train. We have descended 100 feet from Aksakal, and are now 89 feet above sea level. The land is now pastoral, with few trees.

We have a brief glimpse of Bandirma harbour down below on our right, before we plunge down in 1 in 40 through a short tunnel to Bandirma Gar (Station) on the west of the town. No one gets in or out at the little station under the cliff. Our second driver has already taken up his position at the rear of the train and soon we are signalled away by the stationmaster. We have become so used to this that it is a shock to realise he is the last of hundreds of Turkish station masters in Asia, to see us away. Instead of starting off quickly, we creep away, almost lapped by the water, for the 2 km. extension to the port. There is sand between the rails - seashore sand, and presently there are stone sets and we are in the road. The last 500 metres are double track, and between us and the shore is the local, its steam engine resting in the roadway.

We join the mad scramble to the little ticket office in the side

Minarets and winter sunshine for this Darlington-built 2-8-2 seen on November 5th 1970 on the outskirts of Izmir. Photo: Paul Cotterell.

of the archway leading to the pier, for surprisingly few people seem to have through tickets. Our own resplendent yellow pass is strictly a TCDD affair and of course invalid on the Turkish Maritime Lines.

We walk along the pier, surfaced with large uneven boulders, to the quay at right angles to it, parallel to the wharf where the railway ends in the road. People are madly busy trying to load a steamer which is keen to get away on time, though resigned to not doing so. Everything has to be manhandled over the uneven stones, for this is an old fashioned, time honoured route. Frightened horses stumble on the slippery quay; people hurl boxes of fish about. Fully laden donkeys jostle with the passengers. Bandirma, which looks charming enough from above the tunnel, is not yet on the tourist map, and from the recently built, white painted boat, it assumes an air of strange remoteness, despite our new found knowledge of the warmheartedness of the Turks everywhere.

Bandirma must be unimpressive going the other way, struggling off the gangway and rushing for a seat on the Marmara Mototren. It is reminiscent of Fishguard, Holyhead or Dover, just a port on the way to a more important city.

Already the steam train is creeping back along the road to the station, where it will wait 48 hours before the next packet arrives from Istanbul. The steamer hoots and steams away, as dim street and house lights appear on the receding waterfront. Behind the facade, Asiatic Turkey has now lost its eastern mystery, the

nearer the shore, when the light-house begins to shine a little more forcefully than the rest, one marine light among all those land ones. Istanbul may be banned as the Turks official capital, but it is still their dream. Now there are ghostly black shapes of passing vessels, occasionally with a tiny riding light; more are anchored, waiting for morning to pass up to the Black Sea. At last we are near enough to see the tiny opening, curving round so that the lights of Scutari and Uskudar no longer form the continuous crescent. The Turkish flag, of course, has historic origins, but might symbolise this crescent of light, of which the city itself is the star of the land. There is a relative absence of harsh, fluorescent lighting, and most of the lights shine in a golden, old fashioned way. There is no place like Europe, with its ancient civilization. The Bosphorus is so dangerous to shipping that we proceed right up it. The skipper calls angrily for the searchlight, and when at length it is switched on, sure enough there are barques and dhows moving about without lights of any kind. We pass the Golden Horn, looking a little less golden than the Marmara sea front, and round the corner of the Bosphorus, drawing level with the Uskudar Ferry. Here at last we turn and cross the stretch of water to the European side, directly below our hotel. How strange it must seem to visiting Turks, coming this way for the first time, who have never perhaps seen a city this size before. We move back down the Bosphorus again, to the Golden Horn and the steamers and ferries tied up alongside the Galata Bridge, with its pontoons. But instead of joining them, we pick a berth at a jetty surrounded by a dark background, formed it seems of trees, a place specially reserved for the Bandirma steamers. The quay is anything but deserted; already Istanbul begins to show its scrum and jostle, ready to prey on tired, bewildered travellers. The steamer has been slow on arriving, for fear of colliding before the searchlight was rigged up. The taximen have had a long wait for fares.

For some reason everybody tries to rush off the boat at once. There is of course only one gang plank, and ashore there is an almighty traffic jam of honking taxis, as there is only one exit uphill onto the road. As this is a purely domestic service there is no police check nor customs to pass.

We are now accustomed to the taximan assuring us of extra fares payable as it is after midnight, and to our surprise we find we now know enough Turkish to make ourselves plainly understood. The Turks, as has been said before, are hardworking and hospitable, so a welcome awaits us at the Gezi Hotel, even though it is so late at night. The Gezi Hotel is comfortable enough by any European standards, and comparatively cheap, by Hilton standards. So it does not need to call itself Palace Hotel, though it does. Turks rather overdo that word: but then, we've been to Kars.

excitement of being unexplored. Instead, still more exciting, is that these wonderful people are not just going to sit down and wait for the next earthquake, Middle Eastern Style, but rather explode into the twentieth century. They will dig up the minerals found by prospecting Turkish engineers in remote, inaccessible mountains such as the Erciyas Dag above Kayseri, the next generation will have better education and the illiterate, still a big problem for the Turks, will grow fewer.

For the first few minutes the outline of the hills glows in the twilight romantically. Then all is dark, save for the ship's lights. But there is Raki in the bar, unlike railway diners which may only sell Vodka, and this quickly warms the travellers, especially the Air Force, going on leave to Istanbul. The regulation photograph of Ataturk beams down benignly - as in all Turkish Maritime Lines steamers, which are of course state run. The steamer journey takes four and a half hours, which is not long enough to settle truly into a ship, but long enough to become tedious. Yet once more, the sense of briefly sampling the country's attractions presents itself. To do Turkey justice you should stay two months, weeks at a time in one of the more delightful ports, for the country is unsuited to hurrying, though it is purposeful enough.

To arrive at Istanbul by day is notable for the minarets. But come by night. A whole crescent of light glitters, when the steamer is half an hour's journey away. Out of the blackness a whole arc beckons, civilisation beckons. How really enticing it is, after the dusty plains and plateaux of Asiatic Turkey, no wonder so many have made such a fuss about it. How different too, to our arrival by the Balkan Express, when the place itself seemed thoroughly Eastern, with its minarets and hurly-burly taximen. Now it seems gloriously European, with lights everywhere, brightening as the ship nears its destination.

The Bosphorus is so narrow that you cannot pick it out; Istanbul, Sirkeci or Haydarpasa, is one great curve of lights. Nor is it easy to see which one guides our steamer, until we are much

VII The Direct Orient/Marmara Express, Istanbul - Paris

There is every sort of light,
You can make it dark or bright,
There's a handle that you turn to make a breeze.
There's a funny little basin
You're supposed to wash your face in,
And a crank to shut the window if you sneeze.
T.S. Eliot

In 1966 the hall porter at the Gezi Palace Hotel was relatively new to his job. For years he worked for the Wagons-Lits Company, and he made no bones about describing Eastern Turkey as 'another world' compared to Istanbul.

He finished his service as Chef du Train on the Taurus Express, which conveyed the Company's Restaurant, Sleeping and Baggage Cars right through to Baghdad during the whole of World War II. There were also two TCDD coaches working through in the train, instead of the single Sleeping Car and Baggage Car of today.

But long before this, he was working on the Simplon Orient Express, with a flat in Paris near the Gare de Lyon, and travelling not only home to Istanbul, but between Paris and Bucharest, and Paris and Athens as well. By using Turks, the Wagons- Lits Co. were able to carry on the service without change of conductor during the early part of the war. He has strong memories of Dijon at the outbreak, leaving Paris in the evening that war was declared.

The Simplon Orient Express still retained its glittering lustre of peace-time, and food shortages had not hit the diner. As he stood on the platform by the steps of his car, a troop train came in on the opposite line. A French Captain asked him where this magnificent train was going.

"Istanbul, Monsieur" he said.

The Captain looked at the rich clientele enjoying themselves at dinner, and remarked bitterly: "For this, and for such people, we go to war." The elegant exclusiveness was somehow shattered by these remarks.

Yet he carried on living in Paris, in his now blacked-out flat, and owing to the shortage of French conductors, due to the war, he sometimes worked a service to Marseilles, or Ventimiglia, and back, in between his week-long journeys to Eastern Europe. As is mentioned in "Grand European Expresses", the Simplon-Orient Express not only carried on, it even conveyed the Berlin - Istanbul sleeper south of Belgrade, and the French wartime notice "The enemy's ears are listening to you" was never more appropriate, save perhaps in the Yatakli-Vagonlar of the Taurus and Anatolia Expresses.

By 1942 the Wagons-Lits was hard put to it to find work for their French conductors, to keep them out of the Todt Organisation, or forced labour in Germany. For many of the services in France, including the newly started Berlin - Hendaye Sleeper for German diplomats bound for Madrid, were operated by the Mitropa Company with their German personnel. But Mitropa was kept out of Italy, (at that time a loyal ally of the Germans) and all sleeping cars run between the two countries were those of the Wagons-Lits. The French personnel were not permitted to travel beyond Italy, so the Turkish contingent were moved from Paris to Milan, where they took over the train, working through, as before, for the rest of the journey eastwards.

Marshall Tito's guerrillas, and other partisans in Yugoslavia made the journey from Trieste to Zagreb a hazardous business, and in 1943 all the Turkish employees came back to Turkey. There was plenty of scope within the country. The British and American Embassies had a sleeper permanently on private charter to operate between Ankara and Adana in the Taurus Expresses, for example.

The Wagons-Lits service has always been a vocation to many of those who work for the Company, a sort of international passport. Changes and upheavals were slower to take place in Turkey and in the services running to Istanbul from other countries, than elsewhere in Europe. A Royal special train for the King of Rumania was one of the services this conductor worked, though I am not certain as to where it ran, and whether the King left Rumania permanently for neutral Turkey, on this particular occasion. Our conversation, conducted in French most of the time, suffers from translation trouble whenever either of us is lost for words, as a mixture of German, Italian, English and Turkish is then resorted to, and there are frequent interruptions to attend to the needs of the other guests of the Gezi Palace!

Istanbul itself now seems extraordinarily different to when we first arrived. It is easily discernible as the pulsating business heart of Turkey, controlling commerce or at any rate retail goods throughout the country. Some 70 per cent of the Turkish population live on the land, and compared to some of the places we have come from, Istanbul seems highly civilised, European, a goal attained. Whereas for me, at any rate, the prospect of another lengthy Wagons-Lits journey back to Paris, gives the city the added exciting atmosphere of a jumping off place, rather than the end of a quest.

This time we visit the Grand Bazaar on our own, and with our smattering of Turkish and the vendors commendable English, we soon have them trying to sell their wares to us. They are not to know we have experience of such places in Cairo thirty years ago. We pretend we do not want the goods, walk away, mutter darkly that the goods were half the price in Kars, knowing full well that these Istanbul traders will never have been there, and are thus ignorant of the fact that Kars has almost neither a bazaar nor tourists!

Even after a stay of a month, and travelling widely in the country, the visitor is likely to come away from Turkey with the feeling that he has only scratched the surface of the country, or

2-10-0 no. 56502 takes over at Halkali, 28 kilometers from Istanbul.

Photo: D. Trevor Rowe.

seen it through a plate glass picture window. There is a strong feeling underlying every impression of the country, that there is much more to it, an unknown enigmatic charm, the Turks remain charmingly enigmatic.

We depart early from Istanbul, in order to call on the Divisional Manager of the TCDD, and the Wagons-Lits Section, at Sirkeci Station. The Turkish Conductors attached to this section are an elite, who do not transfer with those across the Bosphorus. They all speak Bulgarian, and one other language, usually English or German. The Chef de Section takes us to see the Sultan Abd-el-Aziz's original German-built tank engine, of 1874, and elegant four wheeled carriage, supplied to the Oriental Railway for his use, now mounted on a plinth.

Once again barriers, passports, and customs examinations, separate Turkey from the departing international train. But now all seems much more friendly, instead of bewildering, as is definitely the case when arriving. Special platforms are reserved for the through trains. But these trains stop at many places in European Turkey on the way, and there is nothing to prevent families coming on to the platform to see off their relations. All this seems very Turkish. All the soldiery, and they are plentiful, seem almost superfluous. As usual, they are as friendly as ever with everybody. Yet, in that quiet Turkish way, they are smart and efficient in a manner no Arab could ever attain. And of course further checks take place on the train, after it has started. Only the word 'Edirne' on the shoulder flash of certain army personnel, distinguishes them as travelling frontier police.

Our sleeping car conductor this time is a Turk; the Bulgarians take turns with the Turks in operating the service, but they have only five conductors; Sirkeci Section has many more. Carefully he collects the passengers passports, and as carefully returns us our troublesome transit visas, which we had to get in Istanbul, (and which were abolished for 1967 as the Bulgarian contribution to International Tourism Year). We are mildly surprised.

"The Turkish Policeman might easily lose it" explains our conductor in excellent English. Like him we are getting off at Sofia. Our sleeper is bound for Munich as there is no Paris car on this particular day. The Turkish Railways would really like a daily Paris sleeper, but that is impossible, as the Yugoslavs will take only one car beyond Belgrade in the Direct Orient Express, so that they can run a sleeper of their own between Belgrade and Trieste. The Paris sleeper now runs twice a week from Istanbul and twice a week from Sofia.

In the corridor, a Turkish business man and his wife stands with handkerchief at the ready, to wave as the train passes the back of his seaside villa. We move off easily enough, behind the electric engine, quickly efficient this time. So the journey beside the Sea of Marmara seems much shorter, the setting sun glowing red over the water which stretches westward to the horizon. On the other side of the train lies dusty Yenikoy Airport, busy with jet airliners, and all too soon we are running up the inlet to stop at Halkali station. Only one steam engine backs on here.

After Halkali, the great rolling plains which seemed so harsh and bare coming out, now seem almost green, and luscious compared to Anatolia. Trees are sparse by European standards, but plentiful enough compared to many parts of Turkey.

The darkness which descends so swiftly in this part of the world, swallows up the scene. The train is much as other Turkish trains; next to our sleeper there is a Wagons-Lits diner, not advertised, but running all the same, to Uzunkopru. Only the absence of Mr. Imre's jovial countenance, pressing another olive upon us, reminds us that our Turkish journey is at an end. Yet we are still the guests of the Company, and, in 1966 they still ran the car. So we take our places in it, to the sound of the dinner bell which symbolises that impeccable Wagons-Lits service, which has inspired the elan of the Orient Express.

The diner boasts a crew of only two; so the chef himself serves the meat, and the conductor is kept busy, for foreigners on the train do not load themselves up with picnics, as Turks do. Tomorrow, Bulgaria awaits in total mystery. But tonight we are in the free world, where Turkish hospitality and pride in the job persists to the last.

Such are the vicissitudes of the Oriental Railway's construction, that we do not reach the frontier at Uzunkopru until midnight. Instead, I fall asleep contentedly listening to the shrieking whistle, the short rail joints, and the pounding steam engine, romantic attributes of rail travel which some tourists now go many miles to enjoy.

Later in the night we return to modern reality, after the ancient Greek engine, lurching over the poor track, hoots its whistle and lumbers across the Iron Curtain. 3.30 in the morning, the hour of policemen. Bang, bang, on the door; passport, visa; yellow station lights listless in the early dawn, Bulgarian carriages are shunted on, for now we are the morning workers train, as well as an International Express.

Presently we move off. For the first time we rush along, instead of meandering; gone the rhythm of the rail joints, for they are welded. Up in front the powerful steam engine sets off after every stop with heavy wheel slipping, so popular with the record-makers. People in jeans rush at the train, half-asleep, and just succeed in catching it. The whole area is grey; grey dawn, grey factories, grey gloomy people. They look sad, dejected, overworked; a few spare a cold contemptuous glance at the "wicked" capitalists (like me) luxuriating in bed. Mostly we are discreetly hidden by drawn window blinds.

In Turkey the colours are bright: orange, pink, azure blue, glaring snow-white, or almost black from heavy storms, but rarely grey. Greyness, indeed, is conspicuously absent. So are factories. We stop at a large town, Dimitrovgrad, named after the great Bulgarian leader. Swarms of children get on here, in their best dresses. They crowd into the luggage van as the coaches are full.

At Plovdiv there is a general stampede as they all get out again. The majority of local passengers get out too, but other people join the train. It is 8.30 in the morning, but of course there is no breakfast car, these days, coming on at Svilengrad frontier, and running to Trieste and Lausanne. Such is progress.

I am out on the platform looking at the great passenger locomotive, which is uncoupled to make way for a modern electric engine, and which is Swiss-made, running with the precision and efficiency of Swiss engines everywhere. Fit for a King: maybe the late King of Bulgaria drove it, as was his wont from time to time.

Our train is electrically hauled for the two and a half hour run to the capital, Sofia, where this time we are to break our journey. Soon we climb steadily up through a gorge, and at the top, pass slowly through a wayside station whose name, conveniently written in European as well as Cyrillic characters, catches my eye: Pazardjik. It is an uncanny experience to be miles from anywhere in a totally strange, communist land, and pass through a place with a name so familiar from historic associations. What on earth must it have been like, in the 1880s, to be tumbled out here in a snowstorm, onto a creaking diligence? For such was early Wagons-Lits travel. The Bulgarian line, with its through sleepers from Paris, ended at this wild outpost, with only a coach and four through the mountains to the wobbly terminus of the Oriental Railway at Plovdiv, part of Turkey when first constructed, and called Phillippopolis then

We glide through at a stately thirty miles an hour, for the gradient is appreciable. Then the line enters the great Bulgarian plain. It is 108 miles from Plovdiv to Sofia, and on this section of the line, the trains have now been speeded up, so that the capital is still reached just before noon, though the train does not now leave Plovdiv until twenty past nine, after a quarter of an hour there in which to change the engine.

Along our route, there are several junctions, and at each there is a large steam engine, shunting or waiting to work the local goods trains. Even though the main line is electric, some of the freight trains still seem to be steam hauled. Sofia itself, boasting two large engine sheds, abounds in great locomotives, the largest tank engines in Europe, running on the standard gauge. Our Turkish conductor comes along his car, handing out the passengers tickets and passports, before leaving the sleeper at Sofia.

We are met on the platform by a porter. Luggage portering is evidently not beneath the dignity of a communist, as I had always fondly imagined. A porter in a people's republic is still not a servant, but works at an agreed tariff, which is decidedly costly in terms of English money, and foreigners had better not try and carry their own baggage, unless it be lightweight. That is blacklegging.

The porter deposits our bags on the square, receives his recompense, and leaves. Thunderous trams come and go, turning round a circle of shiny grooved rails, under some trees. But they have impossible cyrillic destination blinds-even if we knew where we wished to go, we could not ask if they went there. Belatedly we think of taking a taxi but all have gone.

In spite of the Iron Curtain, travellers from the west appear to be perfectly free to wander unescorted in Sofia. No one takes the slightest notice of us, nor interest in us. Matters would have been easier had we known whether or not we were expected. Toujours la politesse is not the motto of the Wagons-Lits Co., but it could well be. We ponder, wondering whether Cooks and/or the Bulgarian Tourist Office is as uninterested in us as the general public evidently are, when the Wagons-Lits conductor, now in civilian clothes, comes out of the station with his colleague who arrived from Turkey on the Istanbul Express sleeper a few hours earlier. In a mixture of French, English and Turkish, we soon decide that we all might share a taxi, and when one comes, we are now able at least to hail it in Bulgarian.

We make for 177 Boulevard Giorgiu Dimitrovski, which is a villa in a wide suburban road, lined with well matured trees. The villa looks quiet and unassuming, just like any other in the row; save only that in gold lettering on a black glass plate that has evidently been on the wall since the days when the Boulevard was unashamedly called Marie-Louise, are the magic letters KUK, which any fool can understand, even in cyrillic. Leaving the Turkish Wagons-Lits men to stop the taxi driving off, I go in to explore.

The place is quite unlike any travel office I have ever been in before, but then I soon found that the Wagons-Lits/Cook organisation has opened a smart new bureau in the town centre at 10 Rue Legue. The villa remains what it has always been, the unobtrusive administrative headquarters of the Company, very probably housing their Bulgarian Representative as well.

This gentleman proves to be away at the timetable conference in Madrid, but his assistant, Monsieur Kusmenov, insists on coming with us to the Balkan Hotel. This swagger-looking establishment - "all luxury and no comfort" as my father would have said, is full to bursting point with western businessmen attending the Plovdiv Trade Fair. This is Bulgaria's top event of the year (and accounts for all those children descending from the luggage van). The town's bedroom capacity is overwhelmed by it, so many businessmen stay in the capital, and travel over daily. All the same, the Wagons-Lits Co. rise to the occasion. They have secured us a room for the night.

The Balkan Hotel appears to be the only one to cater for western visitors. Our Turkish Wagons-Lits conductors go on to a less pretentious establishment, where, no doubt, their fluent Bulgarian is quite essential. We are an incontinentally long time depositing our bags, because the lift is liable to jam; unlike Turkish lifts, which though less ornate, work perfectly.

There is a magnificent staircase, with low tread marble steps, created with no expense spared. On each landing wicker armchairs are provided, handy for policemen wishing to arrest the guests, perhaps, as well as for guests to use when meeting each other. But there are no policemen sitting in them, so perhaps this is but a figment of my imagination.

Bulgarian steam. 2-8-2 no. 02-03 at Plovdiv, BDZ. Author's collection.

There is nothing imaginative about the bedrooms, however, except the inability of the magnificent plumbing to work. A private bathroom is obligatory. Four taps protrude through the panelling which conceals what they do. A change over handle is thoughtfully provided, that does not condescend to say, in any language, which position works what. Apart from a sudden cold shower, totally unexpected, no showers are working; though two types are provided. The hot water is not working either, but then, the hotel is totally full.

The Balkan Hotel caters for everything and everyone. Downstairs there is a courteous but costly foreign exchange, where you may exchange your needed specie for levas, but cannot change them back again.

Wide streets in which to saunter between high, spacious, but totally impassive and unmoving buildings, are almost devoid of traffic. An occasional bus, a passing car, usually a foreigner's, and now and then a lorry, bears down upon pedestrians frequently enough to prevent them actually jaywalking in the roadway. The silence after Istanbul's honking, bustling traffic, is striking. Trams grinding along, or gliding along, are equally a contrast, now that Istanbul has none. Some are very modern, articulated vehicles; others are very far from it, solid, sturdy, and towing one or more trailers. They dominate the streets.

In Sofia, the Wagons-Lits Cook Officers are kindness itself. The head of the Divisional office, Monsieur Kusmenov personally takes us on a tour of the city, showing us the huge cathedral edifice, and the equally huge Ministerial and Parliamentary buildings, grey, impressive, and orderly, and devoid utterly of the pulsating gaiety that makes up a city with a waterfront on the Eastern Mediterranean, that some might call an 'Oriental' atmosphere in bygone days.

We are perfectly free to move about, and it is purely a personal premonition that makes me feel I am unsafe. Monsieur Kusmenov steers us away from an interesting-looking church, declaring it is closed. But we are shown all over the big state departmental store in the main square, close to our hotel.

This has everything in abundance, including customers. Few of these seem to have enough money to buy. They look, wistfully, at the consumer goods. There are rows of modern kitchen ranges, with built-in ovens. Massive wrought iron constructions with enamelled oven doors, they seem very Bulgarian. In the west, the emphasis would be on gas or electricity, yet no doubt these are far more suitable here. On the dour faces of the unsmiling populace, it is easy to read in their eyes the comparison of these nice new gadgets with the old tumble-down range at their homes, legacy of the days of poverty stricken capitalism.

A sense of order, of cleanliness, of decent, cautious behaviour, of care for the sick and the suffering, and baby clinics and maternity patients, matters as dull as they are important, pervades Sofia, as no doubt it does in other communist lands. If there is nothing much to show off, there is nothing to hide, so we are free to roam about. Yet Monsieur Kusmenov leaves us with his telephone number, and his night telephone number too, in case of difficulty.

The Balkan Hotel is provided with a basement where there is Tsigany styled music, and wine, and alcoves, most suitable for western visitors. We are treated to the spectacle of a Balkan wine cellar, its waiters and band in Bulgarian national dress, though the pitchpine panelling and seating is as obviously modern as the Balkan Hotel itself. Like the bathroom plumbing, and the lift, this basement lives up to the Hotel's Balkan name. It was, therefore, adorned with Bulgar pimps, one discreetly or maybe genuinely assuming the status of a Bulgarian field officer off duty, who with a thoroughness of an agent provocateur, steers the conversation round to the desirability of exchanging the surroundings of the hotel for those of his flat, somewhere in Sofia.

Language difficulties prevent him understanding that he is coping with an Irish mentality as well as an English one; and in any event we are devoid of identity, since the Bulgarian police have gone off with our passports the instant we arrive, ensuring that we would not stray far from the permitted tourist circuit.

Precisely what happened next is not clear. It is unwise to go out late at night unescorted and without identity papers in communist capitals, in my opinion. Outside I believe the Bulgarian received a thump. Having extricated myself back into the marble hall, I am offered my passport by the Hall Porter, and have the luck to obtain both of them. I reach the seventh floor just in time to see an arrest being made in the courtyard below.

When I get down into the yard, it is utterly deserted. The arrest is in storybook fashion, police and victim are spirited somewhere, leaving the brain whirling. It is such a commonplace occurrence these days that the sense of 'it couldn't happen to me' lulls the free into a ridiculously false sense of security. It has happened. It is all very real. Wait until it does to you, and you will not find this such boring reading.

I pin everything on the passport. I decide I am not going to bother Mr. Kusmenov at two in the morning, because above all I am going to be on the Direct Orient Express the next day. In the morning I will seek out the Consul and deliver the passport. But I do not sleep. In spite of all their flocks of geese, the Bulgarians have no idea of how to make a comfortable pillow. Those stuffed with straw that we used in pre-war army cadet camps were infinitely softer than this nobbly thing that might have contained horsehair.

I suddenly remember that the police often take three days to trace a missing person, especially when he is in prison; yet I cannot say to them "try your prisons", without being invited to try one of them myself.

So wearily I dress again, to screw up my courage to report to the hotel that a guest is missing. All the time there is the gnawing thought that the arrest down below could be somebody else. But as this happened an hour or more earlier, it seems to me there must be a reasonable chance of somebody soon discovering that our papers are no longer in the hands of the police.

I open the door just in time to see Vincent approaching down the corridor, escorted only by an old porter. Apparently his only crime has been to desecrate a People's Fountain. All the same such an experience is to be recommended to all those with a penchant for communist doctrine. Next morning, sure enough, the cane seats on the mezzanine landings of the elegant marble staircase with such shallow treads, are occupied by police with revolvers in their belts; but it is not us they bother about.

In the morning I repair to the same People's State Supermarket to which we had been dutifully taken by the redoubtable Monsieur Kusmenov the day before. Instead of admiring the heavy kitchen ranges, I go to the grocery and food department, downstairs. Plenty of people buying here; queues form, just like horrible capitalist queues, the odious substitute for service. I resent queues at meat counters, (or for that matter at bus stops - as readers of "Gone With Regret" may have gathered), but when at last I reach the assistant on the ham counter, I encounter a difference. "Ticket" says this Bulgarian wench, and of course I have no ticket.

The people in the queue are extremely kind and friendly; a foreigner is evidently an unusual change. In sign language ("Ticket" seems to mean the same in every tongue) they explain that a ticket is necessary, and soon I am queuing again, outside a little ticket window. I put down my remaining 2 levas, changed at an abominable rate from spare German marks left over from our DSG breakfast near Munich, and having seen the quoted price. Nearly ten shillings for a little bit of ham; still, I am not going to starve on the Direct Orient Express, like Michael Barsley.

So I queue yet again, grimly; there is plenty of time to reflect on progress; on the erstwhile Svilengrad - Trieste diner in the Days Before the Queues, and on what an awfully grim time the Bulgarian proletariat must have if their food is all as expensive as this ham apparently is. After what seems like an eternity, I arrive once more in front of the female behind the counter, this time triumphantly waving my ticket at her. I point at the ham, at my ticket, and not being able to swear in Bulgarian, glare at the People's Republic server of ham. A kindly middle-aged lady, four paces in front, harangues the girl, bless her, while thoughts about Communism circulate round my brain. "Communism, so far as supermarkets are concerned, is just like Britain", while the girl, instead of serving me, harangues back at the middle-aged lady. The latter, realising that she is tainting herself by getting mixed up with foreigners, gives one more riposte, and leaves.

Shrugging her shoulders, the girl at last turns her attention to me, and I realise that after all Communism is not just like Britain; in Britain at this juncture, the girl would have put up a board marked "Closed" and gone off for a tea-break; whereas this girl is serving her country, not just the customers. Instead, she begins piling "slices of delicious ham" onto a piece of greaseproof paper, at a positively alarming rate; I think she'll never stop! Nothing induces her to do so, while the queue look on sympathetically, realising that I am not really a wealthy capitalist, nor even a greedy capitalist, but just a poor stupid foreigner who does not understand the ticket system nor that the price tag is for a kilogram. They persuade her to stretch the rules about short measure, and throw in a tube of mustard as a make weight; how could they know, poor things, that I detest mustard?

I decide I am very lucky to have got out of that supermarket unscathed, with a tube of mustard for which I have not paid, thereby cheating the People's Republic of Bulgaria, and after the narrowly averted disaster of the previous evening, my main concern is to clamber securely into one of the two Wagons-Lits in today's Direct Orient Express, when in due course they arrive. At least taximen cannot quibble about the fare, when they are communist taxis.

But they can and do quibble about the destination. This driver knows precisely where we want to go: "Airport" he says gaily and helpfully, driving away in exactly the opposite direction to the station. I feel like spitting, but, being sure this is an indictable offence, I refrain, and say "Station" in every language I can think of, trying him with Turkish "Gar" and German "Bahnhof" for a start. With relief, the taxi turns about. In the good old days there were no iron curtains, nor airports nor airliners nor republics, all of which totted up to my having to mess about with these ham and rolls - Bulgarian rolls, which I reflect, I had indeed once eaten before at dinner in Yugoslavia, between Nis and Belgrade, in the Wagons-Lits diner in 1937.

Our baggage is seized by a porter for whom I doubt if we have enough levas, for the official tip. When we said farewell to Monsieur Simeonov, in charge of Cooks office, (who prefers air

Right: Bulgarian Bo-Bo electric loco no. 40-12, built in Czechoslovakia by Škoda, takes over at Plovdiv.
Photo: D. Trevor Rowe.

Below: Austrian-built BDZ diesel Bo-Bo no. 0432.
Photo: D. Trevor Rowe.

presently it is followed by the Direct Orient Express, with its two blue Wagons-Lits coupled together, one for Paris and one (like yesterday's) for Munich. Hundreds of people again bale out of the Polish luggage van, which I thought was there for the carriage of mails. The Turkish conductor of our sleeper gets down, and a gloomy Bulgarian climbs aboard. By the time Mr. Kusmenov shows up, we are installed in our cabin, our haven for the next thirty six hours. Outside the window, the enormous steam engines which are the non-advertised tourist attraction of Bulgaria, come and go in profusion; they are quite easy to photograph from the security of a Wagons-Lits, but I do not get my wife's camera to function properly. The BDZ place one of their new diesels at the head of our train, after the modern electric engine has moved clear. The thirty four minutes allotted to the train at Sofia, passes more quickly than anticipated, and with a hoot of the chime whistle, a last "Au Revoir" to Monsieur Kusmenov (though "Adieu" would perhaps have been more appropriate), we are off.

Immediately the blue uniformed figures begin to saunter along the train, inspecting passports. Though they appear casual, they have to be quick, for they have less than an hour before reaching the frontier at Dragoman, the last place, going in this direction, with a truly Turkish name. We can hear the pounding of the diesel engine as our train climbs steadily up from the great plain into rolling rather bare hills, covered fairly well in places with scrub, and inhabited here and there by goatherds.

travel) he assured us that Monsieur Kusmenov would be there to see us off, so no doubt he will do the honours if need arises. Had he not even given us his night telephone number the evening before? Little did he know how nearly I had invoked its use. Mr. Kusmenov is not, however, there, while the porter dumps our bags on the wrong platform and goes off. There are splendid engines to be seen, and loud speakers are bawling Bulgarian gibberish, of which just two words: 'Orient Express', are quite distinctive. No wonder people get so worked up about its romantic traverse of Europe.

So we stand in anticipation on the great stone flags of the too-narrow platform, on which (I discover afterwards) King Boris had often stood before us, while the wrong train comes in, and

We stop for eight minutes in the large, modern station at Dragoman, where anyone unable to leave Bulgaria has to get off. The station looks as though it could contain some cells. On the other side of our carriage are great rows of Eastern European goods trucks waiting for customs clearance. Where the Bulgars keep their famous big locomotives is not obvious. Sofia is under thirty miles away so perhaps Dragoman has just a small servicing depot; at any rate we can see nothing of it.

A further seventeen miles separates us from the station on the Yugoslav side of the frontier which is one of those impenetrable ones with no notices or lines of wire or anything to show you where the actual boundary lies among these inhospitable mountains, with stumpy fir trees. The railway is single track, of no especial interest. All the first part of the way is clearly in Bulgaria, but presently the line runs downhill and then some single storey low lying houses in front indicate Dimitrovgrad. On our left is the engine shed and sidings; on our right the single platform station.

During World War II Bulgaria as Hitler's ally, occupied this part of Yugoslavia, but after the country became Communist under the leadership of Dimitrov the area was handed back to Marshal Tito. Maybe this is the reason for the name Dimitrovgrad, which is just 202 miles west of the Bulgarian Dimitrovgrad which the Direct Orient Express calls at, early in the morning on the way to Sofia.

The blue-uniformed policemen who have been so thorough on their section of the journey, suddenly become human, relaxing on a bench in the afternoon sun, as they wait for the next train to take them back to their country. They do not say one word to the brown-uniformed Yugoslav frontier police, who attack the train with a severity quite equal to their Bulgarian colleagues. Up in front, in place of the Austrian-built BDZ diesel, I expect to see an American built one, but, instead, first one great Yugoslav express steam engine comes smokily from the shed, and then another proceeds proudly past us, to double-head the train. They are very slow about it, and we leave late in consequence.

It is lunch time, as here we put our watches back an hour to the timekeeping now called British Standard Time, which all Central Europe and most of Western Europe now uses. It is hot and stuffy in the train and we climb down on to the cinders beside the track, for coming along the train is a snack-vendor. But there is also a ferocious female frontier guard who makes it very plain that it is forbidden to get out to buy snacks. She takes pernicious pleasure in delaying, and if possible depriving us of a means of quenching our thirst.

At last the JZ has sorted out its engines, and we start again. The Dragoman Pass is one of the most spectacular sights of the whole way, and, for once, it is daylight. At first we descend through upland pastures, calling at various stations serving medium sized villages; then we suddenly rush down a gorge through tunnel and corniche for mile after mile. It is as spectacular as the Taurus but the mountains are more visible as they are lower.

Two ladies stand in the corridor, admiring the view of the gorge. One is Turkish, going to Milan to meet her Italian fiancée. The other is an English lady from remotest Lancashire. It is the first time on this journey that any other English people have been on board the sleeping cars in which we have found ourselves, and we fall into conversation.

"Nobody speaks on this train", says the Lancashire lass, almost plaintively. Indeed, why should they? I think to myself. But it is clear that the modern British tourist, anyway, prefers the comradeship of a party to the splendid though isolated privacy which a Wagons-Lits cabin offers its occupants.

"That Italian gentleman", she goes on, "he does not say a word".

"Perhaps he does not speak English".

"He is totally silent to everybody", comes the rejoinder, "although he seems to know people all along the line".

"It is so different to a Turkish train", says her companion, "where everybody is so friendly. Have you been on Turkish trains?"

We admit, cautiously, that we have; all the way to Kars, in fact. This breaks the ice. The other people may be as cold and aloof as the Bulgarian conductor, sitting on the big armchair at the end of the corridor, and staring moodily out of the window. His is a very easy task, with no beds to make up or undo, and only tickets to collect. Passengers kept their own passports at the frontier.

But our two compartments take on a sort of Anglo-Turkish camaraderie; in the free world everyone talks and cheerfully mucks in. It seems that the two ladies are travelling singly, and have never met until the afternoon before; but twenty four hours in a Wagons-Lits compartment is time enough to get acquainted. Their compartment is replete with food; melons, bottles of Turkish mineral water, peppers, bread, far more than they really need, and in true Turkish style they proffer it on us, poor travellers who have boarded at Sofia.

It seems pretty obvious that this lady from Lancashire is not new to the Orient Express, or Turkey either. For her contribution is quite as large and as Turkish as that of her companion. We enjoy a slice of melon, and then return to admiring the gorge. As the line is steeply graded and we are free-wheeling down the hill, the engines do not smother everything in coal dust, when passing through the innumerable tunnels. All the same, Turkish, Greek and Bulgarian steam have left their marks on the compartments.

We pass through the tunnels with just the Blue Light on, contrasting with the sun on the smoothed rock edge of the gorge, shining pink, and very bright. In spring, great spates of water must come tumbling down it. Then all at once the gorge ends, and we run into dusty Crveni Krst.

Here the diesel engine is waiting for us, and also a snack-vendor of the Kola za Spavanje & Restaurancje though his services are not advertised in Western timetables. There are a number of ragged looking youths hanging around the station. The KSR man with his heavy boxes, eyes the youths uneasily, and seems relieved to be aboard without loss: though as all the people getting out seem to be frontier police, his wares are safe enough.

Outside the sleeper, the depressing sadness of youth without opportunity; inside, the gaiety of middle-aged travellers. We talk of Istanbul as the train makes its way towards Belgrade through scenery so very different to the Dragoman Pass. Our new found friends share our view that tea would be nice, it being tea-time. Since this is Yugoslavia, all we can offer is Slivowitz! The English lady confirms that it is her second trip by train to Istanbul. Like so many who visit Turkey, she says it is very difficult to get people in Britain to believe how hospitable and friendly the Turkish people are, how genuinely pleased to be helpful to visitors. She also says people do not know how to get the best out of the Wagons-Lits services. I show her the Guide, and recall my previous trip along here, with ten Wagons-Lits and a Wagon-Restaurant, and not a single ordinary carriage.

Darkness falls and we think about "supper after Belgrade". We are now lucky to have all this ham with us, so that at least we can match the hospitality of the next door compartment. The train approaches Belgrade over one of those complicated networks outside a terminus that are very hard to follow. Going out again from the station, you are suddenly aware of being on a different line without noticing the actual junction.

When we draw into the station, five cleaners in Wagons-Lits uniform descend on our car and make up the beds, while the dour

Bulgarian hands over the car and its documents, and the laundry to a dapper little Yugoslav. The Munich car, next to us, has a Yugoslav conductor travelling right through from Sofia to Munich. The Yugoslavs work sleeping cars to Thessaloniki, Venice, Vienna, Munich and Sofia, and only a few of the Sofia - Belgrade runs have Bulgarian conductors.

The train from Athens, nowadays called simply the Athens Express, has followed us up the line from the junction outside Nis, but arrives a little late, so that there is a great rush, as various people change between the two trains. For these are re-marshalled into the Direct Orient, and Tauern Orient Expresses. Bewildered Greeks and Turks, bound for work in Germany, stumble along the platform or even on to the tracks; presently the work is done, the new train engine attached at the leading end of each formation, and only the ticket inspectors know how many unfortunates, this time, are on the wrong train! In 1966 the Direct Orient left before the Tauern, which overtook it at Zagreb. So anyone bound for Germany on the wrong train, had a chance to retrieve his mistake. In the current tables when this book appears, this is no longer possible, as the Tauern gets away first.

Amongst the pathetic melee of people, losing bundles, losing each other, plaintively crying, while the loudspeakers crackle in unknown Slavonic, it is possible to get down, buy and post a postcard, if you have some Dinars. The snack operators will take any currency, except Bulgarian Levas. All this money changing adds a zest to the simple purchase of a sandwich or a roll, which is part of the ambience of the Orient Express. Another part is the undoubted serenity which two nights running in a Wagons-Lits gives you. You can retire or rise when you wish; and you can watch the world go by literally as well as figuratively.

So we cross the river and watch the glittering lights of Belgrade's lesser suburbs, beside the tramway on which there never seems to be a tram, until the country begins again and there is blackness outside the window. Then we switch on the main lights and start on the ham. Alfresco certainly but pleasant enough, with beer in the tooth glasses, served on the table top formed on the wash basin.

We reach Zagreb after midnight, and Zidani Most, where our route diverges from that by which we came out, in the small hours. After this, the country changes. Cyrillic lettering, common in the south, is forgotten about, save only in the JZ's rolling stock. Now the mountains begin, forming the border with Austria to the north, the extension of the Dolomites that joins them to the Dalmatian coast. The mountains are limestone, bare and waterless, with a thin covering of earth. Towards four in the morning, we enter Ljubljana, where the overhead wires stretch without a break for 874 miles to Paris - rather further than from London to Inverness. In 1968 they begin at Zidani Most.

The electric wires are Italian in style, with rounded poles and angled tubular supports not seen elsewhere in Europe save in these countries. This is because the Yugoslavs had no electrified railways until they acquired some with the former Italian territory which they took over at the end of World War II; so when they extended the electrification to Ljubljana, naturally this and their new locomotives had to conform to existing practice.

It is light by the time we pass non-stop through Rakek, the old frontier station, and run down the steep escarpment to Postojna, noted for its grottos, which, last time I travelled this way, was the point where Mussolini's railway military police climbed aboard.

Only the extraordinary large number of lengthy sidings at these two little wayside stations, now almost wholly deserted, give any indication of their former status.

The present day frontier is Sezana, where we arrive about half past six in the morning. There is forty seven minutes wait here, before crossing the Iron Curtain. So the new-looking Yugoslav electric engine comes off, and is soon heading east again on a goods train, over the 73 miles back to Ljubljana.

For the Yugoslavs do not, in 1966 anyway, seem to have many electric engines, and all the shunting is still done by steam. Black smoke rises from the stacks of the ex-Austrian goods engines, hissing as they shunt a mixture of Western and Eastern Europe wagons. The mountains rise behind them, as a backcloth, while in front, the land undulates with rock outcrops, bushes, stunted trees and small walls. This is the Carso, a most inhospitable place to fight on, and easy to get lost in. No wonder the Yugoslavs were keen to make this their new boundary.

The brown-uniformed frontier guards are silent and efficient, and much smarter than those at Dimitrovgrad. Though they come along the train, they do not wake the passengers in the sleeping car, but take the passports from the conductor. Indeed it is difficult to believe that this is the "wicked Communist barrier" that you hear so much about in the west. It is western reaction to Communism that makes it sinister. No refugees are caught escaping this morning, and long before we are due to start, the Guards decide they have had enough. They stand alongside the train, to make sure nobody attempts to board it at the last minute, and they chat to the many local passengers who are going through to Trieste in the JZ coaches that will come off there; in 1967 the KSR have provided their own additional sleeping car for such people, from Belgrade to Trieste.

Down the line an engine whistles - an Italian whistle, with all the nostalgia of erstwhile English Great Western Railway, now that BR whistles are all standard two tone horns adopted from GWR diesel cars. Round the corner comes a goods train, with an Italian goods engine at its head. It is in some way moving to see an easily recognisable engine again, and it is clearly going to take our train back over the frontier to Italy as there is no other electric engine in the station. But as it draws level, so comes the surprise; for the engine is no longer Italian, but a war-reparations one, handed over by the Italians along with their sections of electrified line, such as that which once ran from Sezana to Postumia, as they call Postojna.

The rostering of the locomotives is a clever arrangement by the Yugoslav Railways, because in this way, their new and powerful locomotives are not kept waiting for the customs, while the elderly ex-Italian ones, very probably not the very best examples of the types concerned, but more likely the most decrepit, are naturally ideally suited to running over the lines of their former owners.

The journey through the Iron Curtain takes just nine minutes. There are no signs of life, just scrubby trees, and rock outcrops, also the walls of the little rough fields dating from the times when the land, like the railway line, was all under one nationality. Just before Poggioreale station, the great line which was once the Austrian Sudbahn, joins in on the right, and gives the newly reconstructed station an air of grandeur and importance worthy of a change of name from Poggioreale Campagna - a mere country place - to Poggioreale del Carso. People in a hurry still call it

Poggio, or Poggio C. to distinguish it from other places in Italy or Sicily called Poggioreale. And now it is called Villa Opicina in 1968.

And what a difference to the tight-lipped communist Yugoslavs. Here, people shout loudly, and light blue uniformed Italian frontier police rush about excitedly in their squashy peaked hats which give their uniform an unavoidable sloppiness. They are as fussy as in Mussolini's day, and (oh joy!) they have actually found an unfortunate Yugoslav peasant whose papers or packages are out of order. Do these innocent bundles really conceal leaflets recommending Black Power? We shall never know; for though the train waits an astonishingly long time at Poggio for customs purposes, the unhappy man does not re-appear.

All the same, Poggio is a bit of a shock; it is the first time it has been brought home to me, that it is the West who are on the defensive, for whom the frontier means so much. N.A.T.O. seems to me much more fussy about the border than are the communist representatives. All the same, it is impossible to feel free in their countries. The brown-uniformed Yugoslavs have come with us from Sezana, and they now get off the train, while the "bogus-Italian" engine, with its 'JZ' in Roman and Cyrillic, is driven round the train by its Yugoslav driver, but with an Italian shunter. At the other end of the station, there are more engines of the same class, and based at Poggioreale. Italian (FS) ones, they are not nearly grand enough to haul the Direct Orient Express inside Italy, and there now arrives one of those really odd local trains that the Italians often run. A single carriage, hauled by a huge articulated electric express engine, which looks as though it has come up to Poggio from Trieste, especially to collect us, as it has! Along the platform, as on every Italian station, the buffet trolley slowly perambulates, Chianti bottles dangling from its corners. The man in charge is shouting of course, and after all these unpronounceable 'z's' and impossible letterings of the east, it is a pleasure to be able to shout back. There is one item on the trolley, not to be seen in Turkey, Bulgaria or Yugoslavia: Bananas.

There is ample time to buy the bananas, and wine too, but at last we start. At first we go on through the harsh countryside of the Carso; then on the right, there is a large viaduct of local stone to be seen, and our train suddenly swings sharply to the left, into a cutting. This is a triangular junction called Aurisina Junction (Bivio d'Aurisina) and for the next fifteen kilometres we run in a corniche, high above the Adriatic. Here you can open the window, and blow away the cobwebs of communism (not to mention the frowstiness of the night) with the sea air, just as you can between Halkali and Istanbul, going the other way. There are glorious places at which it would be nice to stop and spend a holiday, such as Grignano Miramare or Barcola.

Trieste Central station is a terminus, alongside the docks, and separated only by a road (with rails in it) and some sheds. A whole hour is provided here, in case the train from Yugoslavia is running late, as it usually is; in our case we had about half an hour. It is at Trieste that the Direct Orient Express loses its Balkan character. The splendid city which is still full of reminders that it was Austria's seaport until 1918 - in its buildings, its trade and so forth - has Yugoslavian territory almost reaching to its suburbs. So the station yard has many Yugoslav coaches, which are modern in profile and austere and functional, as regards the seating. The Yugoslav sleeper from Belgrade (not in our train in 1966) comes off here, together with the remaining Yugoslav coaches. More coaches come on in their place, including a French one with Calais as its destination. In 1966 the plan to abolish steam from the Italian railways had not yet extended to Trieste station, and for the last time, we are steam hauled. One of the ubiquitous little steam tank engines which so short a time ago could be seen everywhere, all over Italy, hurries us out to the sidings, where two more of the Company's cars, from Rome and Genoa, are being cleaned. For a change they have the Wagons-Lits title painted in Italian, instead of French, German or Turkish.

The engine that now heads our train is even grander than the one which brought us from Poggio, and is painted in the silver grey and green livery which has replaced the khaki-brown for new main line engines. Just as the engine from Poggio was too grand to belong there, and came up from Trieste, so this one belongs at Mestre, the great junction serving Venice. While we wait to depart, men come and clean the windows of our sleeper while two more men in dapper suits, are standing by the lowered window of the speechless Italian gentleman, who now talks freely enough.

He is an elderly man, impeccably dressed, and as soon as we start, becomes affable and charming. Perhaps he has been goaded by the English lady, who has been continually saying "he does not speak" although he seems to know English perfectly. More likely the posse of civil servants who met him at Trieste with diplomatic papers, have re-assured him that once again his trip has passed off without a hitch. He has to leave us at Venice, he says, to go home to Rome. Time was when he shared his monastic style journeyings with the Queen's Messengers, but Mr. Harold Wilson, personally, it is said, stopped them travelling by Wagons-Lits and commanded their conveyance by air.

Our train leaves by the way we came in, continuing on by the sea past Auresina junction to Monfalcone, where we turn inland through flat, rich country. "Sunny Italy" is decidedly chilly for September and it begins pouring with rain. The electric wires for many years ended at Cervignano, and parts of the line on to Venice are now single track. The journey takes three hours, as stops are frequent and there are connections with branch lines that lead, through Udine, to the Austrian frontier at Tarvisio. To while away the hours, the Wagons-Lits provide a roving snack-vendor, from whom we obtain coffee. It is of course Espresso, so very different from that in Turkey.

What gives this journey its particular romanticism is the kaleidoscope of countries, of glorious holiday places through which you pass, wondering what on earth made you go all the way to Turkey. Yet the urge to return is strong, and shared by all the passengers. Safely in Italy, the western world, passengers talk much more freely. Among them is a middle aged successful American businessman, going home to his wife and children, after visiting his parents for the first time for twenty-five years. He is perhaps typical of the profound change which affects the generations of humanity. For his parents are not American but Yugoslav, and he was last seen by them, heading for the woods with Mikhailovitch's partisans. Severely wounded, he left his native land in a British Motor Launch of the Royal Navy, who took him to Italy. Unable to return to communist Yugoslavia because of his association with the wrong brand of partisan, he emigrated to America and became an American citizen after the war was over. Looking back as the train rolled inexorably onward, he said that perhaps it was worse than if he had not made this ostensibly touristic visit to Yugoslavia. For now his parents were old; they had lost the family farm, and the parting this time, they knew, was the final one. It would have been quite hopeless for them to try to leave with him, yet he had to return to his family and his business. So the son was grimly trying to forget his mother's distress, and was looking forward to a few days relaxation in Lausanne.

This sad tale was made sadder by the weather. Teeming rain fell upon Jesolo station as we pulled into it, splashing on the tarmac of the long road leading down to the shore where Jesolo offers the usual Italian attractions of sun, sand and sea. Jesolo is making an all out effort to capture more tourists, too many of whom choose other resorts on the Italian coast for Jesolo's liking. Facing south, with an estuary as the focal point, it is rather odd that it does not do better, when it is so close to Austria and Germany. But it is not too well placed to an airport, it is a very long way from Rome, and an hour or more beyond Venice by train for tourists coming from Britain.

The Direct Orient Express at the time of writing has managed to clip an hour off this part of the journey, achieved partially by omitting a long pause at Mestre. Mestre has a growing importance as a business centre and oil refining town, handily served by Venice's road and railway communications. Lines radiate north, south and west from the station, and trains come and go frequently. To the east they mount the long causeway and bridge leading to Santa Lucia station, that joins Venice to the mainland.

Santa Lucia is another terminus, though goods wagons can be ferried over to the Lido (which gave its name to other Lidos everywhere). Our sleeper draws up alongside the carriages which will be used to strengthen the train for our journey on to Milan, and across the platform, opposite our very doors are the familiar features of the Wagons-Lits diner. So, I nip out, present myself to the dining car conductor, and obtain two seats for luncheon. Then we have the best part of an hour to explore the precincts of the station.

Santa Lucia has been rebuilt and is now one of the clean, marble faced modern stations that do so much for the prestige of the Italian Railways, giving a sense of well being so lacking in many other countries. Venice alone among stations takes you out of the building down some steps straight into a gondola. Even though this is what you imagine ought to happen, the fact that it actually does so always seems to me a romantic excitement.

This morning something very odd seems to be happening on the Canal; people are shouting destinations and touting for traffic But the customers in their elegant expensive clothes, that are very noticeable to travellers returning to the west, are stepping daintily into dirty coal barges, and there seems to be a total dearth of vaporetti, those lovely canal steamers with special non washmaking propellers and the motor boats that turn Venetian tranquillity into constant turmoil, and the lapping of whose wash is said to be about to destroy the place completely.

Not to stop and see Venice seems almost criminal; the famous Rialto Bridge is to your left as you walk down the station steps but out of sight round a corner. It is the canal bends in Venice that make it so attractive. Mysterious little canals start out under bridges and wind about; though there are not as many as there used to be, as it is these that caused pestilence and disease, and so, for far too much of Venice, you have to go on foot. The Scalzi Bridge over the Grand Canal is an old fashioned one with steps up to the crown of the bridge, and, opposite the station, the Diedo and Foscari Palaces give a tantalising idea of what the rest of Venice is like. It would be nice to go down the Grand Canal to St. Marks, or round into the Giudecca Canal with its shipping. This and more, can be done by travelling to Turkey by way of the Turkish Maritime Line's steamers which begin their voyages at Venice.

The charm of Venice is that apart from the railway station and the multi-storey motor garage, it is virtually unspoilt by modern buildings. No cars are allowed , jet planes keep away, and so do visitors in the winter, when Venice assumes a foggy, almost ghostly air. Not surprisingly Ward Lock & Co. have picked Venice as one of the places to

Venice, St. Mark's Square and the Grand Canal. Author's collection.

choose as a subject for their 1968 World Tourist Guide series, which achieves very well the creation of a sense of difference. Venice is still Venetian; there is also Italy, and it is time to return to the train.

Our sleeper has donned an imperceptibly different air, subtly subdued and quietly chic. In place of the alert, unassuming young Yugoslav in charge, we have a modest Frenchman, Monsieur Perrot. Young, agile, Monsieur Perrot is Parisian to his fingertips. Though this is to be the last of our eleven nights of Wagons-Lits hospitality on this journey, it is the first night with a French conductor. He is sorry that they do not put Evian on the train at Venice, but there is Fiuggi to be had in the diner. An hour and a half has gone by since we were last in Mestre station, yet here we are again; this is perhaps the oddity about the Direct Orient, which takes so long and goes so far, often at very high speeds, as we see as soon as we leave for Padua.

This elegant place is only 17 miles further on, and it is possible to make the journey in the Burchiello canal steamer from St. Marks in Venice to the Bassanello landing stage at Padua, with a stop for lunch at Oriago. For those who like beautiful villas this is a splendid trip, for on either bank there are the residences of the rich of an earlier age. But we have not got all day to mess about with canal boats; instead we enjoy the Wagons-Lits luncheon, which begins after Mestre. The diner is one of the newly reconstructed ones with air conditioning, that were first shown at the Munich International Transport exhibition of 1965.

At Padua we overtake a steam-hauled train from Venice, bound for Ravenna. It is the last steam train to be seen on this journey and steam becomes romantic by its absence. Electrification of this line has marvellously speeded the journey across the flat delta of the Po river, its rich land feeding the historic towns, Padua, Vicenza, Verona, at which we stop, one after the other.

The first Italian meal is always an exciting change. The next and subsequent Italian meals in Italy are usually depressingly familiar. Minestrone soup, a vast plate of spaghetti, followed by veal cutlets, all enhanced by that Parmesan cheese, so carefully matured in the Wagons-Lits stores at Rome and Milan for over two years before serving. Could anything be more Italian?

The ten minute pause at Verona's big station, where we cross the main line from Rome to the Brenner, is handy for serving the coffee which follows the ice cream (have you forgotten that ices are an Italian national dish? How nice they were before they were all made in factories).

The Porta Nuova station is outside the walls of Verona, which are almost complete, and conspicuous from the train. Next we run beside the south shore of charming Lake Garda, stopping at Desenzano, the resort at the corner nearer Milan, and just under 100 miles from Venice. On the horizon to the right the Dolomite mountains, scarcely visible before Verona, approach nearest to the line at Brescia, another town with touristic attractions. All these towns have churches or cathedrals that are worth a visit.

Milan is fifty-one miles further on, a run of about an hour. To the right, the mountains recede again. Back in the sleeper, our neighbours have been lunching Turkish style, and now they are getting ready to leave. The Turkish lady prepares to meet her fiancée, and we have suggested to her companion that if she moves into the Milan-Calais car, she will not have to get up at six thirty in the morning at Paris. Our own sleeper is half empty now. This is because no bookings are taken on it between Venice and Paris, in case it is running late. Sometimes it misses the Direct Orient Express altogether, and runs instead in the Simplon Express. This train, better known as the Simplon Orient Express between 1919 and 1962, was created in 1906 by the Wagons-Lits especially to run through the Simplon Tunnel. Its extension into the Simplon Orient Express was the work of the Versailles Treaty.

After the demise of the Simplon Orient from 1962, until 1967, no sleepers ran in it beyond Trieste, and for most of the time, all of them ended their journey at Venice. In 1967 a daily sleeper was introduced into it between Paris and Belgrade, reached in under 24 hours, lasting till May 1969.

The flat fields of Lombardy, luscious with crops, give place to the outskirts of vast Milan, hot, humid, pulsating, industrious. We draw into the huge 22-platform terminus, where an hour and a quarter is available for the reorganisation of the train. Milan has a large network of standard gauge tramways to serve the city. But the trams are not running today, Monsieur Perrot points out, because of a strike of municipal transport workers. Had we not noticed the absence of vaporetti in Venice? So this explains the coal barges, touting for passengers to St. Marks.

Luckily the railwaymen, if they were going to strike, had so far not done so. We hunt up the Calais conductor, and get the last available compartment in his car for our friend. She is very impressed by the modern vehicle, after the Direct Orient Cars which have many years service to their credit.

Milan is almost as good as Basle's splendid railway scene. The Italian railwaymen in their grey speckled dustcoats reaching almost to their ankles, go about their work with gusto. Why they have these coats which look so very cold in winter, and dreadfully hot in summer, I do not know. In forty years of Italian travel I have never seen a railwayman looking smart in one, and the material looks dirty even when it is straight from the laundry. Chatting with the French Wagons-Lits conductors, I feel somehow foreign, for the first time on this journey, as opposed to non-Turkish (European not Asiatic).

The man from Calais has met me before, in Switzerland. He has his relief with him, who arrived from Calais on this morning's Direct Orient. As it is a seventeen hour journey, he will have 24 hours off in Milan, after we have left.

Though Milan Central is one of the largest railway stations in Europe - it was the very largest when Mussolini had it built in 1931 - the Italians have just opened another 20 platform station, which also serves all the lines that terminate in the Central Station. This is the Porta Garibaldi, a through station. In these days of electric traction, terminal stations, bottling up engines, and demanding the provision of either another locomotive, or some shunting, are not as useful as through ones. Porta Garibaldi can be reached by a new underground line from the Venice, Rome, and the Gottard approaches to Milan Central, and from Turin and Switzerland by a surface line already existing. In keeping with its date, 1961, the station is fitted with two platforms for car carrying trains.

The rain has caught up with us once more, and the Istanbul sleeper is the leading carriage in the train from Milan on to Brigue. It stands next to a lift for moving wagons down to the cellars of the Central Station, which are used for parcels. From an enthusiast's point of view, the sleeper is well placed to look at what is going on in the vicinity of the station, that a mere platform visitor cannot see.

But now we start. For the first time on this journey, I really know the way, and it seems slightly unreal to be travelling in the same carriage that took us from the mysterious People's Republic of Bulgaria, over the same embankment where 20 years earlier Italian partisans took pot shots at me for daring to trespass on it, just because I was wearing British Army Officer's uniform on that occasion.

Along this stretch of line "Express" is perhaps not quite the right word, we stop half a dozen times and take almost two hours for the 78 miles to the Swiss frontier. In a curious way, our speed seems to be in keeping with the title 'Direct Orient' that is no longer used on the eastern European portion of the journey. The first part of the way, out of Milan to the west, non stop through Rho, is much as before. Then we turn north west and stop at Gallarate, still down on the plain, an industrial town, brilliantly lit; or it seems brilliant, after the dimly lit places in Yugoslavia. It is unfortunate that, as usual, the train chooses to go in the dark past the beauty spots. At the next stop, Sesto Calende, the train arrives at the bottom or southern end of Lake Maggiore, the big lake, whose other end is in Switzerland. For the next twenty miles or so we follow its western shore, turning north now, and travelling along a corniche. The splendid view is on the right, and to our left the Alps begin to tower up. Here there is that sense of finality as the northern European leaves the Mediterranean climate. Arona, Stresa, and Baveno succeed each other, vying in enticing attractiveness, while the moon shines benignly on the lake and lights glitter delightfully on shore. After Baveno we follow a smaller north west arm of the lake and stop yet again, at Verbania-Pallanza, whose town looks out at us across the water.

At each stop, tourists returning from holiday climb aboard, though they stare blankly at the leading vehicle, our nearly empty sleeper, with its destination board proclaiming Istanbul, that now seems very far away. Yet it was only yesterday that we were promising our neighbour from Lancashire, that in return for all this Turkish style hospitality, melons, cake, biscuits and so forth, that this night it would be our turn, and that the Swiss Dining Car Company's dinner would comprise, potato soup, veal with button mushrooms, salad, assorted Swiss cheese with Jacob's Cream Crackers from Liverpool, and creme caramel if desired.

Thus are the Swiss predictable, whereas Italy is full of surprises. "Did I not know" asks Monsieur Perrot, our helpful French conductor, "that Domodossola water is the best on the whole line?" No, I certainly did not - I have other less attractive, but impressive associations with the place. The last eighteen miles up to it present no problem today, though in days of steam, they were a long struggle for the two engines needed for the hill. The customs are perfunctory, as the Swiss do not bother about through passengers. There is ample time to empty from the carafes, that stale stuff brought round in Jerry cans at Belgrade, and refill them from the fountain on platform 2, gushing fresh alpine water. The sudden arrival of a Swiss goods train, hauled by the very latest engine of the Bern, Loetschberg Simplon Railway, is another matter. The BLS though nationalised, was still running independently in 1966 it seems, and this sight, which eluded me all the time I was writing "Railway Holiday in Switzerland" so carries me away that I almost miss the Direct Orient's departure, which glides out of the station with that slick, speedy and silent efficiency that is the difference between the Swiss Federal, and other countries trains.

There is forty minutes in which to wash, while the train climbs up the steep grade to Iselle, a curious line owned and maintained by the FS, but operated by the SBB, as the Swiss Federal Railways are usually known. After Iselle we thunder through the cold Simplon, Europe's longest railway tunnel under a natural object, which was completed in 1906, and pass from Italy to

Switzerland.

In the days when the Wagons-Lits Company provided the diner on the train, one could enjoy dinner in the bowels of the Alps, instead of having to wait until after eight o'clock for the car to be attached. We have a fleeting glimpse of it, next to a little electric shunting engine, as we run out of the tunnel into Brigue station, the only stop, the whole way from Istanbul to Paris, where people speak German. The Swiss railwaymen on the train, who all come from Lausanne, all speak French.

Instead of the train of sleeping cars only, with diner car running through from Svilengrad, the Swiss put their restaurant on the extreme rear of the train. So we alight at Brigue, and walk along the platform from one end of the train to the other, collecting our friend in the Calais sleeper on the way. The diner is a surprise, for it is exactly like the one running between Istanbul and Uzunkopru, and is still painted in Wagons-Lits colours. Somehow it seems very fitting that this should be so, though the crockery proclaims the name of the new owners, the S.S.G., themselves a subsidiary of the Wagons-Lits Co.

The Swiss Restaurant Car Company's menu is exactly as predicted, and we have but started on the potato soup, when the conductor returns from issuing meal tickets down the train. He is Monsieur Thiemard-Baltenschweiler, a splendid Franco-German name, in keeping with his calling.

"And where have you come from this time?" he says, as soon as he sees me. The English people at the next table, are distinctly surprised. How does he know me, a mere holidaymaker?

"Istanbul" I tell him nonchalantly, as though it were any old place just down the line, and the people at the next table are completely flabbergasted.

"And what about you? A change of uniform, but still your car after 32 years in the Wagons-Lits service. I cannot really imagine the post-war Istanbul train without your diner".

We have a couple of hours for dinner, while we trundle down the Rhone Valley, stopping at Sierre, Sion, Martigny, Bex and Aigle. At the last three places there are tantalising little narrow gauge electric railways or quasi-trams, some starting in the streets but turning themselves into mountain railways, often with rack-rails to assist on the steep gradients. After Montreux, where the line skirts Lake Geneva, our friend retired to her sleeper. Chillon Castle, which we pass before Montreux, shining in the moonlight strikes me as quite as excitingly impressive as any of the sights of Istanbul.

Our train makes one more stop, at Vevey, resort for the not-so-young, and perhaps a Mecca for Milk Chocolate eaters. It would be nice to alight and explore the nearby railway museum line from Chamby to Blonay. A former branch of the CEV (Veveysan electric) narrow gauge line which starts beside our track, it is a flourishing co-operative run by Swiss Railway enthusiasts. The staff are taking the cloths off the tables. The diner is empty now, all the other passengers having retired. We ourselves stay only because we feel it is easier to regain our sleeper at the opposite end of the train in the six minutes stop at Lausanne.

Although we have but a short night's rest, I find I cannot sleep. Up in front the great Swiss engine is heading inexorably into the Jura mountains to the frontier at Vallorbe, and this journey is almost at an end. It would be nice to do it all over again, perhaps, though the excitement of exploration would be lacking. Soon jumbo jets will reduce the cost as well as the time in flying to

Turkey itself - provided the resorts are properly developed as befits city people. Perhaps it has dawned on the Turkish authorities that tourists will spend foreign currency just to travel by steam train - not because they particularly wish to come to Turkey to sample Turkish trains, but because Sir William Stanier's last locomotive will have stopped running on home rails by the time this book appears. The Turks do everything else possible to encourage tourists.

But will the long distance trains survive into the jumbo jet age? There is no doubt that in the late sixties, with overcrowded motorways, new restrictions and increasing costs piled onto motorists, that people are becoming tired of motor cars, and turning again to trains.

How much more comfortable, to doze in the crisp mountain air of Vallorbe, while the engines are craftily changed by the sophisticated device of passing different kinds of current down the same wires, than it is to be turned out of a night flight at four o'clock in the morning. Here all is still, save for the church clock, booming midnight. At Vallorbe the train waits longer than it takes to travel thither from Lausanne. Perhaps it is too still; steam sizzling round cylinders and brake pumps belching smoke from the International Tunnel, great PLM engines in pairs, and a dinky little Swiss tank engine from the private line, is how Vallorbe remains in my memory. Just a dream. Whereas Turkish steam travel is still reality.

Is the train too expensive for ordinary travellers? Perhaps: yet the reduction in the fare by several pounds, on the night ferry service - albeit the most expensive Wagons-Lits route in terms of mileage - is a step in the right direction and a precursor of the second class sleepers to Turkey. Here we can but show how best to enjoy regular train travel; whether groups of people in special trains with sleepers and couchettes and meals will be accepted for travel across all Europe by the railways concerned, is anybody's guess.

A bang on the door; five thirty in the morning. We are back in reality - such is modern "progress" that we rush swiftly up the main line from Dijon to Paris, and this Sens, time to get up. Dream if you wish for five minutes of the pleasurable breakfast car that graced the Simplon Orient and reflect, as you plug in your electric razor, that whilst this pleasure is too expensive, at least you do not have to wrestle with a cut-throat, as father did before you.

Expresses zoom up the mainline from the Riviera, at approximately three minute intervals. So there are no niceties about remaining in your sleeper until a civilised hour at the Gare de Lyon; hence there is much to be said for going on to Calais, rather than spending the day in Paris and catching the Night Ferry. It is time to put away those comfortable slippers and put on the smart suit in which to say good-bye at the Company's head office. As the Direct Orient Express rolls on towards the French capital, through the "fair fields of France" which look decisively autumnal and northern, at five thirty on this October morning, I find myself musing on the irony of progress, by which our high speed electric engine now dumps us in the Gare de Lyon in the small hours (06.24 according to the timetable). What an ignominious arrival; it is as though the operators of this train wish to keep quiet about its existence.

Yet with the departure of steam, tourists are turning back to trains. They are really much cheaper than air travel, especially when group travel is used. Belatedly the railways themselves are turning to tourism. The SNCF, DB and NS (Dutch Railways) already have their own tourist subsidiary companies. It is dawning on the railways that the couchette car - abhorred in Britain where the term is unknown - is not good enough for the 1970s. In Sweden and in Norway special sleepers are attached to ordinary trains, as well as being run in special trains. The Wagons-Lits have their large reductions for travel agents hiring sleepers for the season in most of Western Europe.

At the moment of writing, the airlines are worried by lack of hotel beds. With train travel you can cut out the hotels and still enjoy real beds. Perhaps the idea of reclining seats and open coaches, complete with canned music, so dear to the hearts of urban minded railway operators, has passed its zenith, even though BR is considering introducing such vehicles on the Night Ferry, displacing some of the Wagons-Lits Cars in the process.

For now, it is becoming in vogue to seek to "get away from it all", to peace and quiet and seclusion, such as can be found in country cottages, lesser developed Mediterranean shores (such as Turkey) and also, though only devotees know it, in the cabins of the Wagons-Lits, where the arrangement of the intercommunicating doors is all that most people could desire.

The author's Wagons-Lits dining car bills.

Lay down your rails, ye nations, near and far
Yoke your full trains to Steam's triumphal car.
Link town to town; unite in iron bands
The long estranged and oft-embittled lands.
Blessings on Science and her hand-maid Steam!
They made Utopia only half a dream.
*   Charles Mackay (1886)*

Our route from Paris to Vienna is all electric to-day, though the piece across the Rhine from Strasbourg to the German frontier station at Kehl was only wired up in 1966. We start from Paris behind the French Railways SNCF Bo-Bo No. 16073, from Strasbourg shed. These were built for express service on the 25,000 V A.C. lines in 1958, and cruise in the region of 85 m.p.h.

The Wagons-Lits sleepers are scattered through the train, with the one which we travel, 3909, in the centre. It is Belgian built, but has an Austrian RIC plate. The interior is panelled in shiny dark mahogany. Originally this class were classified YT, signifying that the end compartments had three berths for tourist class passengers, unusable as a double compartment. These are all redesignated YU, or "Y, type Universal". The difference is that the end compartments have been adapted so that the tourist class centre berth has two sleeping positions, and the end compartments can be arranged for single, double or triple berth occupation. Single and double berth compartments in these cars can only be occupied by holders of first class railway tickets.

The RIC plate is displayed on all Wagons-Lits stock except those operating wholly within Turkey, and also Spain and Portugal. RIC stands for Regolamento Internazionale delle Carrozze which has been functioning since World War I (or possibly earlier) and this perhaps explains the use of Italian for the words International Carriage Regulations rather than some other language. Every Wagons-Lits car is allocated to a railway which is responsible for checking the technical details such as brakes, overhauls etc., within the specified time laid down for such checks and overhauls, and these railway administrations have the power to withhold permission for the cars to circulate on other administrations lines if this is not done. The Italian State Railways are perhaps the most meticulous in ensuring that the Wagons-Lits for which they are responsible, comply with the rules.

The two sleepers in the train for Salzburg comprise one of the recent MU type, No.4734, French built, and with a South East Region (F5) RIC plate; and an older Y class car, No. 3705, with Eastern Region (F1) RIC plate. Up in front, the Paris - Stuttgart Car, was in 1966 an Lx 20 class car. These have wider berths in the compartments than the Y but not the MU (which are longer than the older cars). The Lx class also lack any sort of pantry, because they were designed for the days of trains of Wagons-Lits, with a diner incorporated. For this reason they remained as the backbone of the Blue Train formation for many years up till 16th December, 1968. From 1967 the Y class car between Paris and Salzburg, which inter-worked with the Paris - Bucharest car to provide a daily Paris - Salzburg operation in addition to the MU car and the Paris - Vienna car, was withdrawn. Instead, the Paris - Bucharest operation was altered from class Y to YU, and based on the Austrian Division at Vienna, instead of the Inspection Est at Paris. The car was then worked in conjunction with the Paris - Vienna car which in effect was extended to Bucharest three times a week in winter, daily in summer.

Our train covers the 107 miles to the first stop, Chalons-sur-Marne in 1 hour 43 minutes (now reduced to 1 hour 39 minutes) and here is the first sight of steam, one of the ubiquitous Mikado class 2-8-2 mixed traffic engines built in America to French specifications for use after World War II, the 141 R class. Steam persists on the Chaumont-Chalons-Laons-Amiens-Boulogne-Calais line, over which, in the pre-war days, the Orient Express sleepers from Calais ran to join the main train at Chalons.

The Orient Express stops next at Nancy, and then Strasbourg, reaching Kehl, six miles beyond Strasbourg, at 3.25 a.m. Here our train is taken over by the German Railways (DB) E41 class Bo-Bo locomotive that has brought the Orient Express going the other way, from Stuttgart, its home shed. After a run of about 13 kms. the train takes the left hand fork of a triangular junction to join the south-north Rheingold route at Appenweier. It then follows the same tracks along the Rhine as those of the famous Rheingold Express, pausing for one minute at Baden-Oos, (junction for Baden-Baden) and passing through Rastatt, grey in the early dawn, to reach Karlsruhe, the Divisional headquarters of this part of the German Railways.

In May 1963, the DSG (German Sleeping Car Co.) set up their central food supply depot at Rastatt, and dining car supplies are sent out to cars operating all over Germany. The depot is similar to that at Olten of the Swiss Dining Car Co., but larger. In many ways it resembles the Wagons-Lits Co. arrangements at the Maison Raoul Dautry for the supply of their French-based diners, and the restaurants at the airports. Where Paris has a Charcuterie, Rastatt has a Wursterei or sausage making factory. Wine bottling for the DSG until 1963 was carried out at Traben-Trarbach but this too has been re-established at Rastatt. Cars operating into Austria draw wine and various other supplies at Vienna from the Wagons-Lits Co.'s Viennese depot.

After stopping at Karlsruhe Hauptbahnhof, we pass slowly through the large Karlsruhe Durlach station, where we swing away from the Rhine main line, going east once more. Before the next stop, Pforzheim, (30 km. from Karlsruhe) we cross from the Karlsruhe Division into the Stuttgart Division at Wilferdingen. From Pforzheim we run non-stop to Stuttgart, joining the main line followed by the Tauern Express from Ostend to Munich and Salzburg, at Muhlacker.

Our next engine, a blue E10 class Bo-Bo from Munich shed, which is waiting to back on. In 1967, DB replaced the E prefix by 1, for electric classes, and prefixed 0 to steam classes.

The E10, E40 and E41 class Bo-Bo engines all look exactly alike. They have square fronts, but the faster ones are painted blue. The E10s and E40s are very similar in size, weight, output but E10s (which are blue) have higher gearing than E40s (which are green) and the latter are used for mixed traffic. The E10s date from 1956, the E40s from 1957 and in the same year the E41s appeared, of lighter weight and slightly lower speed than the E10s: 66.4 tons, against 86.5 tons, and 120 kph. instead of 150. In 1965 the E10s ceased to be the DB's crack express engines when the 03s appeared, with Co-Co wheel arrangements, rounded ends, and a top speed of 200 kph. (125mph.).

We leave Stuttgart past Stuttgart Bad Cannstatt, the home of Mercedes Benz, passing next through Esslingen, where several classes of DB steam engines were built. The line is four track, and is said to have Germany's most dense traffic. At Plochingen, it becomes double track, as some of the traffic diverges here for Tubingen. We pass through Goppingen, where Marklin have their famous model railway factory, and after Geislingen climb over the watershed to the Danube at Ulm, up a gradient of 1 in 45, which requires banking engines for the goods trains. The goods engines are usually the E50 class Co-Co, the bankers the E93s built for the line in 1933. Some of the goods trains are hauled by the E94 class, an articulated variety of Co-Co, with great snouts fore and aft. This class was introduced to the Arlberg route in Austria when the German Railways took over the Austrian State Railways, after the Anschluss in 1938.

After calling at Ulm, we pass from the Stuttgart to the Augsburg Division of the DB, Augsburg itself being the next stop. Then on to Munich, crossing the next Divisional boundary at Malsach, for of course a place as large as Munich, with fourteen running lines over the section from Munich passing into the Hauptbahnhof, on one of which we run, naturally has its own Division.

Munich is different in many ways from anywhere yet met with in Germany. The great green carriages of the DB mingle with the blue ones of the Touropa, couchette cars maintained by the DB, but actually belonging to the consortia of German travel agencies. Such an arrangement might well develop on British Railways. In addition there are the foreign carriages, Austrian, Belgian, French, Dutch and Italian. There are red Deutsche Schlafwagen Gesellschaft DSG (German Sleeping Car Co.) sleepers, a brown Yugoslav one from the Yugoslavija Express that runs to Belgrade, and finally, more Wagons-Lits, from Italy. One is a blue U type, built in Germany as war reparations, with a DB RIC plate, running to Rome; the other is a P class aluminium unpainted sleeper with 20 single berth compartments in two levels, running to Milan, where it is based. In 1968 a second type U took its place.

There is some steam to be found at Munich, with some non-electrified line trains hauled by the 38 class 4-6-0s, a Prussian class originally, which has given good service over the years, all over Germany. Electrification first came to Munich in 1925, and so the shunting of empty stock trains is performed by elderly 1-C-1 rod-drive E32 class engines. There are 1-Do-1 class engines of distinctive appearance, three classes all told, E16, E17, and E18, which were not found at places on more recently electrified routes until 1967. Much of the shunting is done by the standard V60 class diesel shunters which are painted bright red, and the whole place is under the control of one colossal signal box which recently replaced 17 separate cabins!

Many readers, perhaps exchanging the Tauern Express from Ostend to Munich and Salzburg, for the Tauern-Orient Express from Munich and Salzburg to Istanbul, may decide to change here and spend the time watching the trains. All is set out in J.H. Price's excellent book "Railway Holiday in Bavaria".

The next engine turns out to be none of the kind already described, but a Co-Co, No. 1010.14 of the Austrian Federal Railways (OBB), running all the way through to its home shed, Vienna Westbahnhof. They have a top speed of 80 m.p.h., and weigh a hefty 109 tons! The DB and the OBB have retained the close links they had when the old Reichsbahn owned them both, and recently they made a through working agreement for engines, which saves much mileage for both country's systems.

We move out of Munich through Munich Ost, and go nowhere near the carriage works of the jointly owned subsidiary of the Wagons-Lits and DSG, at Neu Aubing. The Wagons-Lits have other repair shops in Paris (2), Rome, Milan, Ostend, Vienna, Calais, and Athens as well, for the stock in Western Europe, and also at Haydarpasa for Turkey, described later on. In Paris the larger works is at St. Denis, on the Nord main line, which has room for about 38 vehicles at once. Villeneuve-Prairie, on the South East Region main line, is slightly smaller but more modern, having been rebuilt since the war, when it was partially destroyed.

Our Austrian engine, 'awfully arrayed', seems to run faster on the DB than on its own metals. Perhaps it has a DB driver for this part of the journey or at least a pilotman of the German Railways. The Krauss Steam Tram is not at home at Prien, as we tear through - more's the pity. Freilassing, boasts a different Bo-Bo, class E44. These 44's at Freilassing have a few special features for working the Berchtesgarten branch.

There is one of the 1670 class in Salzburg when we arrive now, its squat windows, so much smaller than most windows on electric engines, giving it the distinctive look of OBB ponderance. Fore and aft there is a short snout, but a high one, coming up to the narrow windows. Austrian engines have remarkable great pantographs, and they seem to wobble, at least on the older engines, for this is how they are sprung.

At Salzburg we are already in the Linz Division of the Austrian Federal Railways. Outside the station the line to Innsbruck swings away to the right by a triangular junction. I never pass Salzburg without a certain regret for the departed Salzkammergut Lokalbahn. Incidentally, it was the discovery of this narrow gauge steam line, marked up in a manner just as important as any other in Cook's Timetable, which led me to believe that the present editor was rather different to any of his predecessors! Nowadays, he is well known to readers of railway, and more especially tramway, literature. But at the time, I was immensely impressed with its inclusion, in the hope that this would attract traffic and help to save it. Maybe it had always been in Cook's Timetable, but I rather doubt it.

There is time to muse thus, on this placid, yet swift, journey, which rushes through stations such as Vocklamarkt en route from Salzburg to Attnang; this place has a narrow gauge electric Lokalbahn to Attersee. Compared to the twenty odd minutes' wait at Salzburg, the two minute stops at Attnang, and at Wels, which comes next, seem very short. Peasants scramble out of the second class, but the OBB has in recent years made efforts to distinguish important International trains from those for Austrians, and have succeeded in speeding up the former.

Attnang Puchheim, an important junction for Bad Ischl and Stainach Irdning to the south, on the line linking Salzburg with Graz via Bischofshofen and Selzthal, seems curiously quiet. Nothing appears to be happening whenever I stop here. Bad Aussee is the principal place along this line, but it is Bad Ischl, home of Dr. Fritz Stokl the noted Austrian railway author, and the former Salzkammergut Lokalbahn terminus, that is perhaps best known. The Austrian Postal Buses, not as well known as the Swiss ones, but with quite as much an aura of tradition and service, now replace the erstwhile Salzkammergut steam trains, but running right to the famous White Horse Inn at St. Wolfgang, instead of attempting to serve it from the wrong side of the lake.

There is silent progress on the all electric line to Vienna. Occasionally there are other trains, hauled by the same class of engine as ours. For long Austria has remained aloof from the rest of Western Europe with its Trans Europ Expresses; only one penetrates OBB metals and that is an Italian diesel train from Milan to Munich and back, using the short Austrian section from Brennero to Kufstein, through Innsbruck. In 1967 faster inter-urban trains have been instituted, utilising the vehicles for the Vienna-Basle 'Transalpine' Express that has been displaced by more modern railcar sets, and other newly built or modernised stock. These trains have considerably speeded up the inter-urban Austrian services saving about twenty minutes compared to the Orient Express between Salzburg and Vienna, which takes three hours fifty minutes.

At Wels the double track runs in on the left, coming from Germany at Passau, the route followed by the Ostend-Vienna Express, which in pre-war days was an integral part of the Orient Express group of sleeper operations. Linz is only 15 miles further on, where the Danube rejoins us.

Fifteen miles beyond Linz, we pass through St. Valentin, junction for the line to Vienna via the left bank of the Danube, and pass out of the Linz Division into the Viennese one. Amstetten is the next place of importance, with yet another line south to Selzthal, used by trains to it from Vienna. St. Polten, with a fair sized engine shed, is the outer end of the Viennese suburban area, though picturesque country extends the whole way, right to the edge of the city.

Apart from the connecting line, reached by a triangular junction, going south to join the line to Graz at Meidling, and continuing, near the Wagons-Lits works at Inzersdorf, to link up with the main line from Vienna to Budapest, there are no other lines running into Vienna West. Inzersdorf works is long and narrow, bordered by railways, so that the Company was moved to buy a battery electric shunting engine of its own, instead of using capstans, or sending for a railway administration shunter, as is done at other works. The Wagons-Lits in its heyday had built a railway (to serve the Tatra Ski-ing resorts on the borders of present day Czechoslovakia and Poland), and bought a tramway (on the Riviera), yet Inzersdorf remained the only place where the Company ever moved its rolling stock about with its own engine. The engine is over 60 years old, and built by Austrian Oerlikon in 1903.

From Vienna, our engine is Co-Co 1141.16, which looks outwardly exactly like those working on the main line to the west. In fact this class was specially built to combine the high speed needed over the plain to Wiener Neustadt and Gloggnitz, with the traction for climbing up the Semmering Pass. The class accom-

plish both with apparent ease, and at Murzzusschlag, on the further side, 118 km. from Vienna, we pass from the Viennese to the Villach Division that extends to the Yugoslav frontier.

In 1966, the last 29 miles from Graz to the border had not yet been electrified, and the OBB were using 78 class 4-6-4 tanks (with Giesl chimney) for this portion of the journey. Here our train was taken over by a Yugoslav 33 class 2-10-0, easily recognisable as the DR52 class "Kriegslokomotive", of which we shall find many further on. The DB (West German) collection have now all been scrapped or disposed of to other countries. Though the class seems to be ubiquitous on the standard gauge in Eastern Europe, they belie the fact that these countries are filled with a delightful variety of steam classes.

Zidani Most shed, beside the gorge of the river, in a narrow location, had two 2-10-0s ready for the road when we passed by. One was class 33, the other a JZ 29 class of Austrian pre-war design, left over from the days when this part of the country was Austrian, up to 1918. Other Yugoslav steam engines appear from time to time on the long and rather dull journey to Belgrade, which we made behind a GM A1A-A1A Diesel. Reversal is necessary at Zidani Most (though there is a triangular junction) the station itself is on the west side of the bridge that gives the town its name.

Belgrade's main station is the habitat of class 62 0-6-0T shunters built in Yugoslavia at Slavonski Brod to a basic Baldwin design. Their larger cabs and coal bunkers easily distinguish them from their American prototypes, of which there are also about 100 in service. These are identical to those which, in post war years, shunted the coaches in Southampton Docks. British 'Liberation' class 2-8-0s built at the Vulcan Foundry, Warrington, are also prevalent in Yugoslavia, with UNRRA painted in large letters on their tenders.

Suddenly we flash past the narrow gauge steam shed at Paracin. That is to say I think it is Paracin; though I strained every nerve to see it again coming back, it eluded me. A host of tantalising steam engines, 0-8-2s with tall chimneys, and smaller 2-6-2 types reposed beside our line, mostly in steam, while their single track ambles away to the right, giving the impression that it goes on for ever, plunging deeper and deeper into the Dalmatian mountains, whose mysterious presence one can feel, but not see from the main line.

Nis main line shed, much further on, is on the right as the train forks to Crveni Krst. There are several of the class 05 Pacifics here, as well as 2-10-0s and 2-6-2s. The latter hauled the international expresses in pre-war days to the Greek frontier, and the 4-6-2s then, as indeed now (whenever there is a diesel shortage), took the main line trains from Belgrade to the Bulgarian border.

Our sleeping car, No. 3808, is one of those converted to Universal type compartments. The compartments are all steel with the partitions finished in a rough mottled surface. Even the steel ladder, upholstered in the usual mottled plush material, seems utilitarian. Built in 1939 by Linke Hofmann as type Y, some of this series was destroyed during or scrapped after the war, or written off as missing. There are 12 compartments with three berths, and the centre berth has an upper or lower position, on an ingenious crank fixture, that permits more head room when the compartment, as in our case, is being used by two people only. The top berth is arranged with a piece of wedge-shaped rubber, placed in the luggage rack to form an extension to the berth itself.

UNRRA 2-8-0 no. 38-037 is piloted out of Belgrade on a goods train by one of the long hood units built for Jugoslavia by General Motors, JZ no. 661-143. 1st September 1961.

Photo: D. Trevor Rowe.

This arrangement, enabling the rack to run the whole width of the compartment, handy for use with less than three people, has now been superseded on most of the U class.

At Dimitrovgrad, where the JZ hands over to the BDZ, the engine shed is easily seen from the train immediately on leaving the station, to the right of the running line. It appears to be a kind of jointly occupied dormy sub shed, JZ engines from Nis and beyond and BDZ locomotives from Sofia, sharing the facilities.

The high pitched boilers, the chime whistles and the cow catchers of BDZ engines contrast with the lower pitched boilers and absent cow catchers on the JZ. Perceptibly, one has moved further east, as the change in the time emphasises. Our Bulgarian engine appears to be a 13 class 2-10-0, as far as I can make out in the dark. This class is made up of ex-Prussian G12 type 2-10-0s, some of which were handed to Bulgaria by the Reichsbahn during the war. For at that time, Bulgaria became an ally of Germany, and took over a slice of Yugoslavia, but on becoming communist, handed the territory back to the Yugoslavs, though the engines supplied for operating on the Athens main line between the Greek Frontier at Gevgelija and Grdelica (between Skopje and Nis), were removed back to Bulgaria itself. Our engine, I discover on the return journey, was apparently deputising for a diesel. The BDZ has of course many 2-10-0s of its own and of more recent wartime vintage, some 265 'Kriegsloks' being in use, together with some DR50 class 2-10-0s (BDZ Class 14) acquired after the war. During the war they had been on loan to Bulgaria for hauling military traffic. Some of the Kriegsloks, which are class 15 in BDZ nomenclature, came long after the war, from Russia.

The run through Bulgaria took place entirely in the dark, so that the engines used from Sofia to Plovdiv (electric) and on to Svilengrad (steam) could not be annotated.

From Svilengrad to Pythion, the Hellenic State Railways engine is a Kb class 0-10-0 of Austrian design. They live either in a small shed at Dikea, on the right of the track, or in an equally small one at Pythion, in the middle of the station!

Owing to the ancient construction of the Oriental Railway and the low axle weight permitted on it, the DR Kriegslokomotives are the largest engines able to operate on this part of the TCDD, the 6th Division, which covers all European Turkey with headquarters at Istanbul Sirkeci Station. The class in Turkey are numbered 56501-53. In Turkey the wheel arrangement defines the numbering, the first numeral indicating the driving axles, the second the total number of axles. 2-10-0s, the most numerous kind of wheel arrangement, are thus '56'. If the engine is a tank locomotive, its number will only be four figures long instead of five, but a 2-8-2 and a 4-8-0 are both classed as 46. Nevertheless they are easily distinguished in classes, as can be seen in the appendix.

Compared to the ancient 0-10-0s, and the weedy track of the SEK, the TCDD presents the arriving traveller with a much more modern appearance. Though at Uzunkopru, No. 33502 was the oldest TCDD antique that we saw on the whole journey; built at Wiener Neustadt in 1875, it is one of the standard Austrian outside-framed 0-6-0s. Similar engines can be seen in Austria reposing on the plinth outside Linz station. Despite its age 33502 seems to be in good condition, shiny as any engine of the Dart Valley Railway, its brass as finely polished. At Alpullu, a sister engine, 33501 was still at work in 1966. Its portrait appears in Durrant's "Steam Locomotives of Eastern Europe". Non-standard class engines of more than 40 years of age are a rarity in Turkey, apart from the Izmir area, and concentration on standard classes grows rapidly. All the same the old retainers look as though they will go on, here and there at least until the new line avoiding Pythion is completed.

The journey from the frontier to Halkali typifies engine working on the TCDD. One engine and a regular crew travelling very long distances taking about eight hours or maybe more, followed by an overnight stop at a distant shed, and then back the next day. The attraction of the railways as an employer is the benevolence of the Administration towards their employees. There are sickness schemes, hospitals, holiday camps, and houses provided for the workers, as well as security, and the virtual absence of any reservist military training, after the period of conscription, because the railways are so important to the army, and to the country as a whole. There is no health service in Turkey as there is in Britain. The TCDD has its own hospitals, with a total of 900 beds, at Ankara, Sivas, Izmir and Eskisehir, and Sanatoria at Yakacik and Buca.

1968 Bogazici express at Haydarpasa. GM diesel no. 21525.
Photo courtesy of TCDD.

From Cerkezkoy, our 56500 class engine is assisted over the 1 in 66 over the watershed at Kurfalli, dividing rivers flowing to the Black Sea and Marmara. The pilot is a 46 class 4-8-0, built by Henschel in 1926-27 for the Ottoman Anatolia railway. From Halkali, three electric Bo-Bo locomotives Nos: 4001-3 suffice for the International trains, local trains being multiple unit stock. Steam occasionally works on towards Sirkeci, for local goods traffic etc., but Halkali shed has grown from being a small shed for banking or pilot engines to becoming the main depot for steam of this division. The modern shed is easily seen as the train approaches Halkali, on the right, alongside the track. The overhead wires begin beside it.

Turkish coaching stock (1180 carriages and 483 fourgons in 1965) has the name of the home station where each coach is based, painted in full on the underframe. The RIC plate, with the exception of the six Swiss-built first class carriages used on some international trains, is totally missing. Turkish wagons do not apparently work out of Turkey either, though those running through to Edirne have a large T painted on them, to make sure that they do not mysteriously vanish on to the Greek railways. Wagons and empty coaches are moved by special rail ferryboats, (one is appropriately named the Demiryolu - Railway) and the quayside lines are shunted by little 0-6-0 diesel engines built by Krupp.

Sirkeci station is devoid of steam. The local trains use one set of island platforms, the through trains use others which include the original station building and platform, where customs examination takes place.

Until electrification and the doubling of the line between Halkali and Yesilkoy, the latter place had a small shed. The large shed at Sirkeci was transformed for electric working and all electric stock is based there. Signalling is by colour lights operated from a tall box between the running lines and the sidings, which is something of a showpiece in a country where, mostly, trains are

controlled by telephones, telegraph, and flags with no block system at all. Sirkeci was the first electric installation with a diagram of the track and the usual relays. Elsewhere mechanical signalling with German pattern semaphores are used, at important places such as Ankara or Izmir.

The Bosphorus passenger ferryboats are operated by the Turkish Maritime Lines, whose large liners have exactly the same livery. The train ferries run only by day, and the nasty swell which can get up in the Bosphorus, plus the heavy traffic between the Black Sea and the Mediterranean, still large even though the Suez Canal is closed, slows up the movement of railway wagons. So the decision to build a new bridge over the Bosphorus, besides speeding up all Istanbul life, and relieving the car ferries, should speed up rail freight too.

Electrification from Haydarpasa to Adapazari is not yet completed. So the local trains are steam hauled though expresses and main line trains are entirely in the hands of the red GM C-C1900 h.p. diesels. 37 class 4-6-4 tanks look after the local trains. These are Prussian T18 type engines. They were built in 1925 specially for Turkey, not supplied second hand. The Limani quay at Haydarpasa is one of the many harbours run by the Railways, who do not, however, have a very large port establishment at Istanbul. At some other places by contrast, they own and work the entire harbours.

The Wagons-Lits workshops at Haydarpasa date from 1926, when the 40 year contract was obtained for operating sleeping and dining cars in Turkey. Up until then there had been about half a dozen Wagons-Lits sleepers in Turkey.

At first there were no third class sleepers. The SG class of car, with modified internal arrangements so that certain compartments had extra large washrooms, were built in Birmingham specially for Turkey. Later some of these were converted to SGT type, as were some ordinary S type cars, while others of the SG class were withdrawn from Turkey. The SG class later worked the Vienna -

Warsaw service, in 1966, but none remain in Turkey. After World War II new Y class cars were supplied for Turkey from Belgium (built by Nivelles), and this was the first time that the Y type had entered Turkey in Asia. Originally they had double glazing, but dust and grime tended to enter between the two windows, and the second set of glazing has been removed at Haydarpasa works.

These cars were first brought into use for the Ankara Express, the new name for the previous Wagons-Lits stock only train between Haydarpasa and Ankara, previously carried by the Anatolia Express. The advent of the GM diesels enabled the two trains to be amalgamated again. Though the present day Anatolia

Express is no longer Wagons-Lits stock only, it was shown as such in the Wagons-Lits guide, until 1968, when the change of policy accompanying the change of the Company name, radically altered that splendid publication with blue cover and gold block lettering. During the life of the Ankara Express, one sleeper and a diner ran in the Anatolia. Today the formation of the Anatolia Express, is 1 TCDD Fourgon, 5 TCDD ordinary carriages, the diner, four sleeping cars and one extra run with the permission of the TCDD, if required for traffic offered. In 1966 the two Expresses were

WR 3401	WR 3402
WL 3902 Vre 1	WL 3837 Vre 1
WL 3892 Vre2	WL 3888 Vre2
WL 3901 Vre3	WL 3890 Vre3

The train is run in style. When the Company was still running the diners, the WR opened its doors at 7 p.m., as soon as the train arrived from Haydarpasa sidings (alongside the works) although it was not timed to leave until 8.40 p.m. The sleeping cars are upholstered in the grey green plush, that originally distinguished Y class cars from the blue plush of the previous S class. The antimacassars are plain, not ribbed, there is a glass panel above the wash basin, for anti-splash protection. The Alarm Signal is in the usual four languages, but not Turkish. A notice, found only in the cars based in Turkey, in Turkish and French reminds passengers that 8 per cent is the expected tip and it is collected by the conductor personally. It mentions that he will take your ticket from you when you get in and return it on arrival. It reminds you that all Wagons-Lits cars are provided with a chain, and urges you to put the chain up on your door. Lastly the notice urges travellers to demand a bill for all payments made in the dining car, whose location, as in Wagons-Lits cars elsewhere, is indicated by a board with an arrow, pointing in the right direction. In Turkey they are lettered Lokantali (Restaurant). The Turkish Division staff were continually stressing how there were robbers on board all trains, but because of the alertness and caution of the conductors, this was quite impossible to guess. Throughout our journey the atmosphere was totally the same as in Wagons-Lits everywhere, a superb sense of security, superiority, aloofness, which of course does not prevent a party travel atmosphere beloved by modern travellers.

All these services are based either on Istanbul or Ankara, and Haydarpasa works carries out the usual Wagons-Lits routine, described in Grand European Expresses. The running repairs (Petit Entretien or PE) at Haydarpasa are not separated from the overhaul shops, but all come under M. Etel, the works manager (Chef d'Atelier). The principal on which the services work is that as cars go away for about a week at a time, on return they are refurbished for the next week's run. The few cars based in Ankara have running repairs seen to from the store, which is No. 1396, an old teak diner. There is also a running repair department at Sirkeci for the sleeping cars arriving in Istanbul from Western Europe.

All the fleet appears to be able to operate if necessary to Syria and Iraq, although in practice this is confined to the SGT class and always has been, save only when SGs were used. There are no RIC plates, as mentioned earlier.

Now that the Company no longer run diners, the 'HP' code painted on the ends of the cars to indicate where the maintenance has been carried out is a little superfluous, as normally cars from other European countries are never sent to Haydarpasa for repair, nor mingle with the Turkish fleet.

The works are situated on the right hand side of the line leaving Haydarpasa station and are approached from the road carried on a bridge over the main tracks. They have a curious, old-fashioned external appearance, perhaps due to the fact that the workshops are the most conservative element of the Company's many businesses. Because of the - one might almost say loving - care bestowed on the cars, accidents are few (there was a notable exception in Austria recently), and the works people have for years traded on the need for good relations with the railways and the public by turning out cars in proper condition and keeping them that way. The Representative for Syria reports a broken window, and great concern is taken about tracking down the car and ensuring its replacement.

Haydarpasa works is small. There is thus no need for a transporter and cars enter the buildings from the station end only. There are two roads, painting being done in the main shop, at one end. The usual leather shop, upholstery shop and foundry (small) adjoin. The first thing you notice on entering is the dry cleaning department for the disinfestation of the cars. The passengers are not, however, the scruffy bug-transporters that perhaps some of them were when the works was opened. TCDD coal dust is the principal target for this department today.

Next to the dry cleaning and disinfestation machinery, there is the laundry (which supplies the Ankara section cars in bulk). Meticulous care is taken over the linen, to ensure it is kept up as well as in Wagons-Lits centres elsewhere.

Laundries and liquor go side by side in the Wagons-Lits scheme of things, but the revictualling store, close at hand, was taken over a few years before the dining contract ended, by the Migro-Turk organisation. This is a subsidiary of Migros, the Swiss multiple chain food stores. Their lorries are to be found all over Turkey, and the end of local buying in the Istanbul markets saved the Wagons-Lits a great deal of money. Even so the diners made enormous losses, 50 per cent of which had to be born by the Company under the contract.

Maintenance of the cars is divided into Minor Overhauls (PR3) and (PR6), Petit Renouvellements every three or six months, and Normal Overhauls (RN). Haydarpasa, far from other works, is largely self supporting. The central engineering department of the Direction Generale in Paris controls the activities of all the workshops, but by its location, the Turkish fleet is isolated. Pending the decision to renew the contract, rubber mattresses, to take one example, had not been introduced to the Turkish sleeping cars, though they are now found all over Europe. In Europe various changes have been made in arrangements for overhauling the vehicles. At Ostend for example, the works are no longer used to full capacity, and major overhauls to the cars are carried out in Paris, or Munich or Vienna instead. Decisions as to which car is repaired where, are taken in Paris, as are those appertaining to transfers of stock from one Direction or Division, to another.

These decisions are limited by all manner of factors. I always believed, for instance, that the reluctance of the Italian railways to taking sleeping car passengers on tourist class railway tickets delayed the implementation until 1968 of tourist class facilities on the sleepers of the Direct Orient Express. Standardisation of the fleet has never been a strong point with the Company - indeed there have been over 500 types of sleeper, and in 1968 there are in fact fifteen or so types. The Company has been handicapped by the difficulty of tourist class sleepers as opposed to couchette cars, operated by the railways. Only in Belgium, Holland and Switzerland (except Swiss services to Germany) have the Company taken on the couchette operations of the railways. Now the French Railways (alone at present) have permitted the introduction of the T2 type of sleeper, shown at the Munich International Transport exhibition in 1965. Further changes have been made in fleet transfers, so that Spain now has some of the Lx class, for the first time as a result of this.

To return to the Turkish railways. In 1965 there were 870 steam locomotives, 107 diesels, 3 electric engines, 31 diesel, and 30 electric-multiple units, with 29 diesel railcars. These run over five thousand miles of route (nearly all of it single track), of which only fifteen have been electrified, though the Haydarpasa - Adapazari electrification will soon be completed. Adapazari has recently built some new Pullman-style air conditioned day cars for the Haydarpasa - Ankara main line, where steam is now almost eliminated, save for the four 3-cylinder 2-10-2 banking tank engines operating from Bilecik.

Ankara shed is beyond the station going east, on the left side of the line. Prominent on the shed are the 46201 class USA 2-8-2s which operate the suburban services, running tender first towards Eskisehir for the most part. For the Dogu Express, one of the Czech built 2-10-0s of the 56117-66 class is produced, replacing a GM diesel that had come from Haydarpasa. The famous Henschel 2-8-2 passenger engines have gone from Ankara, though the children's railway has a scale model one. Varied classes are to be seen using Ankara shed, and among those noted were one of the 56300 Vulcan Iron Works (USA) 2-10-0s from Zonguldak shed, bound for Zonguldak, piloted by a 56080 class 2-10-0 built by Vulcan Foundry (GB), from Ankara.

Trains to and from Sivas seem to have one engine working right through, though there are sheds at Irmak and Kayseri. Irmak seems to have nothing but USA 2-10-0s with mechanical stokers. Kayseri has a variety of engines, mostly used on the line to Adana.

East of Sivas, the 2-10-0s employed are mostly oil burners.

Diesel hauled Taurus Express approaching Ankara from the east with WR 1396 on the right. The loco is 20.004, a General Electric type U18C built in the late 1950s. Photo: W. Middleton

Sea, and the narrow gauge line at Samsun that appears to run through the streets between the docks and the station. The Black Sea ports are developing as tourist resorts, reached amiably enough by Turkish Maritime Lines steamers, so let's hope Turkish Tourism and the State Railways understand that in their line to Carsamba they have a first class attraction for visiting foreigners, armed with foreign currency, and run some excursions instead of three trains a day, the first one at 6.30 a.m. plus two short journeys.

Shall I return in time to see those mysterious, Henschel built 2-6-0 Tanks of 1924 plodding across the delta to Carsamba? Or the even more mysterious Russian built narrow gauge 0-6-0 tanks, called 'Kalominka' of which two, 33014 and 33920 are said to be lurking somewhere on the line (or in one of its two sheds)? Maybe the 2-6-0Ts, 34801-34804 will survive; especially if this explains to Turkish officials the need to make the most of this attraction.

Our difficulties with the landslide, too, prevented inspection of Sivas works. The TCDD run a comprehensive apprenticeship scheme, with boys beginning between 12 and 15, starting with ordinary schooling and general mechanical training. Elder generations of Turks have had to acquire their railway skills abroad, mainly in Balkan countries. The training programme lasts four years, and in the last two the apprentices diverge to the specialist trades they intend to take up. Housing, free lunches, summer camps on the Marmara and elsewhere on the coast, as well as free medical attention are some of the benefits of working for the TCDD. The Railways have their retirement schemes, insurance schemes, arrangements for clothing supplies, life insurance - handy in a country where landslides and earthquakes can occur, but more so when such amenities are not provided by the State for everyone. Some 850,000 people work for the TCDD in one way or another, or are eligible for TCDD benefits.

Coming from Ankara, the station at Sivas is on the left, the works to the right. Sivas foundry in the TCDD works is one of the largest in the country. It is well equipped, too, and turns out tank wagon parts, ore wagon parts, machine tools, parts for cranes and bridges and various other castings. In 1961 the works built a new locomotive, like Eskisehir, but this is exceptional as engines have usually been supplied from abroad. Rebuilding them, and renewing all parts is more in the works line; they also build boilers for heating, radiators, cranes, and other things for various state departments, including scales and small weigh-bridges.

As is often the case at places where there are main repair shops, there are a variety of engines available for shunting and local work, forming reserves, or awaiting repairs. The extra turn round needed, because trains were not running beyond Sivas

Eventually the plan is to have only oil burning steam engines on this part of the system. As far as Erzurum, Sivas shed provided another of the Vulcan Foundry 2-10-0s, which gave place to an oil burning Kriegslok, No. 56539 for the final run to Kars. Here the permanent way seems to be lighter, and this class to reign supreme on all passenger trains. Remarshalling of the train at Erzurum was carried out by one of the TCDD's 0-6-0Ts (numbered 3311) built by Nohab in 1928, as part of their Erzurum railway-building contract.

For the Saturdays only train to the Russian frontier, Kars shed turned out 55027, one of the ubiquitous Prussian G10 0-10-0s. This one was built new for the Anatolian Railway in 1924, by Schwarzkopff. Another of the same class, in terrible condition, was being shunted into a goods train, to run dead to Sivas for repairs. As engines are normally kept so very well in Turkey, its state was surprising, reminding me of the disarming habit of TCDD railwaymen everywhere of pulling a wry face and shrugging their shoulders, whenever Kars is mentioned. This machine had had a serious blowback in the boiler, and the guard (evidently an Erzurum man) flatly refused to take the engine in its position half way along the train, sharing the same of opinion as other colleagues elsewhere of the abilities of Kars shunters. The Turks never have a heated argument; but after a while the guard had his way, and a third 0-10-0, the station pilot, returned to the goods train to shunt the mostly empty wagons in place to get the cripple next to the train engine.

56539 was again the engine for our return to Erzurum, where the nostalgic clanking, in the dark, of the shunting engine, heralded the arrival of Stanier 8F No. 45160. Another, 45163 was at Erzincan, engaged in removing wagons of loco ash from the shed, which it shared with a representative of a different class 2-8-0, No. 45124 of the far off Smyrna-Kassaba railway, built by Humboldt in 1912.

Our minibus adventures stopped us having a look at the Black owing to the slip, meant using 0-6-0 tank locos; our train was marshalled by 44049, one of a batch of Prussian G8 class 0-8-0s supplied to the Smyrna-Kassaba railway during World War I when this French line was under German control and operation.

For our return to Ankara, we again had a decapod of the Czech built variety. From Ankara to Eskisehir we utilised the diesel Bogazici multiple unit, and at Eskisehir, the Crewe of Turkey, we were again frustrated in efforts to look over the works, Eskisehir builds coaches as well as repairing engines. It also built a new 2-10-0 at the same time as Sivas in 1961 - see the title page; both these engines are oil burners.

In 1968 new air conditioned stock with reclining chairs has been introduced into the Bogazici high speed diesel service which is now loco-hauled, replacing the sets used in 1966. Numbered seating and no non-reserved seats give this service an uplift over the ordinary service. In contrast the Fiat 1961-built second class only sets provide a free for all, but they run well enough, and far more speedily than the steam trains. Naturally until now they are the grandest provided for the Konya line, whose secondary status is rather pointed. Nevertheless goods is worked this way in quantity, particularly transit freight, in Western European wagons. This relieves pressure on the main line through Ankara. Goods trains are therefore frequent on this line.

Alayunt junction has a small engine shed, but when we passed no locomotives were present at it. Kutahya, where we reverse to get back onto our route to Konya, is simply an ordinary through station. Afyonkarahisar on the other hand is a much larger railway establishment. Because of the historical separation of the Anatolian Railway (CFOA) and the Smyrna-Kassaba and Prolongements line (SCP) with respective German and French masters, it was not until about 1934 that Afyon junction was fully utilised. So the SCP shed is at Afyon Town station, the original SCP terminus 1.8 km. from the junction and better placed to serve the community.

The junction station has three platforms, and, of course came to be fully used for war traffic during the first World War. But as the TCDD was briefed to improve communications without the use of foreign capital, it allowed the SCP and the Ottoman Railway to continue to own and work their own lines, using what capital there was for new construction, instead of for buying them out. Naturally the junction at Afyon faces towards Konya, for Baghdad. It was, until 1932, the only physical connection between Istanbul or Ankara and Izmir.

Whereas the standard axle load on the TCDD is 20 metric tons, the same as on the CFOA, on the SCP it was only 13½ tons,

An unidentified example of the class 56001 Turkish standard 2-10-0 built by numerous German, British, and Czechoslovakian locomotive works. The photo was taken at Medain Ekbes on the Syrian-Turkish border and shows the TCDD loco taking over the Taurus Express from a former British War Department 2-10-0, just visible in the background   Photo: K.R.M. Cameron.

and on the Ottoman Railway 15 tons. (It was only 16 tons on the Oriental Railway which is why the Halkali - Uzunkopru line has nothing larger than Kriegsloks on it). When the TCDD had completed the Kutahya - Balikesir line in 1932, giving a much more direct route to Izmir from Ankara, they ordered some 2-10-2 tender engines from Henschel in 1933 to work the line, and these differ from other TCDD engines by having a 13½ ton axle load. One of these was waiting at Afyon. The standard 2-10-0 axle load is 18½ tons metric, and on the USA Vulcan Iron works 2-10-0s it is 20 tons. The 57000 class have the same boiler as the 4-8-0s, and interchangeable wheels with the Prussian G10 class 0-10-0s. 27 of the 2-10-0s were built altogether, supplied by various German builders including Schwarzkopff and Krupp.

Afyon is the location of the concrete sleeper factory, which cost 3,230,000 Lira and turns out 280,000 sleepers a year, saving the need for wooden ones. Though these are available in the Black Sea Area, Turkey is notably short of fir forests or indeed any trees on the plateau, and many sleepers had to be imported. Some still are, for the TCDD renews 600,000 sleepers every year. The TCDD is embarked on large rail-renewal schemes of 46.383 Kg. per metre rail in place of the 39.52 Kg. rails used on secondary lines, permitting diesels, for instance, to work through to Izmir by bringing up the axle weight of 20.2 tons on the Balikesir line. But the goods trains on the Konya line are operated by steam classes in keeping with its lesser status: relegated engines are put to work on this.

So it is to Konya that you should go to see the erstwhile pride of TCDD passenger steam, the Henschel 2-8-2s Nos. 46051-46061, though they are now used on goods trains. The passenger trains are hauled by the 56700 class 2-10-0 engines, one of which, 56703 took us to Yenice. The 2-8-2s have many interchangeable parts with the Henschel built 2-10-0s, 56000-56079; both were supplied in 1937. As these are very similar to the 2-10-0s, already

A 56901 class 2-10-0 is banked up from Bilecik by a 5701 class 2-10-2T, chimney removed for the journey from France to Eskisehir.

encountered it is likely that the 2-8-2s may survive until the end of steam in Western Turkey, or even later, though their express passenger days on the Taurus Express, as shown on page 26 are over.

By contrast the 56700 class are second hand engines, German class 44 3-cylinder locos taken over at the end of the war by the French National Railways. (The 44 class appeared in 1938). They operated on mineral trains in the Valenciennes - Thionville area until the line was electrified in 1955. They arrived on the SNCF, partly during the war, when the German railways provided them to augment traffic, and partly just after the war, when the SNCF, being very short of rolling stock, acquired them by way of reparations. Altogether the SNCF had 117 of them on the East Region. The batch of 48 locomotives, which were sold by the SNCF to Turkey, journeyed to Turkey on their own wheels, though not under their own power as several parts had to be dismantled to clear some of the loading gauges on the way. The photo above shows one of them being banked up from Bilecik on the way to Eskisehir, where they were overhauled and placed in service on the Eskisehir-Konya-Adana line.

Konya station pilot in 1966 was a 2-6-0 tank, built by Borsig in 1905, No. 3401. For the local pick up goods trains between Konya and Ulukisla, the TCDD use some of their allocation of USA 2-8-0s, Nos. 45171-221. The US Army classified them S.160. One of these engines was waiting for us at Cakmak, to pilot us up the hill to Kardesgedigi, the summit where the line actually joins that from Ankara and Bogazkopru. This was based at Ulukisla shed, (one stop further on) but left us very smartly to

return to Cakmak to bank the goods train following us. For we were severely retarded at Cakmak, waiting to cross the only passenger train of the day, and also because the authorities decided that they would prefer our train to be piloted, not banked, and some time was wasted in getting the 2-8-0 to run round, for fear of the approaching train we were waiting to cross. Ulukisla shed also has a stud of the 56500 (Kriegslok) 2-10-0s which act as pilots, on the heavy grade down to Pozanti and Yenice.

At Ulukisla we also encounter one of the earlier diesel 0-8-0 type engines with steeple cab, built by MAK, hauling some of the railcar trailers which were acquired with various diesel cars built in France. One of these, a single car with no trailer, awaits us at Yenice. They have an extremely 'SNCF Autorail appearance' and are painted blue. There is no shed at Yenice, because those at both Mersin and Adana are relatively close by.

Mersin is one of the four harbours of Turkey that are railway run. The TCDD are particularly pleased with their harbours, perhaps because they do not run all the harbours in Turkey, but only those at Samsun, Iskenderun, Haydarpasa, and Derince, on the sea of Marmara near Izmit. The TCDD's Harbours account for rather more than seven million tons of traffic annually. Shunting in the docks is done by some of the five 2-6-2 tanks built by Maffei between 1909 and 1911. The freight trains and the local passenger trains are hauled by the 4-8-0s of the earlier series, with separate steam dome and sand boxes. This gives them a massive appearance, with domes all along the boiler, whereas British engines tended to have just one dome. The 4-8-0s we have already encountered in European Turkey

We are concerned here with Turkey as seen from the train, and it is not possible to understand the Turkish Railway system without an elementary geography and history lesson on the country. For of course the system is far from straightforward (Have you never heard of the 'mystic east'?)

To start with the geography, Turkey is a large country by European standards, but looks smaller on many maps, because of the proximity of Russia in all its vastness. Its area is about 290,000 square miles, and the Asiatic part can best be imagined as a rectangle, 1000 miles long (east to west), and about 400 miles deep (at its widest point).

The top of the rectangle forms the Black Sea Coast - the virtual whole south shore of the Sea; let us forget the top left hand corner for a minute of our rectangle, and go south from say half way along the top. The sea coast has a number of flat, rich but small plains, backed by afforested mountains which from time to time come right down to the sea coast. Once you get over the first ridge, the sea breezes that warm the land in winter and cool it in the summer cannot get through, and suddenly the country becomes bare; dusty with sparse crops or scrub for grazing herds in summer, full of snow and sleet in winter. This is the great Anatolian plateau, which undulates, and all parts look much alike, though it is dissected by river valleys, which are more fertile than the rest of it; these contain the settlements, and often the railways linking them up. As the bottom of the rectangle is also largely sea coast (the Mediterranean), some rivers flow to the south, others north. Among the northern ones may be mentioned the Kizil Irmak (Red River) which starts by flowing east to west, through Central Anatolia, just east of Ankara. In the east of Turkey, the Euphrates and its two tributaries the Kara or Upper Euphrates, and the Murat, provide a means of access for the railways to follow, though they are not navigable except in rafts. Like the Tigris, the Euphrates flows across the Turkish southern frontier, eventually reaching the Persian Gulf. The Tigris in Turkey drains the south east corner of our rectangle, which is not provided with railways.

As just mentioned, the left or west end of the bottom of our rectangle is formed by the coast of the Mediterranean. Starting from the left hand corner, the Taurus range of mountains stretch north east, punctured by the gap known as the Cilician Gates, through which the Seyhan river makes its way from the Anatolian plateau to the sea. After getting through the Taurus, this river forms the flat, rich, Adana or Cilician plain, with cotton and other crops, which benefit from the much warmer climate of very hot summers and mild wet winters. Here is the Turkish Riviera, just being developed, with modern hotels and amenities. The coast is on a latitude equal to that of Tunisia - but unlike Tunisia, it can be reached by train from Europe with only the narrow Bosphorus at Istanbul forming a break of journey.

At the eastern extremity of the plain of Adana, the Mediterranean ends, and the coast turns south on the way to Syria and Israel, reaching Iskenderun, better known as Alexandretta, which with Antioch came back to Turkey in July 1939, after being part of Syria. So the bottom of our rectangle is not quite straight, but follows the north-south coast of the Mediterranean to incorporate Iskenderun, before turning east again. The frontier with Syria is followed from Cobanbey to Nusaybin by the Baghdad railway, which here turns south east into Syria. The rest of the southern frontier lies opposite Iraq, the south east corner of our rectangle being roughly where Turkey, Iraq and Persia (Iran) join. This is the remotest part of Turkey, often entirely closed to visitors.

Some way up the eastern side of the rectangle lies Kotur, just inside Iran, where the new railway linking Ankara with Teheran in 1970, will cross the frontier. So we come to the north-eastern piece of our rectangle, very much Iron Curtain, dividing Turkey and the Soviet Republic of Armenia, and to the north of it, the Soviet Republic of Georgia. One railway penetrates the boundary with a train just once a week. Batum, that well known Russian oil port on the Black Sea, featured in Maurice Dekobra's "La Madonna des Sleepings", in fact is only just in Russia, on the corner of our rectangle where the frontier meets the Black Sea. Continuing west along this coast, we come first to Trebizond, where there was once a 1.050 mm. narrow gauge line to Devizlik. The Turks call this famous outpost of the old Greek civilisation Trabzon. Its existence is due to the caravan (road) route hence, south-east to Persia via Erzurum.

The next narrow gauge line (75 cm.) along the coast, from Samsun to Carsamba, is the only one still working. Samsun is the most easterly place on the Black Sea to be reached by the TCDD standard gauge, which arrives from the South, branching off at Sivas. Further west again, a further line from the south reaches the coast at Zonguldak, where the former narrow gauge line to Eregli has also ceased, giving way to a diesel-worked standard gauge line serving the new Eregli steelworks. The north west portion of our rectangle takes us to the Black Sea mouth of the Bosphorus, whose narrow channel winds down to the Sea of Marmara at Istanbul. This sea extends to form a further channel at the north west corner of our rectangle, the Dardanelles, best known to British people for the ill-fated Gallipoli campaign there, in World War I.

The maps hereabouts are somewhat deceptive. The Sea of Marmara is in fact so large that it is not possible to see across it at its centre. On the southern shore are two ports, Mudanya, and Bandirma. The first of these had a further narrow gauge line, running through the rich fertile coastal plain to reach Bursa, the capital of this district. The city is one of the most beautiful in Turkey, well favoured by tourists from Istanbul. But it is not now on any railway, and so, not on our route.

Bandirma, on the other hand, is visited on the course of our journey, a port whose existence is largely similar to that of one on the English Channel. It is a much shorter distance by rail and ship from Istanbul to Turkey's third largest city, Izmir, by way of Bandirma and thence by rail, than to make the journey by train throughout.

Izmir, as the Turks call Smyrna, lies on the western side of our rectangle, which is formed by the coastline of the Aegean Sea. Some of the Greek islands in this sea, which are themselves well known resorts, are in fact no further off the Turkish coast then is the Isle of Wight from Britain. Resorts in the south west portion

A 1960s post card view showing the Topkapi Palace with a view to the Bosphorus in the background. Between the palace and sea are railway lines and sidings on the approach to Istanbul Sirkeci station.

of our rectangle, where the Aegean meets the Mediterranean, are not served by the railway, as are the ports of Izmir and Mersin. Nevertheless Antalya and other places on this coast are among those most developed for tourists.

Lastly, we must add to our rectangle, the little piece extra on the northern boundary, beyond the Bosphorus. On the further shore lies European Turkey, continuing up the Black Sea coast to the Bulgarian frontier, formed by the Rezvaya river, which here flows into the Black Sea. This is a short river, as rising ground makes the larger one, which forms the frontier between Turkey and north eastern Greece, flow south west to the Aegean, this is the Meric, or Maritza river. This part of Greece was of course Turkey until 1918, and it is by the railway down this river valley that we enter and leave Turkey.

This single line was the earliest railway to be built in European Turkey, starting from Istanbul in about 1869. Like so many railways elsewhere, the pioneering spirits were British. The railway was called the Chemins de Fer Orientaux - Oriental Railway, in French, for in those days French was regarded as the international language of Europe.

By about 1874 the C.O. had connected Istanbul with the Turkish provinces which nowadays are in Bulgaria and Greece. For this reason it did not run straight to Edirne but crossed the Meric, by the large girder bridge at Demirkopru. Beyond this, one branch forked left to Dedeagatch, as the Turks call Alexandropolis, where later a further railway extended to Salonika, in 1894-5. The main line ran in the opposite direction, up the Meric past Edirne, to which a small branch was built, and past Svilengrad, to Plovdiv. Down this line the famous Orient

Express eventually wobbled, five years after its 1883 incorporation, setting out of Vienna on 12th August, 1888. By this time the Russo-Turkish war, which liberated Bulgaria in 1878, had set the boundary of the Turkish empire back to Svilengrad. The very purpose of the railway - military defence - had thus already been defeated, and more was to come after the First World War. The Turks then lost Macedonia, and the frontier between Greece and Turkey was drawn along the Maritza River, except at Edirne, the principal town of the province, that is now the most westerly in Turkey. Because of this, the Oriental Railway became an international company until 1st January, 1937. Then, ten years after the formation of the TCDD in Asia, the part of the railway in European Turkey was taken over, and the remaining fragment turned into a company called the Chemin de Fer Franco-Hellenique. This lasted until the end of 1954, the most mystic of European railways in its remoteness.

Railway construction in Asiatic Turkey began in 1860 with the building of the line from Izmir to Buca. Like many British-built and British-owned lines overseas, The Ottoman Railway Co., or ORC, started from a port to serve a hinterland, indifferent to through connections or indeed any connections with other railways elsewhere. It began in the form of a concession, granted as early as 1856, with a guaranteed 6 per cent interest on the capital outlay, but limited to a maximum annual payment by the Turkish Government of the day of £72,000 Turkish. Starting from Smyrna (Izmir), the line runs to Aydin (1866) Sarakey (1882) Dinar (1889) and Egridir (1912), and carries cotton, fruit, and corn from the fertile valleys to Smyrna. New arrangements for the concession were formulated over the years and as the Ottoman Turkish

Government in 1906 found they could not afford to buy out the British, they extended their concession to 1950.

Meanwhile the line was seized by the Turkish Government from 1914 to 1919, but as it was only of local interest, with no end-on connection to other lines, the Germans did not endow it with more, and larger, engine power as they did the rival concessionaire's line. This line is the one that crosses the ORC on the level outside Izmir, dealt with in a moment. The occupation of Smyrna in 1919 by the Greeks left 186 miles of the ORC railway in the hands of the Turks who supported Ataturk. But when the Greeks were finally defeated and driven out of Smyrna in 1922, the ORC got control of their whole line again, and set about restarting it. On 1st June, 1935 the TCDD took it over, paying £1,825,640 for it in Turkish 7½ per cent Debt Bonds, redeemable up to 1975. In 1936 the TCDD joined up the line to their main route at Afyon (below), with 113 km. of new construction from Karakuyu.

Afyon had already been reached from Smyrna by the French Smyrna-Cassaba and Prolongements Company. This was another British concession originally, obtained in 1863, and built in 1869 from Smyrna to Cassaba, now called Turgutlu, 58 miles away. In 1870 the Government, who guaranteed 5 per cent on the capital, had built an extension themselves to Alasehir, which was operated by the SCP. In 1893 the British sold out to the French company that was formed to take it over, and this concern extended the line in two directions, north to Bandirma on the Sea of Marmara, between 1890 and 1912, and east from Manisa to Afyon. This railway was also seized by the Turkish authorities during World War I, from 1914-18, but because it provided through rail connections with Afyon, and also formed the through route from Istanbul to Izmir, the German allies of the Turks, provided it with a number of engines, while more were ordered for it from them by the Turkish Army. The French company obtained control again in 1919, except that the line from Afyon as far as Usak was in the hands of Ataturks adherents. After his victory over the Greeks, the whole line returned to the French company, and the TCDD took over only in March 1934, that is to say a whole seven years after the TCDD had reached Afyon itself.

Afyonkarahisar, to give the town its full title, is in fact not nearly as important a railway centre as this history would make it. It is now simply the junction of four branch lines. For the Anatolian Railway, the Societe de Chemin de Fer Ottoman d'Anatolie, is the one which has changed the most, through being nationalised.

This began life in 1873 as a narrow gauge line from Scutari, opposite Istanbul, along the north eastern shore of the Sea of Marmara as far as Izmit, 57 miles east of the starting point, where it is at last possible for railways to begin to go south. The line was extended eastward as far as Adapazari, by an extension which may have been narrow gauge. At any rate Adapazari is not on the present main line, which turns south towards the gorge of the Kara Su river, utilised to get up from sea level to the Anatolian plateau. A British group took over control in 1880, but the Ottoman Government had the power to buy back the line at any time. For unlike all the other railways so far mentioned, this one was started by the Turkish Government themselves, with the assistance of some engineers from Europe.

In 1888 the Government exercised the right of repurchase, doing so with the aid of German banks, and thus began the celebrated 'Drang Nach Osten' the drive to the east, which has down the years associated the Germans with railways all over South East Europe, and Asia Minor. The company was carefully given its French name, on 16th March, 1889 which remained until the end. The main line extended to Eskisehir, then turned east to Angora, as Ankara was then called, which was reached in December 1892. In 1893, the C.F.O.A. proceeded with construction south to Konya, which was completed in July 1895. Continuance of the railway towards Baghdad, for access to India, by extending the Angora line to Sivas, Diyarbakir, and Kurtalan (the present terminus), and then on towards Mosul, was looked on with disfavour by Russia.

The British had toyed with the idea, on and off, since 1836, but were diverted from active pursuit of the railway extension by their concern with the Suez Canal route to India. They now returned to the project, so the story goes, by producing a map in solid silver, with the line marked in jewels, as a present for the Sultan. The Germans were more practical. The C.F.O.A.'s construction engineers were a German firm, Philipp Holzmann and Co. of Frankfurt am Main, and their engineers began a survey of the route for the Turkish Government.

Best known of all the Turkish Companies, the Baghdad Railway route from Konya, through the Taurus mountains to Adana, possessed the additional attraction that its construction could take place east and west of that town, simultaneously with that going on at Baghdad. For in January 1883 two Turkish business men obtained the concession for the construction of a line from Mersin, the principal port of the Cilician Plain, through Tarsus and Yenice to Adana, the chief town of the district. They sold their concession to an Anglo-French syndicate who got the line open in 1886. Meanwhile the Deutsche Bank succeeded in obtaining the concession for the Baghdad Railway in an agreement signed with the Sultan on 27th November, 1899. This caused considerable alarm in western diplomatic circles. The route from Adana to Aleppo by way of Iskenderun, was considered too vulnerable to attack from the sea. So the much more difficult route through the Amanus mountains, by way of Fevzipasa, Islahiye and Meydaniekbez was followed instead.

Ankara became the railhead of a branch line, and though railway construction was continued eastward slowly, during the war, the town remained the railhead of Anatolia until after Mustapha Kemal came to power in 1922, changing the name from Angora and changing the city out of all recognition, just as he changed his own name by adding Ataturk, father of the Turks. Meanwhile the Baghdad Railway began to be built from Konya, where it made an end-on junction with its associated C.F.O.A. company, and from Baghdad, though the final section was only opened in 1940. In 1906 the Deutsche Bank bought up most of the shares of the Mersin-Adana line so that in effect it became German, all ready for the Baghdad Railway. All the rolling stock and locomotives were replaced by German-built ones and the metals re-laid with steel sleepers instead of wooden ones. The last 14 miles from Yenice to Adana was used by the Baghdad Railway for its own route.

Naturally the line was indispensable for the Turkish Armies in World War I. The army fighting against the British in Palestine, was served by the line at Aleppo and its southward branch projection towards Tripoli (Lebanon), and also the army fighting the British in Mesopotamia, now Iraq (for whom the railhead was at

Above: An 0-10-0 fireless locomotive on a Baghdad Railway 60 cm gauge line construction train at Bahce, around the period of World War I.
Photo: Philip Holzmann.

Right: 0-6-0T on the Turkish Army Decauville line south of Afyon. The line is recorded as being of World War II period narrow gauge but the loco is one half of a German 'Feldbahn' twin, several of which were supplied to Turkey during World War 1.
Photo: E.L. Bell.

Resulayn at first, about 100 miles short of Nusaybin, the present end of the Turkish State Railways part of the line, which was reached in 1918).

During the war, the British Indian Army which invaded Iraq (then part of the Turkish empire), had acquired control of the line from Baghdad as far as Sammara, which was the furthest point north achieved by the constructors. The difficult Taurus mountains, and the Amanus Tunnel, 4,905 metres long, and 2,400 feet up, by which he line leaves the Cilician plain and reaches Fevzipasa, were not finished until late in the war. The command of the sea by the British, and the dependence of these armies on this half-constructed single track line, pressed construction forward at a great rate. British and Indian prisoners of war were among those who helped to build it. 60 cm. lines joined Ulukisla - Yenice & Karakina - Fevzipasa.

Right in the corner of the Mediterranean lies Toprakkale (the Earth Fort) and hence in 1913, a 37-mile-long seaside branch south to Iskenderun was opened. The main line runs more or less east to Fevzipasa, where it turns south to Aleppo. Thirteen and a half miles before reaching this important Arab city, the junction was made at Muslimiye with the line on to Nusaybin. Trains run to and from Aleppo where they reverse.

During World War I, the Allies made secret agreements for annexing the various pieces of Turkey and the Turkish empire which they thought they would like. Britain, naturally enough, was still bothered with the idea of control of the seas; so she occupied Constantinople (Istanbul), along with the Dardanelles which she had failed to take in 1915, and the forts on the Black Sea protecting the Bosphorus. Italy took Antalya and also the Dodecanese Islands, Rhodes, Cos, Leros, etc., which had a predominantly Greek population, and which became Greek after World War II, when Italy lost her empire. France annexed not only Syria, but also Cilicia, and took over the Baghdad railway from Pozanti southwards. This is the principal town in the heart of the Taurus section of the line about half way down the hill from the Anatolian plateau to the Cilician plain.

If the allies had not been so busy occupying Turkey, perhaps Ataturk would have had less reason for his revolution. Anyway the Societe Imperiale Ottoman du Chemin de Fer de Baghdad was replaced by the Societe d'Exploitation des Chemins de Fer Bozanti - Alep - Nissibine, which also took over the Mersin - Adana, and the Iskenderun branches. While the British and French companies could of course get possession of their Turkish railways again, the C.F.O.A., German for all its French title, and the portion of the Baghdad railway from Konya to Pozanti, were retained by the Turkish Government. There had been no hard and fast rule about operating on each others' lines, Baghdad engines often working on the C.F.O.A. pending the opening of their line, and C.F.O.A. engines sometimes running south of Konya; though in practice each company's engines tended to remain on their own lines.

Ataturk had been posted to Samsun as Inspector General of the Third Turkish Army. Away from Istanbul and with plenty of Turkish troops, ostensibly needed for the internal order of the country, he was well placed for his war of Independence. After a congress at Erzurum for the Eastern provinces, he made his head-quarters at Sivas, where he held another Congress attended by revolutionary delegates from all over Turkey, including the occupied portions. His fundamental change was to set up his capital at Ankara and keep it there, far away from the sea, with its interfering foreigners.

While the Ottoman Government in Istanbul dismissed him and ordered his arrest, Kemal Ataturk began the slow process of attaining independence. This took several years, during which the Turks had losses, owing to the British supporting the Greeks. Fortunately this deplorable policy of Lloyd George is little remembered by Turks or British, though the inherent hostility and suspicion of Greece remains. This is not the place for the full details, but to set out the subsequent ways in which the railways were affected by it.

In 1921 the Turks decisively defeated the Greeks at Inonu, where the main railway from Istanbul to Eskisehir first reaches the Anatolian plateau. After this the Allies declared themselves neutral, and the Italians moved out of Antalya in June 1921. In October 1921 the French withdrew from Cilicia having made a secret treaty with Ataturk, under which they formed the Syrian frontier that placed most of the eastern end of the finished portion of the Baghdad railway just in Turkey. (Often the line runs within sight of frontier, I understand.)

The establishment of Ankara as the capital in 1923, gave great importance to the C.F.O.A.'s line from Istanbul (Haydarpasa) to the capital. New engines for the C.F.O.A. began to appear from Germany and for a year or two private enterprise operation continued. Then, in 1927, the Turkish State Railways were started by taking over this all important line, together with the Baghdad as far as Pozanti. The object of the TCDD was to open up the country with new railways. The railhead from Ankara had already reached the Kizil Irmak river during the war, though the line was half completed. By 1927 the first 47 miles inland from Samsun

had begun, while 380 miles from Ankara to Kayseri had been completed. The extension east of the railway from Fevzipasa to Malatya was begun in 1928 and 138 miles were open by 1929. For this purpose the TCDD took control of the Baghdad line from Pozanti down as far as Fevzipasa, and on 1st July, 1933 the French operating company was finally liquidated.

In its place the French arranged two companies. One was Turkish, the Cenubi Demiryollari or Southern Railway, called in French Societe Turque des Chemins de Fer du Sud de la Turquie; the other, called Lignes Syriennes de Baghdad, operated the Baghdad Railway in Syria, and the piece of the Iskenderun line from Payas which at that time was in Syria. The Cenup, as it is usually called, joined onto the TCDD at Fevzipasa, though a 1934 account says their engines ran through to Adana, and handed over to the Syrians at Meydaniekbez; it partly worked the Cobanbey-Nusaybin piece of the Baghdad Railway. and the Iskenderun branch from Toprakkale to the frontier at Payas.

The return of Iskenderun to Turkey was one of the most coveted ambitions of Ataturk, who had tried to defend it at the end of World War I, but had been over-ruled by his superiors in Istanbul. The area was nominally independent of Syria, and as a result of plebiscites became an independent Sanjak known as the Republic of Hatay, which within a year opted for Union with Turkey. In 1939 the Union occurred, just after Ataturk's death; and with it the Iskenderun branch passed to the TCDD.

Exactly when the Fevzipasa-Islahiye section of the Cenup passed to TCDD hands is difficult to say (about 1940). It boasts one local train a day which is formed by extending the Mersin-Adana train eastward. The Y section of the Baghdad line in Syria (Islahye - Aleppo - Cobanbey) passed to the Syrian State Railways, after the occupation of Syria by the British during World War II, while the rest of the Cenup came to the TCDD in 1948. Though this section was isolated, the extension of the TCDD line from Gaziantep, on to Kharkamis has united it with the main system. The Taurus Express sleeper now runs via Gaziantep to Baghdad once weekly, and via Aleppo once weekly also. The Syrian Railways still have an isolated portion of the line, stretching from Nusaybin to El Yaroubieh, as Tel Kotchek is now called. From recent photographs it appears that they continue to operate this part of the line with the former Baghdad Railway's engines. Until the Gaziantep - Kharkamis line was opened, Syrian engines worked the trains throughout the length of the Cenup railway. A through Syrian diesel train runs Aleppo - Mosul from 1968.

The remainder of the Turkish Railways were built between 1927 and the present time, and the steam locomotives acquired for their use are all listed in the appendix, together with the origins of each class. While diesel and electric engines are of course all TCDD, the wide variety of the railways listed above adds to the charm of Turkish steam engines. For among the slightly old fashioned ways of Turkish life, compared to modern western standards, goes that old fashioned pride in the job. There is a shine on Turkish engines, equal to the spit and polish smartness of the Turkish Army, whom they so often move about. Turkish drivers seem to have their own engines, and to work until their task is done with them. Naturally the loving care bestowed on the machines in their charge, has resulted in some quite startling longevity of life. Equally naturally enough, the Turks are most proud of their modern diesel and electric locomotives and trains, which have cut down the time, and the dirt which Turkish coal unquestioningly makes, despite the most ardent cleaning. Unfortunately it is beyond the understanding of both the Turkish Tourism and Railways authorities so far, that in both their elderly, and quite recent, steam locomotives, they have an in-built tourist attraction, requiring very little expenditure on amenities, as has been necessary for ordinary tourists. Let us hope they hurry up and learn from British tourism's success with steam trains, such as the Tal-y-llyn or Dart Valley Railways.

As the hotels in remoter areas are fairly rough, and as time is always a limiting factor, Wagons-Lits travel combines a solution to both these problems. Every night spent in a sleeping car is one less to be paid for in foreign currency, which is often precious, whenever governments feel that way. Moreover low wages within Turkey, make the supplements charged far cheaper than in some other countries, while the 'old fashioned' standard of service referred to, means that it remains just the same instead of deteriorating. Turkey was not involved in World War II, and the standards of the thirties are remembered and adhered to; many of the staff have twenty-five or thirty years service with the Company.

The full story of the Wagons-Lits is set out in my earlier book 'Grand European Expresses'. Following early successes from 1872 onwards, the Belgian engineer Georges Nagelmackers founded the present company in December 1876, and added the title 'Et Des Grands Express Européens' in 1883 to celebrate the creation of the Orient Express, which at the time connected Paris, not with Istanbul, but with a ferry over the Danube on the Rumanian-Bulgar Frontier, near Bucharest, at Giurgiu.

Following the arrival of the Wagons-Lits in Turkey in 1888, Nagelmackers wasted little time in providing hotels for his guests. The Pera Palace Hotel still opens its doors to visitors in Beyoglu, as Pera is now called. But Wagons-Lits ownership has long since been given up. There was also the Bosphorus Summer Palace Hotel at Therapia, which became a Turkish Hotel School. They were opened respectively on 1st November, 1894, and 23rd June, 1894. The attraction of Bursa for visiting tourists had not escaped Mr. Nagelmackers. The Mudanya-Bursa narrow gauge line lay uncompleted through lack of capital, when Nagelmackers became a shareholder and induced a French group to take over the line in 1891. This company worked the line until 1914, when Nagelmackers was dead, and the war obliged them to cease.

Although sleeping cars appear to have been used during the war in Asiatic Turkey, in his book Greenmantle, John Buchan is careful not to say who ran them. The sudden transference of the Turkish capital from 'the fleshpots of Istanbul' to Turkish Ankara, an ancient town with no plumbing, brought in its wake diplomatic problems. The British, who to the end supported the Ottoman Sultans, and bore away the last one from his Dolmabahce Palace, did not move their embassy at once. Instead the Ambassador established himself in a sleeping car at Ankara Station. By August 1924, building the capital at Ankara had progressed a little, and the Wagons-Lits Co. began their first services between Istanbul and Ankara, leaving the imposing station on the Asiatic shore at Haydarpasa (the C.F.O.A.'s headquarters) every Tuesday and Saturday, and returning on Thursdays and Sundays.

The 1926 C.F.O.A. Guide and Timetable shows how the Wagons-Lits were running a 16-berth sleeper and diner, thrice weekly on the route. It also complains how their line beyond Yenice was still in the hands of the French, who controlled the Mersin - Adana - Islahiye section, as well as the Cenup and Syrian portion, with one Company, the Cilician and North Syrian Railway. The Wagons-Lits company operated a 14-berth sleeper, twice weekly from Haydarpasa to Adana, and the Guide states that a diner would be provided as soon as possible. This sleeper was the fore-runner of the Taurus Express, which followed the route from 1930 until 1935 when it diverted via Ankara instead of Konya.

In 1926 Ataturk gave a forty year concession to the Company for the operation of sleeping and dining cars over the newly created TCDD. At this time the Company had five R class teak sleepers in the fleet, excluding those operating to and from European Turkey. By 1959 this had grown to 60 steel sleeping cars, twenty diners, three bar cars (ex-Pullman cars converted to diners) and eight baggage vans for the international mail contract.

On 1st July, 1927, the Anatolia Express was started. Compiled of Wagons-Lits stock only, Arabic had not yet been abolished, and the sleepers, diner and fourgon, bore in both Arabic and Roman characters "Angora-Paris-Londres" because it connected at Haydarpasa with a ferry to Istanbul, where the Simplon Orient Express waited to bear the passengers, diplomats, and others on to London. By 1949 traffic between Haydarpasa and Ankara overnight became so heavy that a relief train, the Ankara Express, was started, at first just once weekly; then with the advent of new sleeping cars, the Ankara Express took sleeping car passengers only, and the Anatolia Express had one sleeper at the rear of the train, and ran more slowly between the two places. This arrangement lasted until the autumn of 1965, when the advent of the TCDD new diesel locomotives enabled the two trains to be run as one, under the title of Anatolia Express once more.

Then at the end of 1966, the Wagons-Lits Company celebrated its ninetieth anniversary by dropping the title 'et Des Grande Express Europeens' in favour of 'et du Tourisme', though this is not painted on the cars. The new contract provides for a five year operation of the sleeping cars, from 1st April, 1967, though it may be terminated after two and a half years, if either side gives 6 months notice to do so. The TCDD have taken over the diners, and in 1968 built some new ones.

This enables the Taurus Express, created in 1930, to continue its international journey from Haydarpasa to Baghdad, and Beirut. We have already mentioned the new railway being constructed by the Iranian railways to join the new Turkish railway at Kotur, just inside Persia. At present the Wagons-Lits Co. run a sleeper in the Lake Van Express, 'Van Golu Ekspresi' is how it is shown on the nameboard, which runs from Haydarpasa at Ankara overnight, then journeys on through Kayseri to Sivas, reached after midnight of the second night, and through Cetinkaya to reach Malatya next morning. Here it joins the line from Fevzipasa, and then branches off at Yolcati from the Kurtalan line, to pass through Elazig, Mus and eventually reach the Lake at Tatvan, at eight in the evening. A ferry plies all night to Van, the principal town of the area, and hence a new line 74 miles long is being built to Kotur, due to be opened now in 1970. From Kotur, the Iranians are building a new line, 87 miles long, to join their existing Teheran-Tabriz line at Sharifkhaneh, 52 miles from Teheran. Already they have asked the Wagons-Lits Co. to run through sleeping cars from Teheran to Haydarpasa, when it opens, but this is not yet agreed.

Appendix I   Wagons-Lits Car Types and Numbering

The numbers of the cars were allocated by the Company to the builders who were scattered through Europe (and in two cases USA); because of this historical order and numerical order does not quite correspond.

Numbers 1000-1500 were originally allocated to Vans and Gas Transport Wagons (F & R). Numbers 4000-4200 were allocated to Pullman cars which had blue and cream livery, and which were aimed to be distinctive from saloon cars. The very earliest Pullman cars were not included in this numbering. Vehicle livery was varnished teak except that certain cars were painted brown and cream. Cars in Egypt and occasionally in North Africa were painted white. Cars in Spain were for a short time painted aluminium, and the Special class sleepers are unpainted stainless steel (Aluminium colour). Certain Fourgons (vans) were painted blue and cream for running in Pullman trains.

For reasons of space the innumerable variations of seating in the dining cars cannot be shown. Common seating is 56, 48 or 52 or 46; 42 (chairs) or 36 (chairs).

Sleeping car type letters are said to bear some relation to the vehicles, thus:

Pre-war classifications:

S	Steel Sleeping Car; first to be painted blue instead of varnished teak, used on Calais-Mediterranean Express, hence Train Bleu.
ST	As above, but adapted for conveyance of Tourist (2nd class passengers). These were the first steel sleepers (newly built incidentally) taking 2nd class passengers.
STU	A post war variant of the S or ST classes, incorporating Universal type compartments.
P	In the 1920s some sleepers built specially for Poland. See later for modern P class.
F	Sleepers for the Night Ferry (1936) conforming to British loading gauge.
Z	Steel sleepers (1926) with zigzag compartment partition of 24 berths. Modernised to 22 berths plus intercommunicating doors.
M	'Mixte' sleeping cars including some compartments with 3 berths for 3rd class.
Y	Steel sleepers similar to the Z, with 22 berths, but as the designation 'Y' shows, each pair of compartments joins, with intercommunicating doors.
YU	Some Universal compartments at the ends of the cars.
Lx	Steel sleepers of the Luxe type, at first with ten compartments with one berth. Later Lx16 and Lx20 with 2 berths available if needed in some or all.
3	This number was applied to 3rd class sleepers built for use in the Baltic States and Poland, etc. It has subsequently been applied to cars adapted to three-berth compartments throughout, thus M3, R3, Z3, but not S3. (See below.)

After the Second World War this nomenclature continued as follows:

U	Universal. As we have seen, the two position centre berth enables the compartment to be used at will as single or double or tourist. The differentiation here is that previously compartments with 3 berths had permanently less headroom between the lower and centre berths than in a double compartment.
YT, ZT	These were adaptions of the Y & Z with some third class compartments.
M	In the 1960s, the re-introduction of M for Modern (or so I suppose) with 12 compartments instead of 11, and a single vestibule. The M class are only found in Italy, everywhere else the compartments are Universal and the class is therefore MU.
T2	Tourist (2nd class rail fare) berths in two-berth compartments instead of one as in all "Universal" Tourist compartments. Introduced 1968 (November) on Train 61/62 Paris-Nice, and The Blue Train. December 16th (with MU type rep.)

After the war, the practice started of incorporating the initials of various Divisional Engineers whose designs were adopted by the Central Engineering Department of the Direction Generale at Paris.

Under this heading (begun I believe, before the war when the adaption of the S class for Turkey was designated SG after the design engineer whose name began with G), we find the P class cars, designed by the then Chief Engineer, Monsieur Pillepich, for Second class passengers travelling singly. These never really came into their own, owing to the abolition in Europe, of three classes in 1956. Also, the SK, an adaption of the S type designed by Head of the Dutch Division. named Kraal, and the twenty U sleepers in Spain named after the Spanish Director Luis Jamar, but also said to be called Lujo (Luxe in Spanish).

Meantime, the confusion with numbers and suffix letters is made worse by the fact that the original type S were built with the double compartments with shared washroom in the centre in some cases, leaving single berths over the wheels. The latter sort were quickly designated S2, while those with the double compartments (with intercommunicating washroom) at one end of the car, were called S1. As the second class compartments in the original S were numbered berths 4-11, this was kept in the S1, and berth numbers along the car did not run consecutively. When these numbers were altered, so that once more they did run consecutively, the cars were redesignated S3. For Spain, a type S incorporating three shared washrooms for six compartments in three pairs, was produced, called S4. Many of the S2 class were rebuilt with double compartments throughout, thus becoming ST type, though as we have seen some STs were built new. After the Second World War, some S2 class in Spain with other S4 class there, were altered to have Universal compartments, and wide sized zigzag partitions in place of the communal washrooms, with curtains for privacy. Lastly some of she S3s had a Cafeteria for service in Spain, type S3K, so called because they became the only sleepers to be fitted with a kitchen.

What confuses the foreigners in this nomenclature, is that it is predominantly English (Steel, Universal, Kitchen, Third Class, Zigzag are all perfectly comprehensible to an Englishman but not perhaps people whose mother tongue is German).

After 92 years the cars of the Wagons-Lits have had to be renumbered, to bring them into line with the uniform numbering scheme of the International Union of Railways, which includes all Europe except Ireland, Asia except Israel and countries east of Persia that are not behind the Iron Curtain. As we go to press (in 1969) very few of the numbers have appeared on the cars, though the system comes into force for RIC vehicles in May l969, and for vehicles running only within their own countries from October 1970. As no other numbers are permitted on the sides of the cars, the CIWL fleet numbers now appear on the ends of the cars. Certain of the UIC digits must be underlined, and others must not: so the new numbers break the lining-out on the waist of the cars, so that the first four digits are not mistakenly underlined.

The UIC number comprises 12 digits;- 00 00 00-00 000-0. The first two digits specify the gauge, and RIC ability. European gauge cars with RIC are 51; non RIC 50. Cars which can work into Britain via the English Train Ferries carry the digits 66 instead of 51, while cars with interchangeable bogies for working to Spain in the new Paris-Madrid Puerto del Sol train will be 54. The second two digits signify the administration or private company who own the cars. The Company has been allotted its own number, 66, whereas the DSG uses the DB number (80). Is is not clear if the Wagons-Lits diners, running in CIWL livery but sold in 1961 to the SNCF, will carry the SNCF number (87) or if the MU class cars rented from the Swiss Railways will be using the SBB number 85 (Nos. 4776-85).

The fifth and sixth digits, which are the first two underlined ones, show the type of the vehicle, and here special numbers are used, (except for the interior of some communist countries where no private enterprise exists) for privately-owned vehicles as opposed to those of the railway administration. The third digit, 0, indicates this. 00 = Fourgons with mail compartments. 06 = 1st or lst/2nd class sleeper: 07 = 2nd class sleeper; 08 = diner; 09 = Pullman. The next two digits indicate the maximum speed, and when combined also show the type of heating connection avail-able. The seventh digit 4 or 5 = under 140 kph, 8 over 140 kph. 40, 41, & 42; and 50, 51 & 52, and 80, all indicate that the car has independent heating, plus steam heating pipes for the train, plus connections for all five types of current permitted under RIC regulations and used by various railway administrasions, viz:- A.C. 16 2/3 cycles, 1000 volts; A.C. 50 cycles 1000 volts; A.C. 50 cycles 1500 volts; D.C. 1500 volts, and D.C. 3000 volts. In practice Types F, Y, Z & Lx turn out to be 06-41 or (not type F) 06-42; Type U Hansa are 06-51; types MU & T2 06-80.

The next three digits are allocated by the owning company or administration. The numbers allocated by the Direction d'Exploitation Generale or the Services Techniques are dispensed in batches corresponding to the type of car, maker, etc. The last or 11th digit is the individual car number, running in sequence with the last digit of the old CIWL number nowon the ends of the cars. Only on the T2 class are they the same (e.g. 504 = CIWL 5004).

The twelfth digit is nothing to do with the other numbers and is separated by a hyphen. It is there as a check to see if the other numbers are right when taken down, either by hand or by computer or scanning apparatus, and is called "Auto-control". As the numbers are very long and often transmitted by computer or Telex or apparatus known in America as "Kar-Track" to control their circulation, the control number is arrived at by a complicated mathematical formula, since inhuman computers prefer mathematics to simple memorising. To obtain the control number, multiply odd numbers by two, working from right to left. Add the even numbered digits. Then add up all the digits (odd x 2 + even) and subtract the last digit obtained from 10. The figure obtained is the control number, except that if the sum of add x 2 + even digits comes to zero, then the control digit is also zero. This system might be called the loco-spotters' nightmare, because locomotives are going to be included, using the figures 8 as the first of the eleven digits (where carriages are 51 or 66) while railcars or power motor coaches are to have 9 as the first digit.

With the introduction of the new numbering, the RIC plate now only shows the railway administration which assumes RIC responsibility for each CIWL vehicle, together with the letters RIC, and where appropriate, an anchor, indicating that the car is fitted with rings for lashing to Scandinavian or Sicilian Train Ferry decks.

Abbreviations Used in the Wagons-Lits Fleet List		
WL	Wagon-Lits	Sleeping Car
WLM	Wagon-Lits Mixte	Sleeping Car with some ordinary compartments
WLS	Wagon-Lits Salon	Sleeping Car with saloon, large compartment with sofa or several berths
WR	Wagon-Restaurant	Dining Car (with kitchen unless stated)
WRS	Wagon-Restaurant-Salon	Dining Car with Saloon portion
WS	Wagon-Salon	Saloon or Drawing Room Car
WSP	Wagon-Salon-Pullman	Saloon Car with Pullman Parlour Format
WP	Wagon-Pullman	Pullman Car (Parlour Car) no kitchen
WPC	Wagon-Pullman Cuisine	Pullman Car (Kitchen Car) with kitchen
F	Fourgon	Luggage Van
FC	Fourgon Cuisine	Luggage Van with Kitchen or Kitchen Van
FP	Fourgon Post	Luggage Van with Mail Compartment
FT	Fourgon Truck	Container Flat wagon with guards compartment
FF	Fourgon Fumoir	Luggage van with Smokers Saloon
R	Reservoir a Gaz	Gas Tank Wagon
-	Labo	Snack Vendors Van with bunks stores and sometimes kitchen

TYPES DE WAGONS-LITS ET PULLMAN

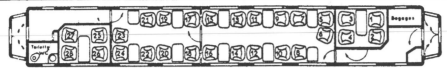

(Diagramme 79)
Wagon-Pullman à 28 places
Pullman-Wagen mit 28 Plätzen
Carrozza-Pullman con 28 Posti

Wagon-Pullman de 1re classe
Pullman Wagen 1-Klasse
Carrozza-Pullman di 1a classe

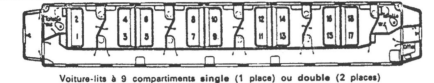

F

(Diagramme 115)
Voiture à 18 places
Schlawagen mit 18 Plätzen
Carrozza-letti con 18 posti

Voiture-lits à 9 compartiments single (1 place) ou double (2 places)
Schlafwagen mit 9 Abteilen single (1 Platz) oder double (2 Plätze)
Carrozza-letti con 9 compartimenti single (1 posto) o double (2 posti)

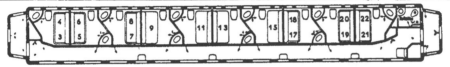

LX 16

(Diagramme 185)
Voitures-lits à 16 places
Schlafwagen mit 16 Plätzen
Carrozza-letti con 16 posti

Voiture-lits à 4 compartiments single (1 place) et 6 compartiments single ou double (2 places)
Schlafwagen mit 4 Abteilen single (1 Platz) und 6 Abteilen double (2 Plätze)
Carrozza-letti con 4 compartimenti single (1 posto) e 6 compartimenti double (2 posti)

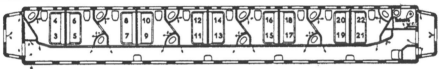

LX 20

(Diagramme 184)
Voitures-lits à 20 places
Schlafwagen mit 20 Plätzen
Carrozza-letti con 20 posti

Voiture-lits à 10 compartiments single (1 place) ou double (2 places)
Schlafwagen mit 10 Abteilen single (1 Platz) oder double (2 Plätze)
Carrozza-letti con 10 compartimenti single (1 posto) o double (2 posti)

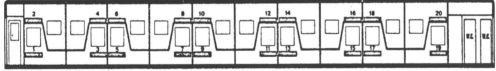

P

(Diagramme 158)
Voiture-lits à 20 places
Schlafwagen mit 20 Plätzen
Carrozza-letti con 20 posti

Voiture-lits à 20 compartiments spécial (1 place). Les numéros impairs concernent les compartiments inférieurs et les numéros pairs les compartiments supérieurs communiquant 2 à 2.

Schlafwagen mit 20 Abteilen special (1 Platz). Die ungeraden Zahlen bezeichnen die unteren Abteile und die geraden Zahlen die oberen Abteile deren zwei je eine Verbindungstür besitzen.

Carrozza-letti con 20 compartimenti special (1 posto). I numeri disperi designano i compartimenti inferiori ed i numeri pari i compartiment con superiori che comunicano due a due.

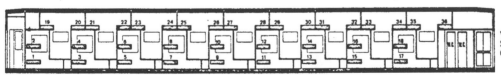

T 2

(Diagramme 186)
Voiture-lits à 36 places
Schlafwagen mit 36 Plätzen
Carroza-letti con 36 posti

Voiture-lits à 18 compartiments T 2 (2 places) accessibles avec billet de 2e classe.
Les 9 compartiments inférieurs (1/2 à 17/18) peuvent être vendus en spécial (1 place) accessibles avec billet de 1re classe.

Schlafwagen mit 18 Abteilen T 2 (2 Plätze), die mit einer Fahrkarte 2. Klasse benutzt werden können.
Die 9 unteren Abteile (1/2 bis 17/18) können als special (1 Platz) verkauft und mit einer Fahrkarte 1. Klasse benutzt werden.

Carrozza-letti con 18 compartimenti T 2 (2 posti) accessibili con biglietto di 2a classe.
I 9 compartimenti inferiori (da 1/2 a 17/18) possono essere venduti anche come special (1 posto) con biglietto di 1a classe.

TYPES DE WAGONS-LITS (suite)

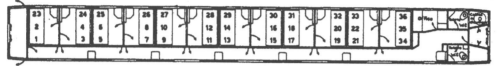

M

(Diagramme 168)
Voiture-lits à 24 places
Schlafwagen mit 24 Plätzen
Carrozza-letti con 24 posti

Voiture-lits à 12 compartiments single (1 place) ou double (2 places)
Schlafwagen mit 12 Abteilen single (1 Platz) oder double (2 Plätze)
Carrozza-letti con 12 compartimenti single (1 posto) o double (2 posti)

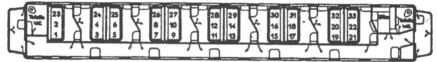

MU

(Diagramme 169)
Voiture-lits à 36 places
Schlafwagen mit 36 Plätzen
Carrozza-letti con 36 posti

Voiture-lits à 12 compartiments single (1 place), double (2 places) ou touriste (3 places)
Schlafwagen mit 12 Abteilen single (1 Platz), double (2 Plätze) oder touriste (3 Plätze)
Carrozza-letti con 12 compartimenti single (1 posto), double (2 posti) o touriste (3 posti)

U

Diagramme 159)
Voiture-lits à 33 places
Schlafwagen mit 33 Plätzen
Carrozza-letti con 33 posti

Voiture-lits à 11 compartiments single (1 place) double (2 places) ou touriste (3 places)
Schlafwagen mit 11 Abteilen single (1 Platz), double (2 Plätze) oder touriste (3 Plätze)
Carrozza-letti con 11 compartimenti single (1 posto), double (2 posti) o touriste (3 posti)

Y
YF
climatisée
(en Espagne)

(Diagramme 84)
Voiture-lits à 22 places
Schlafwagen mit 22 Plätzen
Carrozza-letti con 22 posti

Voiture-lits à 11 compartiments single (1 place) ou double (2 places)
Schlafwagen mit 11 Abteilen single (1 Platz) oder double (2 Plätze)
Carrozza-letti con 11 compartimenti single (1 posto) o double (2 posti)

YU

(Diagramme 161)
Voiture-lits à 26 places
Schlafwagen mit 26 Plätzen
Carrozza-letti con 26 posti

Voiture-lits à { 7 compartiments single (1 place) ou double (2 places)
{ 4 compartiments single (1 place), ou double (2 places) ou touriste (3 places)

Schlafwagen mit { 7 Abteilen single (1 Platz) oder double (2 Plätze)
{ 4 Abteilen single (1 Platz) oder double (2 Plätze) oder touriste (3 Plätze)

Carrozza-letti con { 7 compartimenti single (1 posto) o double (2 posti)
{ 4 compartimenti single (1 posto) o double (2 posti) o touriste (3 posti)

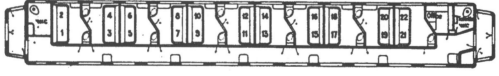

Z

(Diagramme 67)
Voiture-lits à 22 places
Schlafwagen mit 22 Plätzen
Carrozza-letti con 22 posti

Voiture-lits à 11 compartiments spécial (1 place) ou touriste (2 places)
Schlafwagen mit 11 Abteilen spécial (1 Platz) oder touriste (2 Plätze)
Carrozza-letti con 11 compartimenti spécial (1 posto) o touriste (2 posti)

TYPES DE WAGONS-LITS (suite)

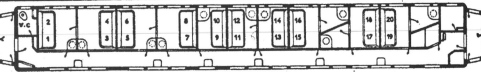

SG
modernisé

(Diagramme 170)
Voiture-lits à 20 places
Schlafwagen mit 20 Plätzen
Carrozza-letti con 20 posti

Voiture-lits à 10 compartiments single (1 place) ou double (2 places)
Schlafwagen mit 10 Abteilen single (1 Platz) oder double (2 Plätze)
Carrozza-letti con 10 compartimenti single (1 posto) o double (2 posti)

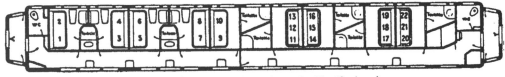

SGT

(Diagramme 100)
Voiture-lits à 22 places
Schlafwagen mit 22 Plätzen
Carrozza-letti con 22 posti

Voiture-lits à $\left\{ \begin{array}{l} 5 \text{ compartiments single (1 place) ou double (2 places)} \\ 4 \text{ compartiments single (1 place) ou double (2 places) ou touriste (3 places)} \end{array} \right.$

Schlafwagen mit $\left\{ \begin{array}{l} 5 \text{ Abteilen single (1 Platz) oder double (2 Plätze)} \\ 4 \text{ Abteilen single (1 Platz) oder double (2 Plätze) oder touriste (3 Plätze)} \end{array} \right.$

Carrozza-letti con $\left\{ \begin{array}{l} 5 \text{ compartimenti single (1 posto) o double (2 posti)} \\ 4 \text{ compartimenti single (1 posto) o double (2 posti) o touriste (3 posti)} \end{array} \right.$

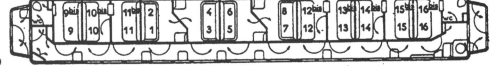

ST
(modernisé
en Espagne)

(Diagramme 46)
Voiture-lits à 24 places
Schlafwagen mit 24 Plätzen
Carrozza-letti con 24 posti

Voiture-lits à 12 compartiments single (1 place) ou double (2 places)
Schlafwagen mit 12 Abteilen single (1 Platz) oder double (2 Plätze)
Carrozza-letti con 12 compartimenti single (1 posto) o double (2 posti).

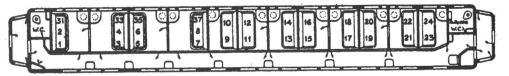

STU

Voiture-lits à $\left\{ \begin{array}{l} 8 \text{ compartiments single (1 place) ou double (2 places)} \\ 4 \text{ compartiments single (1 place), ou double (2 places) ou touriste (3 places)} \end{array} \right.$

Schlafwagen mit $\left\{ \begin{array}{l} 8 \text{ Abteilen single (1 Platz) oder double (2 Plätze)} \\ 4 \text{ Abteilen single (1 Platz) oder double (2 Plätze) oder touriste (3 Plätze)} \end{array} \right.$

Carrozza-letti con $\left\{ \begin{array}{l} 8 \text{ compartimenti single (1 posto) o double (2 posti)} \\ 4 \text{ compartimenti single (1 posto) o double (2 posti) o touriste (3 posti)} \end{array} \right.$

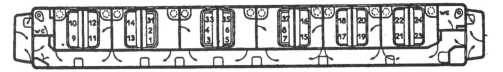

STU

(Diagramme 165)
Voiture-lits à 28 places
Schlafwagen mit 28 Plätzen
Carrozza-letti con 28 posti

Voiture-lits à $\left\{ \begin{array}{l} 8 \text{ compartiments single (1 place) ou double (2 places)} \\ 4 \text{ compartiments single (1 place), ou double (2 places) ou touriste (3 places)} \end{array} \right.$

Schlafwagen mit $\left\{ \begin{array}{l} 8 \text{ Abteilen single (1 Platz) oder double (2 Plätze)} \\ 4 \text{ Abteilen single (1 Platz) oder double (2 Plätze) oder touriste (3 Plätze)} \end{array} \right.$

Carrozza-letti con $\left\{ \begin{array}{l} 8 \text{ compartimenti single (1 posto) o double (2 posti)} \\ 4 \text{ compartimenti single (1 posto) o double (2 posti) o touriste (3 posti)} \end{array} \right.$

TYPES DE WAGONS-LITS (suite)

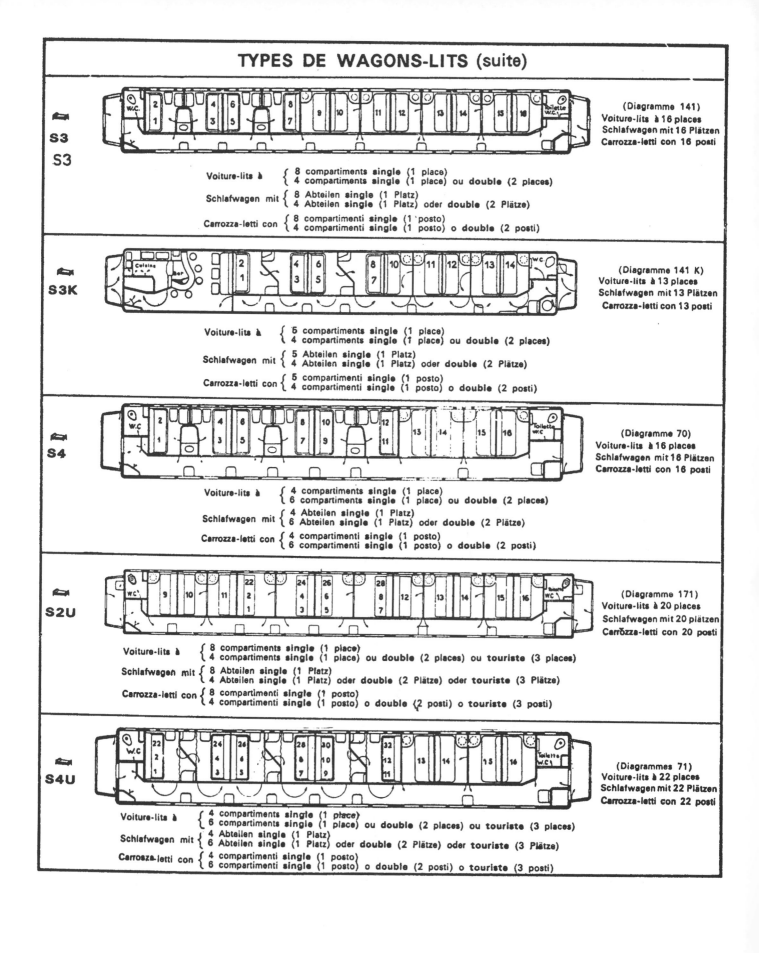

S3 / S3

(Diagramme 141)
Voiture-lits à 16 places
Schlafwagen mit 16 Plätzen
Carrozza-letti con 16 posti

Voiture-lits à { 8 compartiments single (1 place)
{ 4 compartiments single (1 place) ou double (2 places)

Schlafwagen mit { 8 Abteilen single (1 Platz)
{ 4 Abteilen single (1 Platz) oder double (2 Plätze)

Carrozza-letti con { 8 compartimenti single (1 posto)
{ 4 compartimenti single (1 posto) o double (2 posti)

S3K

(Diagramme 141 K)
Voiture-lits à 13 places
Schlafwagen mit 13 Plätzen
Carrozza-letti con 13 posti

Voiture-lits à { 5 compartiments single (1 place)
{ 4 compartiments single (1 place) ou double (2 places)

Schlafwagen mit { 5 Abteilen single (1 Platz)
{ 4 Abteilen single (1 Platz) oder double (2 Plätze)

Carrozza-letti con { 5 compartimenti single (1 posto)
{ 4 compartimenti single (1 posto) o double (2 posti)

S4

(Diagramme 70)
Voiture-lits à 16 places
Schlafwagen mit 16 Plätzen
Carrozza-letti con 16 posti

Voiture-lits à { 4 compartiments single (1 place)
{ 6 compartiments single (1 place) ou double (2 places)

Schlafwagen mit { 4 Abteilen single (1 Platz)
{ 6 Abteilen single (1 Platz) oder double (2 Plätze)

Carrozza-letti con { 4 compartimenti single (1 posto)
{ 6 compartimenti single (1 posto) o double (2 posti)

S2U

(Diagramme 171)
Voiture-lits à 20 places
Schlafwagen mit 20 plätzen
Carrozza-letti con 20 posti

Voiture-lits à { 8 compartiments single (1 place)
{ 4 compartiments single (1 place) ou double (2 places) ou touriste (3 places)

Schlafwagen mit { 8 Abteilen single (1 Platz)
{ 4 Abteilen single (1 Platz) oder double (2 Plätze) oder touriste (3 Plätze)

Carrozza-letti con { 8 compartimenti single (1 posto)
{ 4 compartimenti single (1 posto) o double (2 posti) o touriste (3 posti)

S4U

(Diagrammes 71)
Voiture-lits à 22 places
Schlafwagen mit 22 Plätzen
Carrozza-letti con 22 posti

Voiture-lits à { 4 compartiments single (1 place)
{ 6 compartiments single (1 place) ou double (2 places) ou touriste (3 places)

Schlafwagen mit { 4 Abteilen single (1 Platz)
{ 6 Abteilen single (1 Platz) oder double (2 Plätze) oder touriste (3 Plätze)

Carrozsa-letti con { 4 compartimenti single (1 posto)
{ 6 compartimenti single (1 posto) o double (2 posti) o touriste (3 posti)

Wagons-Lits Cars in the Fleet of the Istanbul Division - Winter 1971-72

Train Name Route	Train Numbers	Frequency	Total Cars Needed		WL Car Type	UIC No.	WL Fleet No.
Anatolia Express Haydarpasa - Ankara	6-5	Daily	8	}	Y	06.20.444	3889
				}	Y	06.20.445	3890
				}	Y	06.20.446	3891
Taurus Express Haydarpasa - Baghdad	4-3	Weekly	1	}	Y	06.20.447	3892
				}	Y	06.20.449	3894
				}	Y	06.20.450	3895
Izmir Express Ankara - Izmir	7-8	3 per week	1	}	Y	06.20.451	3896
				}	Y	06.20.452	3897
				}	Y	06.20.453	3898
Reserved at Ankara			1	}	Y	06.20.454	3899
Reserved at Haydarpasa			3	}	Y	06.20.455	3900
				}	Y	06.20.456	3901
				}	Y	06.20.457	3902
				}	Y	06.41.443	3888
Taurus Express	4-3		3	}	SGT	06.20.093	3414
Haydarpasa - Baghdad via Aleppo		Weekly		}	SGT	06.20.095	3418
Haydarpasa - Baghdad via Gaziantep		Weekly		}	SGT	06.20.101	3435
Haydarpasa - Aleppo		Weekly	1	}	SGT	06.20.102	3436
Haydarpasa - Beirut		Weekly	1	}	SGT	06.20.103	3437
				}	SGT	06.20.104	3438
Guney Express	12-11	4 per week	5	}	SGT	06.20.105	3440
Haydarpasa - Kurtalan				}	SGT	06.20.106	3441
				}	SGT	06.20.107	3442
Van Golu Express	12-11	3 per week		}	SGT	06.20.108	3443
Haydarpasa - Tatvan				}	SGT	06.20.111	3448
				}	SGT	06.20.112	3449
Reserved at Haydarpasa			4	}	SGT	06.20.116	3459
				}	SGT	06.20.114	3454 (withdrawn)
Dogu Express	10-9	Daily	5	}	YU	06.41.338	3911
Haydarpasa - Kars				}	YU	06.41.339	3912
				}	YU	06.41.346	3919
Pasinler Express	714-713	2 per week	1	}	YU	06.41.348	3921
Ankara - Erzurum				}	YU	06.41.350	3923
				}	YU	06.41.354	3927
Reserved at Haydarpasa			2	}	YU	06.41.355	3928
				}	YU	06.41.356	3929
Reserved at Ankara			1		STU	06.40.201	2892 (withdrawn)
Out of Service			1		SGT	06.20.118	3462
Out of Service and Withdrawn			7		STU	06.40.008	2776
					STU	06.40.009	2778
					STU	06.40.012	2791
					STU	06.40.017	2817
					STU	06.40.200	2806
					STU	06.40.202	2903
					STU	06.40.203	2920

List of Turkish Steam Locomotive Classes

Class Number	Type	Date Built	Origin
2201	0-4-0ST	1889	ORC
2251	0-4-0T	1874	CO
2291	0-4-0T	?	Mudanya - Bursa Railway
3301	0-6-0T	1918	Military Order
3311	0-6-0T	1929	not known
3326	0-6-0T	1913-14	CFOA
3351	0-6-0T	1911	SCP
3361	0-6-0T	1888-91	ORC
3371	0-6-0T	1885	ORC
3391	0-6-0T	1894	Feldbahn twin locos 750mm gauge
3401	2-6-0T	1905-09	CFOA
3411	0-6-2T	1911	ORC
3501	2-6-2WT	1909-11	Baghdad Rly.
3511	2-6-2T	1923-24	SCP
3551	2-6-2T	1911-12	CO
3701	4-6-4T	1925	CFOA, Prussian T18 design
4401	0-8-0T	1928	not known
4501	0-8-2T	1911	ORC
5701	2-10-2T	1951-52	Bilecik banking locos
23001	2-4-0	1869-81	ORC
24001	4-4-0	1890	ORC
33001	0-6-0	1890-92	CFOA
33011	0-6-0	1889-90	ORC
33021	0-6-0	1911	ORC
33031	0-6-0	1868/70	ORC GWR Dean goods via ROD GWR nos. 427 & 1084
33031	0-6-0	1890-92	Cenup (same as 33001 class)
33041	0-6-0	1883	ORC GWR Dean goods via ROD GWR no. 2308
33501	0-6-0	1872-73	CO
33901	0-6-0	WW1 approx.	Sarikamis-Erzurum line. Built at Kolomna works. 750mm gauge.
33951	0-6-0T	1916	Sarikamis-Erzurum line. Built by Alco for Poland. 750mm gauge.
34001	2-6-0	1911-14	CFOA and Baghdad Rly. CFOA locos originally fitted with an extra carrying axle.
34019	2-6-0	various	Ex-Prussian Railways class G5, supplied during WW1
34026	2-6-0	1894-98	CFOA
34041	2-6-0	1905	Baghdad Rly.
34046	2-6-0	1912	Cenup
34051	2-6-0	1930	Nohab design
34061	2-6-0	1933-34	Similar to German class 24
34081	2-6-0T	1925-26	Samsun-Carsamba, 750mm gauge
34851	2-6-0T	1911	Mudanya-Bursa, metre gauge
34901	0-6-2T	1913	5ft. gauge, built Kolomna Works
35001	4-6-0	1900-11	SCP
35501	4-6-0	1897-1908	CO
44001	0-8-0		Prussian G8 design
44001-46	various		CFOA, ex-Prussian Rlys.
44047-56	1924		new to SCP
44057-83	various		Cenup, Syria, Lebanon
44091	0-8-0	1906	ORC. Built by Stephenson
44101	0-8-0	1915	Ex-Prussian G8.1 class
44103	0-8-0	1913	CFOA. Similar to Prussian G8
44107	0-8-0	n/k	not known
44501	0-8-0	1910-13	CO
44901	0-8-0	n/k	Russian Ov & Od class. 5ft. gauge
44951	0-8-0	n/k	Russian O class variant. 5ft. gauge
45001	2-8-0	1927-35	Prussian G8.2 design
45101	2-8-0	1909-12	CFOA
45121	2-8-0	1912	SCP
45151	2-8-0	1941-42	LMS type 8F built new for TCDD supplied via War Department Known as the 'Churchill' class
45171	2-8-0	1942-44	USATC class S.160, new to TCDD
45501	2-8-0	1924/27	CO
46001	4-8-0	1927	46001-010 Baghdad Rly. Enlarged version of Prussian P8 design 46011-025 TCDD, two domes.
KL46001	2-8-2	1957/64/71	miniature locos, 600mm gauge
46051	2-8-2	1937	Based on 56001 2-10-0s
46101	2-8-2	1929/32	ORC
46201	2-8-2	1942	USATC/WD Middle East class
55001	0-10-0	1924-28	CFOA Prussian G10 design
56001	2-10-0	1937-49	TCDD standard 2-10-0
		1937-40	56001-079 German builders
		1948/49	British & Czech builders
56201	2-10-0	1961	'Karakurt' built Eskisehir
56202	2-10-0	1961	'Bozkurt' built Sivas
56301	2-10-0	1947-49	Skyliner design
56501	2-10-0	1943-44	Reichsbahn class 52 'Kriegslok'
56701	2-10-0	1944-46	Reichsbahn class 44, ex-SNCF
56901	2-10-0	1917-18	Modified Prussian G12
56911	2-10-0	1926	SCP
57001	2-10-2	1933-37	46011 series boiler on a stretched Prussian G10 chassis

James Vincent Kelly 1931 - 1975

James Kelly was born in 1931, the eldest of a family of five, at Tullow, where his father was the Postman. Tullow is a small market town in County Carlow, in South-East Ireland, on the former railway from Dublin to Waterford, east of Carlow. His mother died in 1943, leaving three sons and two daughters.

While at the local school he often assisted his father as Telegraph Boy, cycling many miles alone in the hilly, rural Tullow area. During World War II there were many telegrams (and few telephones), as many Southern Irish served in the British Armed Forces, even though Southern Ireland was neutral. He was an avid reader who greatly admired Brendan Behan and James Joyce and, like the latter, wore an eye-patch.

At fourteen, in 1945 he went to sea as cabin boy in the last sailing cutter not to be motorised, which plied a coastal trade from Wicklow and Arklow Harbours, and thus he came to know various ports like Liverpool, and also the Channel Islands, the vessel being small enough for such harbours, visiting regularly. Jim Kelly was not distinguished enough a name, so he added the name Vincent and dropped James. He attempted to join the French Foreign Legion, and on his rejection went from France to Jersey in 1958, where his lasting monument is the archway in the fortress wall cutting off the beach, which he successfully constructed so that the future guests of the hotel 'Le Couperon de Rozel' could go bathing. He became Head Porter of the new hotel.

I met Vincent for the first time in the local pub, the Rozel Bay Hotel, where my newspaper was delivered from St. Helier when I was living with my wife in a flat on Rozel Pier. His father died in 1957, so the family home had to be given up, being over the Post Office, and he got both his younger brothers work in Le Couperon. In 1961-2 this was sold, the Kellys moving to Chateau Plaisir, St. Ouen, where he was in charge of the supply of beer etc. for this holiday night club. Lorry loads of drink arrived daily, and he and the proprietor's wife, who also moved from Le Couperon, fell in love. This lasted until 1974, when she died. Vincent spent his last years in a flat in Belmont Road, St. Helier.

In 1964 he came with me to Switzerland where I was writing my second book in David & Charles 'Railway Holiday' series, which I started for them, with France. We stayed with Sepp Meyer at his Sonne, Stafa, hotel, who had been chef at Le Couperon when it opened. Two years later he came with me to Turkey and helped write Yatakli-Vagon, which Jersey Artists published, its second title, in 1969. He was a stalwart companion in Eastern Turkey.

Vincent died suddenly in 1975 having fallen backwards against some stone paving, which was a great shock to me. My last words to him were on the telephone: "See you next Tuesday", about 24 hours before the accident happened.

George Behrend.

Acknowledgements

Thanks due to Mr. E. Hekimgil, Counsellor in the Ministry of Tourism for proposing this visit and this book, to Mr. Y. Mardin. former Director of Tourism London Office, and Mr. O. Kologlu the present Director (in 1969). Also to the Director of Tourism at Ankara, at Izmir (Mr. M. Giz, now Secretary to the Ministry of Tourism in 1969), and the local Directors of Tourism at Mersin and Istanbul, and all their staff.

Thanks are also due so Mr. Fahir Bilce, Secretary General of the Turkish State Railways, for facilities to travel and interview various officials, and for photographs.

For the hospitality of the Wagons-Lits Company, we are indebted to M. Claude Savary, Directeur des Services Administratifs of the Direction Generale, Paris, and M. Fikret Evliyagil, Representant for Turkey. In addition we are most grateful to M. Roland de Quatresbarbes, Public Relations Officer, M. Philip Jefford, Secretary of the Direction Generals, M. Esmail Etel. Chief of the Haydarpasa Works, M.Ilhami Erman, Manager Istanbul Agency, and M. Midhat Ertug, Chief of the Ankara Agency, and in particular to M. Hamil Imre, Controlleur de route, who was instructed to accompany us on all the portions of our journey undertaken by Wagons-Lits within Turkey. I am also most grateful to M. Boris Nedelev, Representant for Bulgaria, and M. Kusmenov, his Office Manager and M. Ivan Simeonov, Chief d'Agence for arrangements in Sofia.

The various people who helped with the means of reaching Turkey we are also grateful, viz: M. Claude Roche, SNCF Paris, Dr. Fritz Karner, OBB Vienna, The Bulgarian State Railways, through M. Gursel of the Bulgarian Tourist Office. London, M. Gassos, CEH/SEK Athens, Dr. Mario Pelligrino, FS Rome, The Swiss National Tourist Office (in particular Mr. Jurg Schmid though one is not supposed to mention names in the SNTO) and the SBB London. To Mr. W.D.C. Cormack, Publicity Manager, Thos. Cook & Son; and Mr. F. Emere also of Cooks in London who assembled all the pieces of the ticket over the portions of the journey for which we had no assistance.

For photographs we thank the Turkish Tourist Office, the Turkish Railways, the Austrian Federal Railways, the French Government and Italian Government Tourist Offices, Dr. P. Ransome Wallis, D. Trevor Rowe, W. Middleton and European Railways, Philipp Holzmann, Redactor Verlag, Paul Cotterell (for this edition), and M. Billy VIC and lastly but by no means least, Mr. J. H. Price, Editor of Cooks Timetable who also very kindly checked the MS. We thank Mr. Ian Yearsley of the Railway Gazette for editing the MS. In spite of all this massive assistance, the book and its opinions are our own, but we also thank Mr. Peter Pears for permission to quote from Armenian Holiday, and to those concerned, so far as could be traced, for the chapter titles. These include Messrs. Faber & Faber for the quotes of Stephen Spender, T. S. Elliot and Randall Jarrell (in UK), and Leslie Frewin for Professor Hopkins "Poetry of Railways".

Thanks are also due to Herr Willhelm Brach, of Vienna, for hospitality and information, to Dr. F. Stokl, Mr. E. Bell and others for information, to Miss D. Love and Mrs. D. Francis for secretarial assistance, and Mr. A. Tanner and Mr. D. Spear for graphics, and I wish to express my gratitude to Paul Catchpole for taking on this book for publication of a second edition.

Lastly, I am indebted to my wife for considerable help in many ways.

Bibliography

Mountains and a Shore by Michael Peteira, Geoffrey Blest 1966 London

Turkey Observed by R.P. Lister, Eyre & Spottiswood 1967 271 pp London

Vista Books Series: Turkey, Andre Falk, Vista Books 1963 167 pp. Also in French. London

Istanbul by Peter Mayne, Cities of the World Series No 8. Phoenix House 1961 118 pp London

Introducing Turkey by Cedric Salter. Methuen 1961 190 pp London

Turkey. Admiralty Geographical Handbooks series, by Professor K. Mason et alia N.I.D. 1943. 1200 pp

The Steam Locomotives of Eastern Europe by A. E. Durrant, David & Charles 1965, Newton Abbot 160 pp

European Railways Magazine. Quarterly, Latest steam engine details always given. (Published by Robert Spark, Cobham, Surrey)

Rollende Hotels by Dr Fritz Stockl. Bohmann Verlag 1967 136 pp Vienna & Heidelberg (German only)

Grosse Expresszuge Europas by George Behrend. Orell Fussli Verlag 1967 232 pp Zurich. Translasion with revision of :-

Grand European Expresses: The Story of the Wagons-Lits by George Behrend. Allen & Unwin 1962 252 pp London

Pullman and the Orient Expresses, George Behrend, published by the author, printed to order.
c/o 9 Station Road, Findochty, Buckie, Banffshire, Scotland, AB56 4PN

List of Place Names with Anglicised and Local Forms

Adana
Adapazari   *Adapazarı*
Afyonkarahisar (Afyon)
Alayunt
Aleppo (Syria)
Alsancak   *Alsançak*
Anatolia Express   *Anatodolu Ekspresi*
Ankara (formerly Angora)
Ararat (Mt.)
Aydin (formerly Aidin)   *Aydın*

Bahce   *Bahçe*
Balikesir   *Balıkesır*
Bandirma   *Bandırma*
Beirut (formerly Beyrouth - Lebanon)
Belgrade   *Beograd*
Bilecik
Bogazici Express   *Boğazıçı Ekspresi*
Bogazkopru   *Boğazköprü*
Bursa

Carsamba   *Çarşamba*
Cassaba (now Turgutlu)
Cerkezkoy   *Çerkezköy*
Crveni Krst (Yugoslavia)

Denizli
Dikea (Greece)
Dimitrovgrad JZ (Yugoslavia)
Dimitrovgrad BDZ (Bulgaria)
Dogu Express   *Doğu Ekspresi*

Edirne
Ephesus   *Efes*
Erciyas Dag (Mt.)   *Erciyas Dağ*
Erzincan
Erzurum
Eskisehir   *Eskişehir*

Fevzipasa   *Fevzipaşa*

Gaziantep
Goreme   *Göreme*

Halkali   *Halkalı*
Halkapinar
Haydarpasa   *Haydarpaşa*

Istanbul (formerly Constantinople)
Izmir (Greek Smyrna)
Izmit

Kara Dag (Mt.)   *Kara Dağ*
Kars
Kayseri

Konya
Kusadasi   *Kuşadaşı*
Kutahya   *Kütahya*

Lubljana (formerly Laibach) (Yugoslavia - Slovenia)

Manisa
Maritza (R)   *Meriç*
Mersin

Nazilli

Ottoman   *Osmanlı*

Plovdiv (Bulgaria)
Polatli   *Polatlı*
Pythion (Greece)

Railways:- Baghdad Railway
          CFOA   Chemin de Fer Ottoman d'Anatolie
          CO   Chemins de Fer Orientaux
          ORC   Ottoman Railway
          SCP   Smyrna-Cassaba et Prolonguements
          Tunel Railway, Istanbul

Samos (Greece)   *Sámos*
Samsun
Selcuk   *Selçuk*
Semmering (Austria)
Sezana (Yugoslavia - Slovenia) *Sežana*
Sofia (Bulgaria)   *Sofiya*
Stresa (Italy)
Svilengrad (Bulgaria)

Tarsus
Tarsus Mountains
Tatvan
Taurus Express   *Toros Ekspresi*
Tavsanli   *Tavşanlı*
Trieste (Italy)

Ulukisla   *Ulukışla*
Urgup   *Ürgüp*
Uzunkopru   *Uzunköprü*

Van Golu   *Van Gölü*
Varto
Venice (Italy)   *Venezia*
Vienna (Austria)   *Wien*

Yenice
Yerevan (formerly Erevan) (Armenia)

Zagreb (Yugoslavia - Croatia)
Zidani Most (Yugoslavia - Slovenia)

LOCOMOTIVES INTERNATIONAL
BOOKS AND MAGAZINES

*To see more details visit our web site at www.locomotivesinternational.co.uk
or write to us the address below.*

LOCOMOTIVES INTERNATIONAL **books and magazines are published by:**
Paul Catchpole Ltd., The Haven, Trevilley Lane, St. Teath, Cornwall, Great Britain, PL30 3JS